The Story of the Chestnut Canoe

150 Years of Canadian Canoe Building

Kenneth Solway

Nimbus Publishing Limited
PO Box 9301, Station A
Halifax, NS B3K 5N5
(902) 455-4286

Graphic Design: Margaret Issenman, Halifax
Photo Credits: Photos on the following pages are courtesy of the George Taylor Collection, the New Brunswick Provincial Archives: 1, 149. Author photo, back cover, by Jack Solway.
Printed and bound in Canada

Canadian Cataloguing in Publication Data
Solway, Kenneth.
The story of the Chestnut canoe
Includes bibliographical references and index.
ISBN 1-55109-221-2
1. Chestnut Canoe Co.—History. 2. Canoes and canoeing—Canada—History.
I. Title.
VM353.S65 1997 338.7'623829 C97-950132-6

Contents

Foreword

Meach Lake Rd.,
Old Chelsea,
Quebec V0X 2N0

Dear Kenneth,

I love it. I cannot tell you how much I enjoyed reading your paper. Your research is fantastic. You've answered so many questions I've had about the origins of the various designs. Congratulations. You've done a great job.

What's the plan for this paper. Will you be publishing it with lots and lots of pictures. (I hope)

What a pity that so many of these shapes have become extinct. You have done a great job of reminding us of the golden age of canoes.

I'll be anxious to know what your plans are for the paper.

My film "Water Walker" is nearing completion. It will be released as a feature film in spring 1985.

I'll keep you informed.

Sincerely,
Bill Mason

Editor's Note:
A handwritten letter from Bill Mason to Kenneth Solway about a paper that was the basis for this book.
(Courtesy: The Author.)

Preface

According to legend, in the early1890s, two teenage boys, William and Harry Chestnut, had luck and serendipity on their side when they set the subtle waves of history in motion. From them, the great Chestnut legacy begins.

… The blistering heat of the sun beat down on the crowded banks of the Saint John River, the shores overflowed with the weekend populous as Fredericton suffered through a scorching heat wave.

Two teenage brothers were leisurely fishing in the middle of the river, taking in the sights around them. They passed a courting couple and admired the hand-caned canoe back rest on which the elegant young woman reposed, protected from the sun by a mounted parasol. The boys recognized the craft. It had been made by a well-known local Indian who had died just two summers earlier. The Victorian seat should have been incongruous, fastened as it was into a birchbark canoe, but such sights were familiar now, as Fredericton began to merge its frontier ways with the onslaught of modern life. Besides, the seat protected the young lady from a good two inches of water, which the boys could see had already leaked into the primitive-looking craft.

The boys' canoe, on the other hand, wasn't leaking too badly today. They had gone over the seams judiciously with roofing tar from their father's store that morning. These birchbark canoes certainly weren't what they used to be, and these two teenagers knew it. The only birch trees left now were so small that the bark skins had to be sewn together from a dozen different pieces. Leaks were inevitable.

Something across the water caught the boys' attention, though it was still far away.

The brothers stared at a canoe coming towards them that stood out from the others. It was a very different-looking canoe, even from such a distance, coloured a solid green from bow to stern. The canoe was paddled by two men neither boy recognized, obviously out-of-towners. The canoe was filled to the brim with skins of deer and other hunters' prizes. One could tell the canoeists had been out in the bush for quite some time; the boys could see that the men had attempted to spruce themselves up, like most proud backwoodsmen, for the big trip into town—clean clothes and cleanly shaven.

"What in the world kind of a canoe is that?" Harry asked.

"I dunno. Never seen anything like it," his brother Will replied. "Sure isn't Indian. Look at the wood; it's all planed and nailed together."

"And look at the skin. It's some kind of cloth. There's not a seam in it."

"The canoe looks dry. Can't be leaking at all."

"And it sure is fast!"

The boys followed behind these strangers, paddling hard to keep up and feeling a little embarrassed of their own old battered birchbark. A few other canoes gathered round into a welcoming party. As the strangers reached the Fredericton docks, one of the men finally spoke.

"Come from the headwaters. Been out five weeks. Taking the train back. Anyone want to buy a canoe?"

Acknowledgements

I would like to thank many people who have helped me over the years with the research to compile this book: Dan Soucoup at Nimbus Publishing, a Chestnut buff himself, for his support and for contributing his own research, the Peterborough Centennial Museum and Archives, the New Brunswick Archives, the Kanawa International Museum (now the Canadian Canoe Museum), Kirk Wipper, Hugh Stewart, Jerry Stelmok, Rollin Turlow, Gerald Stephenson, Jeff Solway, Jill Dean, the Wooden Canoe Heritage Association, the Royal Canadian Geographical Society, Lock-Wood Ltd., and Mount Allison University Archives. Thanks to various ex-Chestnut employees, including Donald Fraser, Carl Jones, and George Birch, who graciously agreed to be interviewed in the course of my original research. Thanks also to those who helped with the archival artwork, to everyone at Nimbus who worked to get this book into print, and others whom I have undoubtedly neglected to mention. Finally, I would like to thank Susan Graves, my wife and fellow canoe builder, without whom this book would never have been completed.

From the Aboriginal's to the White Man's Canoe

Introduction

Canada is a nation indebted to the canoe, perhaps more indebted than any nation can be to a mode of transportation. The canoe is the quintessential Canadian icon, and historically a driving force behind the political, cultural, and economic development in the early days of the nation.

The canoe helped develop Canada's east-west axis. An invention of the aboriginals, it appeared to be ready and waiting for westerly exploration (and exploitation) of the New World. If not for the canoe, Canada as we know it today would not exist, for without the canoe there could have been no fur trade. Without a fur trade, there would have been no rationale for the climate-defying western trek; settlement of Canada would likely first have headed south to less adversarial agricultural lands. The Canadian-American border and the countries' contrasting histories owe their existence to the canoe.

The story of the canoe spans nations and millennia. Basic laws of physics make it no wonder that the classic canoe shape is ubiquitous among aboriginal cultures and among other early watercraft worldwide. Although the story of the evolution of the canoe, as it is generally told, tends to be dominated by the aboriginal conception, it does not end there. The story of "white man's canoe" unfolds with fascinating developments as European technology met centuries-old aboriginal designs and methods to give shape to the canoe as we know it today.

Among the canoe companies to emerge in Canada, the Chestnut Canoe Company survives as the most important in the history of the craft. Yet, the story of the Chestnut canoe lies not in the invention of a radical new construction technique or the advent of a single new style. Rather, it is a story of people, who have used, and still use, those canoes as a means to their livelihood or as a recreational vehicle. In either capacity, Chestnut canoes helped shape the character of Canadians today.

What makes the builders of the Chestnut canoe unique is that most canoe builders and canoe companies were regional, serving the needs of a local public paddling the local geography. The sheer bulk of the craft made the transportation of finished products prohibitively expensive, so that a global market was difficult, if not impossible, to achieve. Nevertheless, Chestnut canoes reached international markets and their reputation was unbeatable.

The Peterborough canoe area companies of the mid-nineteenth century did ship around the world, using a technique Chestnut later copied of packing many canoes together, each one smaller than the last, without thwarts or other encumbrances—those were to be installed later by the retailer. But in the world of wood-and-canvas canoes—the canoes which were the "final version" in this evolution of the white man's canoe—only one company took on the international mandate, building canoes from eleven-foot Featherweights to massive motorized Freighters, building canoes for all needs and all people. That company was Chestnut. It was the culmination of developments, including those made by dozens of other canoe builders for 150 years or more.

To understand Chestnut we must understand its aboriginal predecessors, the Peterborough canoe, the Dan Herald canoe, the Gerrish canoe and many, many more. Chestnut's history is intertwined with that of the Peterborough builders; therefore, it is incumbent upon this book to chronicle as well the Peterborough area development of the all-wood canoes that evolved from the aboriginal dugout and birchbark.

I tell this story with a particular passion and perspective. I grew up in Chestnuts, under the watchful eye of one of Canada's great paddlers, Omer Stringer, and was a grandson of the founder of the first co-ed children's camp in Algonquin Park, Ontario. My lifelong fascination with Chestnut canoes led to deep sadness when the Chestnut Canoe Company was in its deathwatch in the mid-seventies.

At that time, a few of us talked wistfully of trying to buy the company, but we were too young. Later, I received a grant from the Royal Canadian Geographical Society to write the Chestnut story. I discovered that the company, decrepit and scattered across Canada, could still be bought. Eventually, I bought bits and pieces of this relic of Canadian history.

The traditional construction of birchbark canoes depicted here at a reserve on the north side of the Saint John River, c. 1905, was phased out with the evolution of the white man's canoe.
(Courtesy: The George Taylor Collection, Provincial Archives of New Brunswick.)

Since we view the past with different eyes than those who lived it, the facts presented here may take on a new significance. For example, Chestnut produced, what was regarded at the time, a commodity, not family heirlooms or museum pieces. Chestnut was particularly bad at record keeping—perhaps intentionally—as deception, corporate espionage, and sabotage are part of the Chestnut story from its inception. Many of the facts in this book come word-of-mouth, often second- or third-hand, placing the story as much within the realm of cultural anthropology as within that of history.

Admirers of Chestnut canoes have long enjoyed arguing over the Chestnut folklore as part of the tradition around canoe trip campfires. This book does not attempt to be the definitive history of the Chestnut Canoe Company. Indeed, there remains ample room for debate over many fine points in the Chestnut lore; the only difference is that now such debates could be held in the Chestnut Pub, built from the old factory boiler room in Fredericton.

What is not debatable is that Chestnut produced over sixty different models of canoes to meet the needs of people across a country as large and geographically diverse as Canada, along with paddlers in the United States, South America, Europe, Asia, and Australia. What evolved were some of the greatest shapes in the history of the craft. It is these designs and their traditions that I address with reverence.

Sled Lake Forestry Cabin.
Via Big River, Sask. June 12th, 1927

Dear Sirs:

Wrote you some years previous to this regarding a forestry canoe of which I had and still have charge.

This is the thirteenth year for that "Old Lizzie" and, in new canvas and new paint, she looks and is as good as when she came out of the factory and this district with its rapids and miles of portaging is not by any means an easy one on a canoe.

I have seen some fine canoes of other makes up here and appreciate their qualities, but here, where a canoe is more a beast of burden than a pleasure craft, I'll back my double ribbed Guides' Special CHESTNUT anytime and anywhere.

Sincerely yours,
EARLE G. APPLEBY
Ranger

White Man's Canoe Innovations

One of the first white men to report in detail about birchbark canoes was the French explorer Samuel de Champlain. In 1603, he wrote: *"Their canoes are some eight or nine paces [about twenty feet] long, and a pace or a pace and a half broad amidships ... and are so light that a man can carry one of them easily; and every canoe can carry the weight of a pipe [about one thousand pounds]."*

Champlain immediately recognized the advantages of the aboriginal craft. He carried them aboard his ship to use in exploring rivers along the Atlantic coast, and travelled in them on extended journeys inland, learning aboriginal methods of travel and survival. Of the Lachine Rapids on the St. Lawrence he wrote: *"It is vain to imagine that any boat could be conveyed past the same rapids. He who would pass must provide himself with the canoes of the savages."*

With the white man's influence, aboriginal canoes gradually assumed different shapes, styles, and construction techniques. Both the birchbark and the inland dugout served as models for the canoes of today.

The abundant profits of the ensuing fur trade soon displaced interest in the quest for the Orient, providing ample *raison d'être* for colonizing an otherwise inhospitable and unrewarding climate. The canoe, as the principal form of inland transportation, facilitated early pioneering in Canada, which was based on a wilderness economy and European partnership with (as well as encroachment on) the aboriginal peoples.

The cooperation between the Europeans and the aboriginals for the sake of the canoe is an anomaly in history. Colonizing invaders did not often ally themselves so closely with the ways of the natives; however, the aboriginal craft was ideal for trading.

Because its very nature was incongruous with European tradition, some modifications were inevitable.

Indian guide in a birchbark canoe, 1862.

(Courtesy: The George Taylor Collection, The Provincial Archives of New Brunswick.)

Fur traders wanted their canoes larger and stronger in order to maximize their carrying capacity for cargo during the short canoeing season, and the life of the aboriginal canoes was short, usually only one year.

The French first met the demands, and met as well the European penchant for standardization, building two principal styles of canoe in "canoe factories." The *canot de maître* was used to carry goods from Montreal to the head of Lake Superior; they averaged thirty-six feet in length, six feet in breadth, and carried a crew of eight to ten and three tons of freight. The *canot du nord,* used on smaller waterways, was twenty-five feet long, manned by a crew of five or six, and carried up to one and a half tons of freight. When Montreal fell into English hands in 1760, the English were surprised to discover how closely the French had allied themselves with the Indians and their methods: one government storehouse was found filled with six thousand cords of birchbark. The redcoats soon realized that the small town of Trois-Rivières, Quebec, had for over a century been the hub of a canoe building industry.

The English quickly recognized the importance of continuing the Trois-Rivières tradition to ensure preservation of the fur trade. They encouraged both French and Indian craftsmen to continue and expand their work. Soon more canoe factories sprang up in Detroit, Michigan, and in Grand Portage, Minnesota.

A "factory" was not particularly innovative then. The canoes were still made by the aboriginal method. The factory process was mostly a matter of organizing manpower and the use of a standard building bed on a platform of wood to ensure uniformity. A few European tools had been adopted: steel awls and hammer and the plane, which was used opposite to its design, held stationary while the cedar was pulled over it. The principal tool was the crooked knife which to this day can be purchased from the Hudson's Bay Company.

The use and construction of fur trade canoes gradually disappeared as the nineteenth century ended, although some were built as curios as late as World War I. As testament to the functional nature of the fur trade canoe, only one original and parts of another are extant today.

While construction of the fur trade canoe was petering out, North America's newcomers had subtly made their presence felt upon a native vehicle established centuries before. Inevitably, they soon sought to radically change the craft to reflect European craftsmanship and temperament.

The changes came in droves. Canoe history experienced an unprecedented period of change from the 1850s through the 1870s. Three inspirations were afoot in three widely separate locales that would change the image of the canoe forever: In Peterborough, the all-wood planked canoe was invented; in England, the Rob Roy touring canoe emerged; and in Maine, the wood-and-canvas canoe appeared. Each style left an indelible mark on the history of canoe building and the culmination that would lead to the Chestnut Canoe Company.

The Peterborough Invention

The modern-day Otonabee River valley teems with canoes, its topography a spattering of land amid water. Towns across the area sport names synonymous with canoe companies—Peterborough, Lakefield, Rice Lake, and Gore's Landing. Early English settlers had hewn the virgin forest into a rough logging community by the mid-nineteenth century; the valley had wide tracts of land cleared for agriculture; and towns were in the throes of industrialization.

Here, one of the earliest developments in recreational canoeing occurred. Canoes that had been part of daily life in the workaday world were becoming a recreational vehicle. Early informal races blossomed into full-scale regattas, with separate camps that followed the birchbarks and the area's unique basswood dugouts, the latter of which had evolved into strikingly sophisticated craft.

Early dugouts were made by slowly burning out the inside of a tree trunk, controlling the fire inside with wet mud and scraping away char until the shape of the hull appeared. This rough vessel, made pliable with hot water, was then stretched into a flared shape and permanently fixed with thwarts. Such dugouts could be bought cheaply enough from local Indians, but in the bustling mill town many settlers quickly became skilled in the art themselves, hastening the process with adze and auger.

In the early nineteenth century, Major Sam Strickland reported that his first attempt at a dugout "looked more like a hog trough than a boat." By 1857 his son George had perfected a new method of carving sleek dugouts aided by the use of templates. George Strickland's radically new dugout, the *Shooting Star,* drew well-earned attention. Completed just days before the Katchewanooka Regatta in Peterborough, the perfectly smooth, cleanly shaped craft earned top honours in the "log division." *Shooting Star* was the talk of the town.

Among the competitors and spectators in 1857 were two young men with a keen appreciation for this new canoe: John Stephenson and Thomas Gordon. Hunting and paddling companions, as well as skilled woodworkers, they recognized the benefit of the new canoe, but wondered just how far improvements to the all-wood design could be taken. It was only logical that Stephenson, co-owner of a planing mill, should adapt the aboriginal dugout to plank construction.

Although all wood, the new design borrowed from the birchbark concept, incorporating a skeleton of bent ribs covered by thin planking. The design didn't need the bark skin because the finely planed planks were capable of being tacked solidly to the ribs and were waterproof by themselves. The canoe was built in reverse of the "outside-in" birchbark method: ribs first, then closely fitted planks.

The new boat's magic ingredient was a form, over which the canoe was constructed and from which an unlimited number of identical craft could be built. As glamorous and refined as the invention proved to be, the first form was probably an overturned dugout.

Birchbark and wood-and-canvas canoes both use double hull construction. The birchbark is built into its outer skin of bark with the loose planking held in place by bent ribs, and everything is held together with tension and spruce root. The wood-and-canvas has a solid hull built over a form, which at the end of construction is covered with its outer waterproof layer.
(Courtesy: The Author.)

Thomas Gordon was the first to exploit the plank canoe commercially, and quickly established the world's first wooden canoe shop. He was a leading craftsman, a perfectionist with an eye for both beauty and utility. Gordon's legacy was recognized as early as 1866, when he won the Prince of Wales medal for craftsmanship at the British Empire Exhibition in London.

Stephenson kept a lower profile in the public eye, but played a no less important role. It was his patent that an early Canadian entrepreneur, Colonel J. Z. Rogers, purchased to set up what became the Peterborough Canoe Company.

Combining the best qualities of Indian design and fine European carpentry, the new plank canoes flourished. Within a few years, two other men had joined in the business: William English of Peterborough and Daniel Herald of Gore's Landing. The four woodworkers pushed the refinement of their craft at a remarkable pace, searching for the ultimate method of constructing lightweight, watertight canoes. Their wood-joinery developments included board-and-batten, flush-batten, metallic-flush-batten, tongue-and-groove, cedar rib, and the "Patent Cedar Rib." Within twenty-five years, all four men were producing what would later be regarded as the pinnacle of all-wood canoe building—the shiplapped cedarstrip canoe.

In 1876, the Philadelphia Centennial Exhibition brought together the two major developments in canoe building. English, Gordon, and Herald were all in attendance on the 236 acre site, among 6,000 other exhibitors. Another of those exhibitors was J. Henry Rushton, an American canoe builder who successfully modified the British sailing canoe, the Nautilus, derived from the recreational Rob Roy.

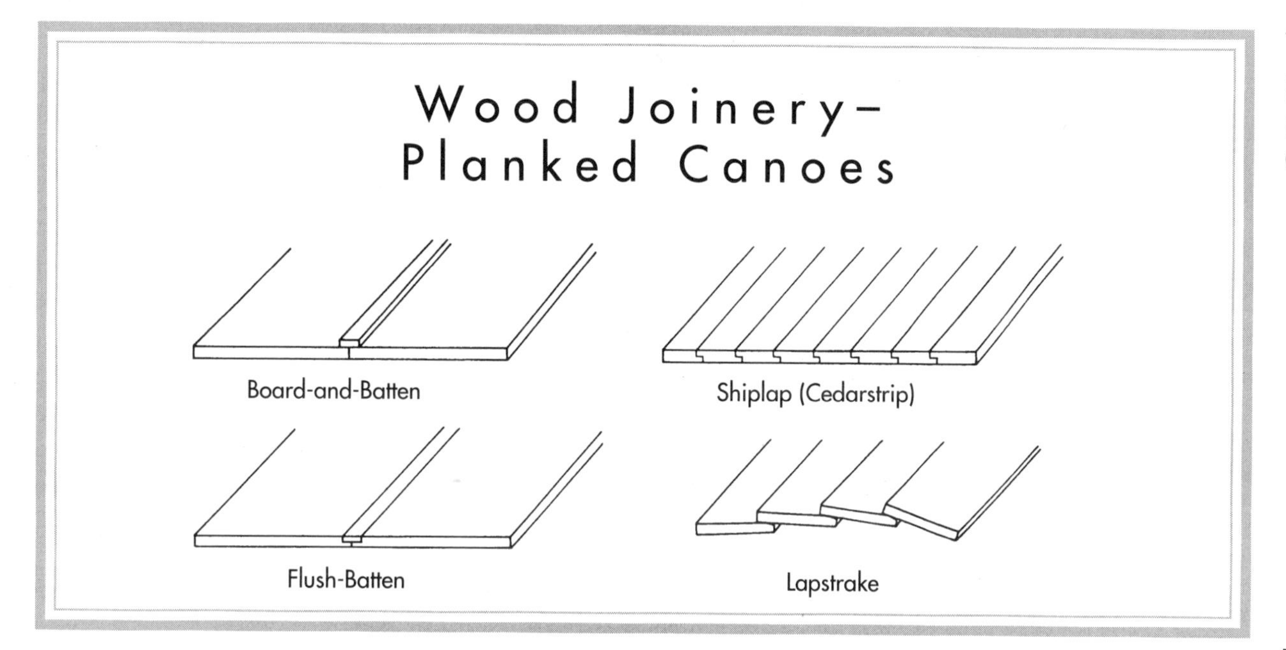

The evolution of wood joinery in canoes is illustrated here.
(Courtesy: Susan Graves.)

Peterborough's Longitudinal Strip Canoe was assembled with the shiplap joint.
(Courtesy: Jill Dean.)

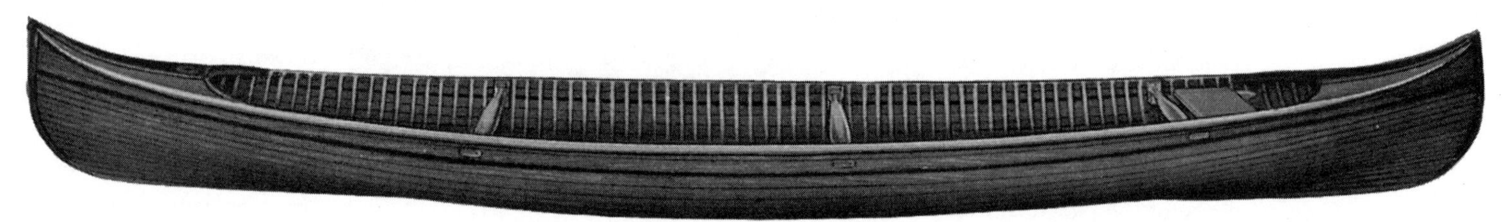

The British Influence

Recreational canoeing does not have its roots in America at all, but in Britain. In 1847 Sir Henry deBathe, a founding member of the Royal Canoe Club, travelled the Thames River in a tin canoe, the first logged cruise in a non-aboriginal canoe design. At about the same time another member of the club, John MacGregor, was experimenting with a canoe made of India rubber.

MacGregor was quite a character: religious zealot, intellectual, sportsman, and explorer. Son of a general, educated in law at Trinity College, Dublin, and Cambridge, he travelled around the world spreading the gospel. In 1859 he crossed the Atlantic. He travelled in birchbark and dugout canoes in Ontario and then headed west to Kamchatka, the Siberian peninsula that all but connects Asia to the Aleutians. There he was particularly taken by the kayaks of the north.

He returned to England enriched by his experience. He wrote his first book, *Our Brothers and Our Cousins*, and built a canoe that was the first of many to be christened the Rob Roy. There was very little evidence of the North American canoe in the craft. It was a hybrid of Inuit kayak design and European shipbuilding. About fifteen feet long, it was a decked canoe designed for cruising, with propulsion either by a double-bladed paddle or a sail.

Rushton copied this Rob Roy design and called it the American Travelling Canoe.

And a-cruising MacGregor did go. With copies of the New Testament and religious tracts he had written and published himself stowed below deck, he set off on a three-month tour of France, Switzerland, and Germany. The literary result of his tour—a small book titled *A Thousand Miles in the Rob Roy*—won canoe converts worldwide. The tome, first published in 1866, underwent untold editions. There were more Rob Roys, more tours, more books: *On the Baltic, On the Jordan* to name just two titles. Later Rob Roys were meant to be lived in and slept in, whether on shore or at anchor. Designs expanded to include complete dining and sleeping facilities, even a canoe tent. MacGregor's influence would earn him the title Father of Recreational Canoeing.

Inspired by the Rob Roy, the canoe craze spread across Britain and Europe. Other designers tried their own improvements. Warrington Baden-Powell, brother of the founder of the Boy Scouts and the Girl Guides, introduced the Nautilus—the first canoe designed primarily for sailing. The boat added both another dimension to the sport and Baden-Powell added another book to the growing library of canoeing best-sellers. By 1869 the British canoe craze reached New York. In 1871 members of the newly formed New York Canoe Club wrote to Baden-Powell and received drawings for the Nautilus No. 3. A local boatbuilder was commissioned to build it, and by the spring of 1872, the club took delivery.

J. Henry Rushton, the pre-eminent canoe builder of Canton, New York, began building skiffs and dinghies in the early 1870s, and built his first canoes half a decade later along the Nautilus lines. There were, of course, other builders attracted to this new design, but Rushton had a flair for business and marketing that brought him early attention. He had the good fortune to establish the right contacts, beginning with his very first canoe order for two boats used in a journey that reached its zenith at the Philadelphia Exhibition. Rushton was prominently written about in *Forest and Stream* (later *Field and Stream*) magazine, especially via the praise of popular travelling journalist George Washington Sears, known as "Nessmuk." He was also a founding member of the American Canoe Association (A.C.A.).

Like many canoe builders of the period, Rushton fashioned "cabinet-maker" craft with exacting finishing touches and luxuries. Rob Roys were a specialty but his line soon expanded to include the cedarstrip "Canadian" canoes. Both the Peterborough builders and Rushton eschewed "cheap" boats. This was, after all, the Victorian era: a time for romantics, when a luxurious canoe was considered an irresistible setting for the ultimate marriage proposal. To serve that purpose, these boats were equipped with comfortable reclining stern seats, decks that virtually enthroned a bow seat of supreme comfort facing the stern, and cabinets that housed liquid refreshment and a built-in Victrola. With a passion for boats such as these—the epitome of the "poor man's yacht"—it's no wonder Rushton resisted for as long as possible the growing trend towards a more utilitarian craft—the wood-and-canvas canoe.

The Maine Wood-and-Canvas Canoe

In Peterborough and Canton, canoe builders catered to princes and lords, writers and socialites. For a few years, their all-wood canoes were used for major expedition work, but the number of underwater seams made them less than ideal. Given the high-society clientele for the all-wood canoes, it is not surprising that so much is recorded about them. By contrast, we know virtually nothing substantive about the inventors of the wood-and-canvas canoe. It emerged unannounced and almost anonymously out of the Maine backwoods.

Of the various white man canoes, the wood-and-canvas has the most in common with its birchbark predecessor: transverse wide cedar ribs that hold in place longitudinal cedar planking, covered by an entirely free and separate outer shell of canvas in the former case, birchbark in the latter.

The principal difference between the wood-and-canvas and the birchbark canoe is how they were constructed. Like the boats from Peterborough, the wood-and-canvas canoes were built on a form. A bark canoe is built from the outside in: an envelope of bark is made, which is then lined with planking and held in place by the ribs which are installed last. Everything is tied together with split spruce roots—a perfect balance of tension and flexibility. This design suited the Indians perfectly. It did not, however, lend itself to European production methods, or to European tools and materials.

The wood-and-canvas canoe is an absolutely beautiful example of a white man's adaptation of Indian technology. Other forms of canoes, from earlier attempts of all-wood construction to modern crafts of molded plastic, all lack the birchbark canoe's wondrous use of a double-layered construction: an outer, waterproof layer covering a rigid frame. The resulting craft is stronger and much easier to repair. The canvas covering stretches to take the shape of the hull, eliminating the "gore" that needs to be cut from the bark in order for the rigid material to curve to the shape of the hull. This single sheet of canvas readily took to the "secret formula" that was hand-rubbed into the weave of the canvas, permanently waterproofing the craft.

Whether use of the form was invented independently or the knowledge was imported from the Otonabee Valley is impossible to establish definitively. There are various theories: a boy found a discarded birchbark canoe and re-covered it with canvas; the Maine boatbuilders who used stretched canvas to cover schooner hatches went one step further; or the Indians themselves began using canvas when bark was not available.

All the above are probably partly true. For example, for hundreds of years the Cree of Northern Quebec had built their birchbark canoes with canvas they had traded with the Hudson's Bay Company. This was born out of necessity—there simply was no suitable bark left in the north—but the canoes were built no differently than their predecessors, from the outside in. To complete the craft the Cree simply painted the canvas with traded Hudson's Bay Company paint.

The Ontario builders had been developing their all-wood canoe designs on forms for over two decades, but there is little evidence that those canoes had much impact on the east coast where the mainstay was still Indian bark canoes. All-wood canoes were too expensive and not rugged enough for Maritime conditions. If not the result of independent "research and development," word of these new all-wood canoes and how they were made might have come to Maine from such places as Boston, where some Peterborough area canoes had been exported. Or perhaps information might have filtered from the Peterborough regatta which the American Canoe Association organized. We don't know.

There is little that can be learned about the origins of Maine's wood-and-canvas canoe, shrouded as it was in backwoods folklore (which is probably the strongest evidence that it was more of an independent development). It appears most likely that a canoe builder by the name of Evan Gerrish, who worked out of Brownville, Maine, can be accredited with the "invention" of the wood-and-canvas design, some time between 1872 and 1880. He did not, however, become a major canoe builder.

However, three significant canoe companies quickly sprang up in his wake in the area surrounding Bangor—E. M. White, B. N. Morris, and the Old Town Canoe Company.

E. M. White's first canoes date from 1889. He favoured large, flat-bottomed models, indicating a clientele of mostly local professional guides. These big canoes with minimal draft, even when heavily loaded, proved ideal on the state's shallow salmon rivers. The often-used name, "Maine Guide canoe," that commonly substituted for the generic wood-and-canvas name is no accident. Old guides, such as Mick Fahey, claimed the twenty-foot White poling canoe was Maine's most popular model. Today, these canoes, built over the original forms, are still crafted by Jerry Stelmok of the Island Falls Canoe Company.

The B. N. Morris canoes date from 1882. Like the canoes by E. M. White, Morris' catered at first to professional guides. By the early twentieth century, Morris was focused on the pleasure market, adopting much of the finery of Rushton or Peterborough canoes: large mahogany decks ringed by an ornamental coaming, flag sockets, and unique splayed stems. Today, a vintage Morris is one of the most cherished wood-and-canvas canoes.

The Old Town Canoe Company holds a special place in canoe-building history because of its longevity. From the end of the nineteenth century to the present, it has built the same wood-and-canvas models, while evolving into a maker of modern plastic canoes.

The wood-and-canvas canoe adopted the stature of its birchbark predecessor as a people's canoe. Regional builders sprang up in every little hamlet, catering to their local markets of regular customers. The canoe was once more accessible to the everyday man in the bush. It was affordable, readily available, durable, and easy to repair. It suited mass production and the development of a commodity market. However, the thirst for profit in such a competitive market brought a laxness of quality control in the later years, hastening the near demise of the wooden canoe industry in 1960s and 1970s.

The Demise of the White Man's Canoe

The wood-and-canvas canoe was the pinnacle of the classic white man's canoe because it was practical and most adhered to its aboriginal origins, and as such it is the primary survivor. It, too, has fallen to a level of artisan obscurity; although the demise of this classic canoe has come in stages. Bicycle madness in the 1890s took much of the impetus out of a developing recreational canoeing industry. Bush planes reduced the far north's dependence on the canoe. Ole Evinrude sputtered into fame with his outboard, and while canoes quickly adapted to use horsepower, runabouts further hampered the canoe industry.

World War II necessitated cheap alternatives to the labour-intensive and by then expensive "oddity." Grumman took its aircraft technology and adapted it to boatbuilding; fibreglass was heralded as the marine cure-all. In the postwar boom of Wonder Bread and a television in every house, a popular notion took hold: "wood was worse."

Ironically, today's highly refined Kevlar and ABS canoes are helping to rekindle interest in the classic canoe. The cost of petroleum products continues to rise, making the price of a classic canoe more and more competitive. As the shapes of difficult to mold synthetic canoes are increasingly refined, the market is becoming more sophisticated and more demanding. Once again, paddlers are more appreciative of the fine shapes attainable only in wood.

Wooden Canoes Today

Undoubtedly, Canadian philosopher and media guru Marshall McLuhan never imagined his popular remark would be applied to a wooden canoe, but it fits rather well: "The medium is the message." Canoes have been constructed of tin, rubber, aluminum, fibreglass, Kevlar, ABS, graphite compounds, even concrete. But these materials are incongruous with the purpose of most canoes as vehicles that transport us into the unknown wilderness of quiet rivers, plodding moose, and the call of the loon.

There is no escaping the contradictory message when sitting in a canoe built of artificial materials—most of which are products of some of the greatest pollution the earth has ever known—while ostensibly exploring the wilderness to enjoy nature. The canoe can help to teach us something about natural beauty and respect for the world around us by giving us harmless access—if we choose it—to pristine wilderness.

Furthermore, wooden canoes are superior in practical terms—the most commonly overlooked element in support of wooden canoes. Ignorance about wood-and-canvas canoe upkeep was rampant in the 1960s and simultaneous with the steady development of new technologies, which led to the mistaken belief that the wood-and-canvas canoe was a leaky, cumbersome dinosaur.

The wood-and-canvas canoe has one unique attribute which simply has been forgotten: two hulls. A structural, naturally floating cedar hull is covered by a single watertight sheet of canvas. This outer covering can be removed to make minor or major structural repairs and then a new canvas covering will make the boat like new.

In the sixties, many of the children's camps abandoned the simple art of canvassing, blinded by the craze for plastic. Hundreds of canoes, mostly Chestnuts, were "improved" with fibreglass covering. Now, years later, those boats are rotting shells because the plastic did not let the wood breathe.

I came honestly by a guides' adage that states: "Give me the seat and I'll rebuild the canoe." Before I became a canoe builder, I began a collection of canoes that included many relics at various stages of restoration and a new Chestnut, one of the very last from Fredericton. It was a seventeen-foot heavily built Prospector. Where it should have flexed, its thick oak gunwales remained stiff, ready to crack. Its planking, ribs, decks, and everything else were too heavy. A canoe that should have weighed eighty-five pounds came off the shop floor at an even one hundred.

With the luxury of hindsight, I see now our first white water expedition in that canoe was an exercise in pure ignorance. The waters of Algonquin Park, where I grew up, are almost entirely placid. (Hence my training, under the "flat water" guru Omer Stringer was entirely in flat water paddling.) The one exception is in the far north of the giant park where Cedar Lake forms the headwater of the Petawawa River, flowing forcibly into the Ottawa and onwards toward the Atlantic.

I was an avid reader of Bill Mason's books (although not quite as assiduous as I might have been), and this was one of Bill's favourite playing grounds. He would spend days paddling in the relatively innocent rapids downstream from Lake Traverse. But as an Algonquin history buff, I wanted to start further up, from the rail stop of Brent, where my wife-to-be, Susan, and I would paddle downstream with portages, to Lake Traverse, following the traditional white pine logging run.

As luck would have it, once we got off the big lakes a strong wind came up. It just so happens that some of the portages along the river's edge follow the rail line, high up on man-made embankments where there is nothing to calm an angry wind. Twice the one hundred pound canoe practically ripped my head off, and I felt my life was in danger if we continued to portage. Any sane person would have set up camp, enjoying the freedom from the bugs—I have since grown wiser.

Far below the high embankment of the portage, the river seemed pleasant enough, but the many bends limited our view. Never mind that I had no topographical maps for anything upstream of Lake Traverse. Never mind that I must have glossed over, no matter how many times I read Bill's book, that short but crucial phrase, "Wind and rapids do not mix." Susan, the wiser one, continued on the portage and wished me well. I travelled on with one pack, much too light ballast for a canoe that size.

I was doing fine until I came suddenly upon a series of three chutes where all the water of the Petawawa charged through narrow gashes in the great Canadian Shield, far narrower than the length of a canoe. But the water was deep, without obstructions. (I later learned from maps that these were called the Devil's Chutes.) The first two chutes went perfectly: Ready, aim, shoot. I have never experienced anything quite as exhilarating in my life.

At the third chute a strong wind blew up from nowhere—little did I know that a tornado tore down the main street of nearby Haliburton that day. My canoe seemed to be lifted from the water. I was dropped back down with the wind pushing me broadside to the chute; a seventeen-foot canoe does not fit broadside through an eight-foot opening in a rock wall. I remember very little after that except the straining of my muscles. Most of what I know now came from my then seemingly would-be wife, who was watching from the shore.

The canoe split in half like a popsicle stick. There is no canoe that would not have done the same—wood, metal, or plastic. The boat and I disappeared below the surface, only reappearing far downstream in the calm of a large pond with no recollection of what had transpired, under water, for such a great distance. When I pulled myself onto the shore, I saw that the bow and stern of my canoe were back to back, both pointing towards the sky.

The moral to this story is that any other canoe would have been destroyed beyond repair; this one was not. Only when we spread open the decks, like spreading the wings of a dead butterfly, did we realize the canvas was still whole. The canoe had simply folded. We cut saplings which we lashed into the gunwales to make the canoe relatively straight again so we could complete our journey. The craft handled well, all things considered, and didn't even leak.

We returned safely home with the canoe, feeling embarrassed since we had just days ago left with a virtually new one. I rebuilt it, making it a foot shorter, and honing it down to that eighty-five pounds. I even re-used the canvas. We still use that canoe regularly.

Though I believe that particular Chestnut was poorly conceived, my experiences with it taught me my most important lessons:

- Canoes meant to be portaged should be built as light as possible; and lightweight does not mean less strong, sometimes flexible is better.
- Unless Prospectors are used for the purpose they were intended—carrying a great deal of weight—I consider them, in most modern paddling circumstances, to be a dangerous canoe.
- I learned why wood-and-canvas canoes seem to last forever—their repairability.
- And finally, I reread Bill Mason's advice in *Path of the Paddle* about wind and rapids.

This wood-and-canvas canoe is still paddled today—after repairing this damage.
(Courtesy: The Author.)

Peterborough Area Canoe Builders

Any story of the Chestnut Canoe Company is incomplete without an account of the Peterborough area canoe builders that preceded it.

The Peterborough region is dominated to the south by the Lake Ontario ports of Port Hope and Cobourg, to the north by bush, lakes, and rivers, including Rice Lake and the Trent and Otonabee Rivers. An hospitable terrain, it was long inhabited by Indians. The Peterborough area's long association with the canoe makes it deserving of the reputation, "home of the white man's canoe." While other isolated forays were made into canoe building using European ideas, such as the earlier plank and the tin boats of master surveyor David Thompson, it is in the Peterborough region that white settlers shared and even competed with the local Indians to produce and steadily improve on a more modern craft. Early European settlers made dugouts as a basic means of transportation, and birchbarks coexisted with dugouts. Friendly cooperation and fierce competition fostered the development of new technologies.

The Peterborough area Mississauga Indians mastered both the bark and small dugout canoe construction—one of the few groups of aboriginal peoples known to have built such different canoes. The simultaneity of the two different methods of canoe building added broad perspective for the European settlers, helping to foster the upcoming innovations. A water raceway that provided power for sawmills and planing equipment led to the transformation of the primitive craft during the industrial revolution.

The first European settlers at the Peterborough area arrived in the early 1800s, primarily from Ireland, England, and Scotland. They farmed the fertile plains, and logged the clear white pines so famous that the area's highland is still dubbed Pine Ridge. Among early settlers, it seems dugouts were the preferred canoes for open water, and the birchbarks were reserved for travel into the backwoods that required substantial portaging. Since weight was not a prohibitive factor, sturdy, rugged dugouts could stand up to constant use and abuse. Shallow Rice Lake—named for its abundant wild rice—was a haven for feeding birds, and the dugouts made excellent hunting canoes.

The early settlers from Lake Katchawanooka to Rice Lake made ample use of dugouts, having traded for them with the local Indians. Basswood was the choice wood for these inland dugouts because it is light, resistant to cracking, and easy to carve. No doubt other woods were used at times. Although none survive, at least one giant dugout, hewn from the massive white pines, is preserved in a written account.

The Peterborough area prospered earlier than similar locales. Canoes here were not only used for hunting, fishing, and discovery, but for recreation as well. By the mid-nineteenth century, Peterborough was attractive to tourists for its steamboat routes, hotels, and cottage sites.

Literary Links to Canoes

From the small community of Lakefield, near Peterborough, a strong connection emerged between two of Canada's early literary figures, sisters Susanna Moodie and Catharine Parr Traill, and the first canoes produced by the English settlers. The sisters' maiden name was Strickland, and along with their brother Samuel, they wrote about their times together in Indian style canoes. Samuel even learned to build them. Later, his son George played a pivotal role in the white man's conversion of the aboriginal craft. In her book *Roughing it in the Bush,* Susanna Moodie indicated that the Moodies' recreational canoe was a small dugout. She described it this way: "My husband had purchased a very light cedar canoe, to which he attached a keel and a sail, and most of our leisure hours were spent upon the water.... I learned the use of the paddle and became quite proficient in the gentle craft."

Catharine Parr Traill wrote about canoes as well: "... Our nearest path would have been through the bush, but the ground was so encumbered that we agreed to go in a canoe. Our light bark skimmed over the calm water, beneath the overhanging shade of cedars, hemlock and balsams...."

The Rise of the Peterborough Canoe

Twenty-five years after his father's first effort at building a dugout canoe, George Strickland devised amethod (using templates) that his brother Henry called the "beautiful Lakefield dugouts." George made his mark at the district canoe regattas, which had become popular. The first one was held in 1835. In June 1857 George easily defeated the challengers in all three Lakefield races in his sleek *Shooting Star.* Three months later, the Stricklands organized another regatta, this time in Peterborough, where their design—probably long and slender, almost resembling a rowing shell—was copied. A paddler named Armstrong raced his *Belle of Peterborough;* the Rice Lake Indians entered their *Flying Cloud.* Both canoes defeated Strickland's *Shooting Star.*

This proved to be the pivotal moment in modern canoe history for watching from the shore at the Peterborough regatta was another canoe buff, John Stephenson. Henry Strickland, secretary-treasurer of this event, would later state to the American Canoe Association that at this regatta, "J. S. Stephenson conceived the idea of the Canadian basswood canoe." (When speaking to a Canadian audience Strickland called this the "Peterborough canoe.")

There were other influences on Stephenson, such as the experience of portaging a two hundred pound dugout on a hunting trip. In an interview with the *Peterborough Examiner* in 1912 Stephenson said he was "resolved that next fall he would have a lighter one, and every foot of the carry served to impress the thought more firmly on his mind." So, a technological race was on in the Peterborough area; Stephenson was in the lead among three other men who worked together as friends, colleagues, and fierce competitors to produce a half century of radical innovation and an unprecedented pace of development duplicated only by the post World War II boom of synthetic designs.

John Stephenson, William English, Daniel Herald, and Thomas Gordon are the four whose influence shaped the eventual Peterborough Canoe Company. Stephenson is most important to the Chestnut story, for not only is he the earliest contributor, but he has the most direct lineage to the Peterborough Canoe Company, and therefore to the Chestnut Canoe Company. English canoes, too, were eventually incorporated into Peterborough. The Gordon canoes are built today, while Herald's business evolved into the Rice Lake Canoe Company, disappearing from the scene in the 1920s.

Pivotal Moments in White Man's Canoes in Canada

1850s . . . . Experiments by Stephenson (Peterborough) and Gordon (Lakefield)
1858 . . . . Ontario Canoe Company established, Peterborough
1858 . . . . Gordon Canoe Company, Lakefield
1860 . . . . Strickland Canoe Company
1862 . . . . Daniel Herald (Rice Lake Canoe Company), Gore's Landing
1887 . . . . Brown Boat Company
1892 . . . . Peterborough Canoe Company established from Ontario Canoe Company, Peterborough
1893 . . . . Canadian Canoe Company
1897/8 . . . . . First Chestnut canoes
1905 . . . . Harry Chestnut obtains Canadian patent on wood-and-canvas construction techniques.
1907 . . . . Incorporation of Chestnut Canoe Company.
1923 . . . . Canadian Watercraft Limited merges Chestnut, Peterborough, and Canadian canoe companies

Innovations in canoe building evolved over time, culminating in modern-day beauties like this one.
(Courtesy: The Provincial Archives of New Brunswick.)

Evolution of Early Peterborough Area Canoe Companies

John Stephenson
1831–1920
Ashburnham (Peterborough)

1857 First experiments with planed plank and rib canoe
1883 Bought out by Rogers to create Ontario Canoe Company
1892 Major fire
1892 Canadian Canoe Company created by Rogers' workmen after fire
1892 Rogers joins as manager of Peterborough Canoe Company
1923 Peterborough buys out English Canoe Company
1923 Merger with Chestnut creates Canadian Watercraft Limited (CWL)
1927 CWL purchases Canadian Canoe Company
1961 Closure; Chestnut on its own

Thomas Gordon
1833–1916
Lakefield

1832 Major George Strickland's "hog trough"

1857 George Strickland's *Shooting Star*

c.1860 Gordon Canoe Company

1892 Strickland & Company

1904 Lakefield Canoe Company via an amalgamation of Gordon Canoe and Strickland Canoe companies

Present day
Walter Walker continues to build Gordon canoes for Peel Marine

William English
date unknown–1890
Peterborough

1861 English Canoe Company

1923 Acquired by Peterborough just prior to CWL merger

Daniel Herald
c. 1833–1890
Gore's Landing

1862 Herald & Hutchison

1892 Herald Brothers

c. 1895
Renamed Rice Lake Canoe Company by Herald's sons

1921 Moved to Cobourg

1928 Closed doors after moving to Montreal

John Stephenson

John Stephenson was born into the life of a backwoodsman. His parents were among the first Europeans to settle Peterborough, which they reached by rowing up the Otonabee River in 1818. Peterborough was hardly a town, with a population of about five hundred people and with stumps still in the streets. Yet, Stephenson was fascinated with mechanical developments. At the age of seventeen he was sent to the town of Cobourg to apprentice with a blacksmith. Upon his return he worked for a combined blacksmith and woodwork shop, and by the 1850s he was a partner with his brother and brother-in-law in a planing and manufacturing factory, the Cragie and Stephenson Mill. John was the inventor among the three partners, a man who tired quickly of repetitive work but was always tinkering with something new. As the *Peterborough Examiner* stated: "It is as an inventor that he has impressed the citizens of the last generation."

Stephenson's canoe invention merged the Indian steam bending tradition with the European technologies of a repetitive building form and machine-milled lumber. The first Peterborough canoe had thin, wide, milled basswood boards nailed to widely spaced elm ribs steam-bent over an existing dugout canoe that was used as a primitive building form. Not invented yet were the metal bands that would clinch each canoe tack as the tack was hammered. With Stephenson's method, the new boat was literally nailed to the old one and had to be slowly and gingerly worked off. Nonetheless, to build a craft from just six extremely wide and thin boards, bending them to take the desired shape would have been much quicker than the lengthy and wasteful process of building of a dugout (although waste was probably of little concern).

While Stephenson's intentions were to build a racing canoe for himself, he found out soon enough that he couldn't keep one; each canoe was bought as soon as it was built. Since repetition was against his nature, Stephenson seized the opportunity to make refinements to his design with every new canoe. Rapid improvements were the result. Stephenson's canoes were becoming well known to the area, showing up at regattas, owned by various paddlers. But his time to build canoes was limited by his responsibilities to the Cragie and Stephenson Mill. Soon other builders were following in his footsteps to meet the demand. It appears there was so much business that there was little need for protectionism.

The building form was the basis of the new construction technique. But still, there was room for improvement. Later, patterns for the planks were incorporated to ensure the uniformity of the craft. Exactly who invented what will remain in dispute, but Stephenson will always appear a leader. Then came various methods of joinery for the seams of the planks, including some radical attempts such as Dan Herald's patented "Double Rib" canoe. The culmination was the narrow planked, shiplapped craft that has come to embody the term, "Peterborough Canoe," then and today.

Thomas Gordon

Thomas Gordon was born in 1833 and died in 1916. (He was twenty-four at the time of the Peterborough regatta in 1857.) He became a boatbuilder and stuck with it throughout his life, building steamboats, rowboats, canoes, anything that would float. He and a partner built one of the early steamboats launched at Lakefield.

As a boatbuilder Gordon would have been familiar with many techniques. In Donald Cameron's 1975 paper "The Peterborough Canoe," Cameron stresses his belief that Gordon was the first to develop patterns, and thus greatly improved the quality of the earliest canoes.

One great difficulty in canoe design lies in shaping the planks uniformly to match the ever changing shape of the canoe, from its slender ends to the wide midship girth. The all-wood canoe, without the benefit of a canvas covering, desperately needed help to facilitate the planking process. It is said that the shop was always cluttered with pre-established planking patterns and that a great fuss was made about them.

Gordon and Stephenson were good friends who frequently hunted together; and some have suggested it was Gordon who actually built the first plank canoe. But Stephenson was three years older and appears to have been more of a "tinkerer" than Gordon. Gerald Stephenson, in researching his grandfather's pioneering work, firmly believes that as a professional builder, Gordon began almost a decade after Stephenson, even after English.

Later Gordon canoes had the "metallic flush batten," in effect one long, flexible zinc strip, formed like a staple and pressed into the wood to hold the seams of the planks together. This method, while successful, required that the batten be supported with more than the widely spaced ribs of the earlier canoes. Thus the canoes also featured many more, narrowly spaced ribs—one of the steps toward the development of the cedarstrip canoe we know as the Peterborough canoe.

Cameron argues, in his same paper, that Gordon is the logical "inventor" of the cedarstrip design on the grounds that Gordon replaced the wide boards with many shiplapped narrow boards due to his familiarity with different types of boat construction techniques. Most other reports favour with Stephenson as the inventor.

In any case, the cedarstrip offered real advantages and proved to be the crowning achievement of the Peterborough area. Narrow planks, while initially thought to be more work, solved the problems created by the ever-changing shape of a canoe. The thin cedarstrips eliminated much of the brute force needed to push and shove the earlier wide boards into shape. It also allows for the eventually popular use of contrasting coloured woods above the waterline, for a striking appearance. (Local butternut and walnut were used, possibly black cherry as well. At least one company later imported exotic woods.)

In 1904 Gordon teamed up with George Strickland and set up the Gordon Canoe Company in Lakefield, precursor to the Lakefield Canoe Company. From 1918 to 1942 Lakefield survived at least four ownership and structure changes. In 1942 the plant burned to the ground, but the forms survived. It is likely the forms were somewhere else at the time of the fire, possibly in storage.

A small company in Lakefield, Peel Marine, which sells and repairs wood and fibreglass outboards and canoes, obtained the Gordon forms. Stuart Peel, founder of Peel Marine, enticed a seasoned all-wood canoe builder, Walter Walker to come out of retirement and build these classic all-wood canoes once again. Walker had started as an "extra" for Lakefied during the beginning of the Depression, and worked in canoe building through the Peterborough glory years. In 1967, at the age of sixty, Walker started to build canoes again, and now in his nineties, he is still building them today.

Thos. Gordon, President — J. E. Richardson, Manager — Chas. Fallon, Secretary

THE LAKEFIELD CANOE BUILDING AND MANUFACTURING CO., LIMITED

By the amalgamation of the old established businesses of Thos. Gordon and Strickland & Co. in the above Company, we have secured the services of men whose experience in the building of canoes and boats is unsurpassed in the world, and the well founded reputation of these firms for the best class of work and superior models of boats will be found to be amply sustained by the present Company.

While we do not profess to compete with the builders of the cheap (in every sense of the word) class of canoes, for which there is a certain demand, we do claim to give the very best value for money obtainable, and guarantee that in every boat sent out from our factory there is good sound material, and faithful conscientious workmanship.

On these conditions we solicit your order.

Respectfully,

The Lakefield Canoe Building and Manufacturing Co., Limited

1

Lakefield Canoe Company Catalogue, 1915.

(Courtesy: Peterborough Centennial Museum and Archives.)

Daniel Herald

Herald shows the greatest amount of movement among the four Peterborough area builders. He ran away from home at the age of eighteen and emigrated from Ireland, first to the United States, and then to Gore's Landing. Gore's Landing, although not nearly the size of Peterborough or Lakefield, would have benefited early on being on the south shore of Rice Lake, closer to the Lake Ontario ports of Cobourg and Port Hope.

In 1862 Daniel Herald set up a partnership, Herald and Hutchison, in Gore's Landing. After Herald's dealth (he was hit by a train), it was taken over by his sons and renamed the Rice Lake Canoe Company. Future moves placed it in Cobourg, and eventually Montreal, where it closed in 1928.

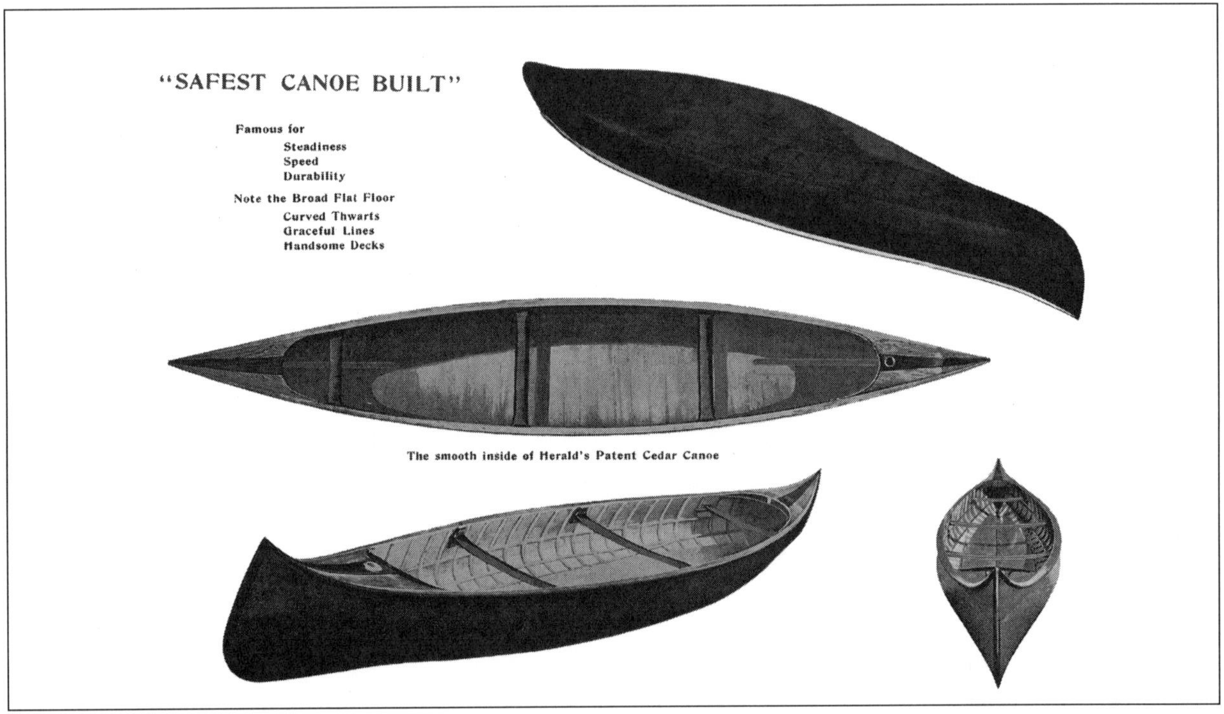

"SAFEST CANOE BUILT"

Famous for
Steadiness
Speed
Durability

Note the Broad Flat Floor
Curved Thwarts
Graceful Lines
Handsome Decks

The smooth inside of Herald's Patent Cedar Canoe

Located on the south shore of Rice Lake, Daniel Herald's unique canoes, begun in 1862 as Herald and Hutchison, were still thriving in the early twentieth century. The greatest advertising zeal is still reserved for the "patented" cedar rib canoe. Page from the Rice Lake Canoe Company catalogue, c. 1918. (Courtesy: The Author)

Herald is best remembered for a unique patented canoe design of his own invention, the Herald Patent Cedar Canoe of 1871. This canoe predates the molded plywood concept, with a solid set of ribs made of wide thin boards identical to the planking, placed crosswise, from gunwale to gunwale, tacked to lengthwise planking. In between was a waterproofing layer of fabric coated in rot-resistant white lead, much like the later wood-and-canvas concept. This made the interior of the hull completely smooth; without the encumbrances of ribs or battens there was no need for the floorboards common on ribbed canoes.

Of course this canoe design, with fabric essential to it, may also have had an impact on the later development of wood-and-canvas, half a continent away. Included in Herald's patent is reference to a method for turning over the tacks in planking the canoe over the form (possibly metal bands). Both Herald and Stephenson laid patent claim to this development. A major collection of artifacts, including building forms and documentation, is held at the Museum of Science and Technology in Ottawa.

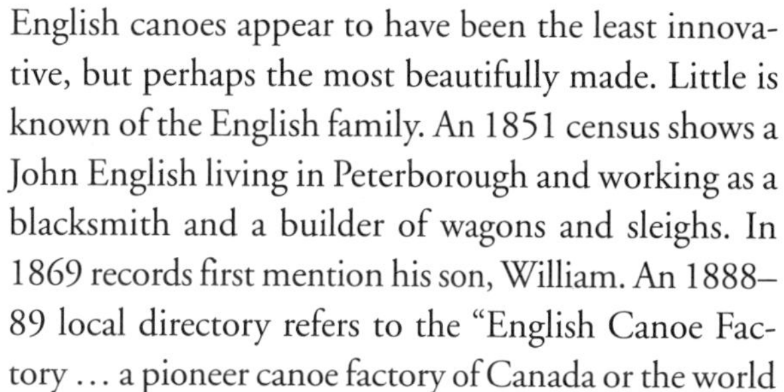

The title Page from the Herald Brothers 1892 canoe catalogue is an impressive early catalogue by Dan Herald. This company became the Rice Lake Canoe Company.

(Courtesy: Daniel Herald/Rice Lake Canoe Collection at National Museum of Science and Technology, Ottawa.)

William English

English canoes appear to have been the least innovative, but perhaps the most beautifully made. Little is known of the English family. An 1851 census shows a John English living in Peterborough and working as a blacksmith and a builder of wagons and sleighs. In 1869 records first mention his son, William. An 1888–89 local directory refers to the "English Canoe Factory … a pioneer canoe factory of Canada or the world in its special line, basswood canoes of all kinds…." The shop was founded in 1861; William would have been about twenty-one, his father forty-five. While there is no indication that the father, John English, was a canoe builder it is highly probable, with his woodwork and blacksmith background, that he had a role in the company's formation.

Other Influences on the Peterborough Canoe

Although Peterborough is clearly the hub of early developments in the white man's canoe, it is important to realize that other influences were at work. There was the continuing aboriginal influence. The ongoing search for a European replacement of the birchbarks still used for rough wilderness travel would eventually lead to a codification of the "Open Canadian" canoe. The club and racing scene was eventually influenced by the Americans through the inception of the American Canoe Association (A.C.A.) in 1880, which continued to influence racing styles, including the twentieth-century Olympic racing canoes. There was a strong British influence as well, emphasizing highly finished crafts with an aristocratic flair, and a passion for sailing rigs—the epitome of the "poor man's yacht."

The English connection began in 1860, when the Peterborough area was visited by Edward, Prince of Wales. He was presented with a beautiful dugout canoe finished in French polish, a gift from Samuel Strickland and his sons. It was a racing design: eighteen feet, a slim twenty-four inch beam, and long decks fore and aft. The prince was hooked. Since then, other canoes have gone from Peterborough to British royalty. In 1948 the City of Peterborough gave then Princess Elizabeth a Peterborough cedarstrip as a wedding gift. More recently, the Town Council of Lakefield commissioned as a gift a cedarstrip canoe for Prince Andrew from Walter Walker. In 1982 an American from New York sent his beautifully varnished cedarstrip made by the Peterborough Canoe Company travelling first class on the Canard liner *Queen Elizabeth II* as a donation to the National Maritime Museum in Greenwich, near London.

In 1866 John MacGregor, innovator of the Rob Roy design, and Edward, Prince of Wales, became the founders of the Royal Canoe Club. MacGregor was becoming a European folk hero, paddling a boat that could hardly be called a canoe. It was assumed by his followers that a canoe had to double as a bed, in or out of water, and be propelled by a double paddle and sail. By 1879 his book *A Thousand Miles in the Rob Roy Canoe on Twenty Rivers and Lakes of Europe* had undergone fifteen printings, with equally popular sequels. Canoes became popular with the affluent youth in England, continental Europe, and the United States, which sustained the impetus for finely crafted all-wood boats that epitomized the Victorian era. MacGregor's popularity helped keep the Peterborough builders inclined towards the fanciful, including sailing rigs as a mandatory element of many canoes. However, the proliferation of the Open Canadian canoes helped to finally end the confusion between the quintessential Canadian craft and this odd European conception.

Peterborough area canoes were recognized worldwide during the pre-wood-and-canvas era. The evidence is in awards garnered by Peterborough area canoes the world over, as seen below. The second half of the nineteenth century is marked by the constant search for a better canoe construction technique. The search was completed with the eventual and universal adoption of the wood-and-canvas design; while the ultimate design for function, it was not considered an improvement in craftsmanship or beauty. Interestingly, these awards suddenly stop with the wood-and-canvas takeover.

1881 .... Fisheries Exhibition, London, England
1883 .... Fisheries Exhibition, London, England
1885 .... The World's Exhibition, Antwerp, Belgium
1886 .... The Colonial and Indian Exhibition, London, England
1887 .... The Colonial and Indian Exhibition, London, England
1891 .... The Jamaica Exhibition
1893 .... The Chicago Exhibition (Gold Award)
1900 .... The Paris Exhibition (Gold Award)
1901 .... The Glasgow Exhibition, Scotland

Stephenson Moves Ahead

John Stephenson had not thought of patents when he designed the original Peterborough canoe, but during the latter half of the 1870s he was more careful. Stephenson left active work in the mill operation and devoted his time to designing a new canoe building technique. On May 17, 1879, a Canadian patent was issued for the Stephenson Rib boat. It, too, included the clinching technique. This was a cedar canoe fully built of wide cedar ribs. Each rib, about one inch wide, was fastened to its neighbour with tongue-and-groove joints. There were no planks; gunwales, keel, and keelson were the only longitudinal members. Of particular interest is the inclusion in the patent of fabric covering—another precursor to the wood-and-canvas designs first of Maine and later of Chestnut, although rarely was this method used over the preferred clear varnish finish. The new Stephenson Hunting canoe, as he referred to it, was first exhibited on a steamboat excursion to Idyll Wild Resort on Rice Lake on May 26, 1879.

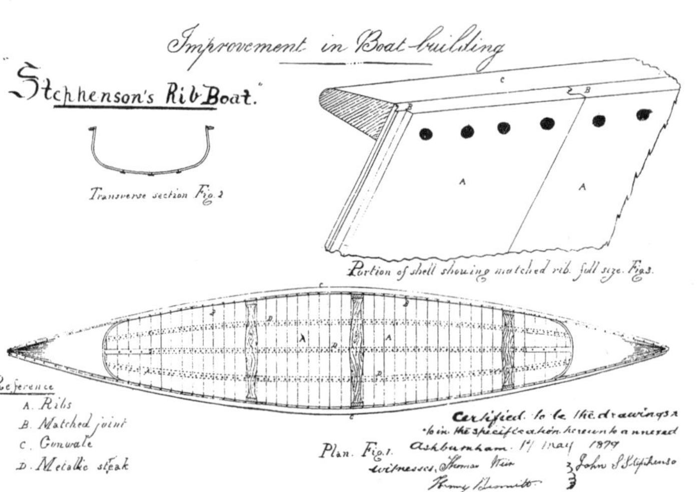

In 1878 Stephenson's patent states: "The second part of my invention relates to the covering of the said hull with paper or cotton or other textile fastened on with waterproof glue [sic] forming a waterproof skin to the wooden hull."
(Courtesy: Canada Patent Office)

It was around this time that Maine builders are presumed to have been working on the wood-and-canvas design; however, a connection has not been traced between the developments on either side of the Canadian/American border.

In 1882 the American Canoeing Association held its annual regatta in Peterborough, where many Americans became familiar with the Peterborough developments, if they were not already familiar. Could this be how the Maine invention was first conceived?

One year later the beginnings of the Peterborough Canoe Company began to take shape. Stephenson suffered two upheavals: His twenty-year-old son died, and the Canadian Pacific Railway built through Peterborough, uprooting his boat shop. It was almost like starting anew: Stephenson got use of a building next to the abandoned Cobourg Railway station and happened to meet Colonel James Z. Rogers, a local businessman, who was interested in his activities, particularly in the new cedar rib canoe. This was an important meeting of minds as Rogers would eventually create the Peterborough Canoe Company proper.

Meanwhile things were brewing south of the border. In Canton, New York, Rushton was making a name for himself building canoes of lapstrake cedar. The American Canoe Association (A.C.A.) held its first regatta in 1880 at Lake George, New York. Peterborough canoeist Thomas Henry Wallace apparently made quite an impression by winning the main event in an open racing canoe that by all accounts would have borne closer resemblance to a racing scull. Apparently, he won, "while nonchalantly smoking his pipe and pausing to scoop a drink of water." His prize, which he brought back to the Peterborough area, was an American canoe, one of the expensive "Rob Roy" types—shorter, fatter, and more adapted to sailing races and double paddles. The win cemented an association with both the A.C.A. and the Rob Roy style of boats among the Peterborough area builders and outdoorsmen.

Stephenson was still tinkering. In the winter of 1882–83 he designed a hybrid of his past experiments. Evolved from the earlier basswood plank canoe, hardwood ribs were still used, but made lighter, steamed and bent sharply and spaced closer together. Then the craft was planked tightly with thin strips of cedar shiplapped and fitted snugly together. It was a fastidious construction, but as patterns were developed to accommodate the complicated curves of the canoe's gore, the method gained popularity. Finally, the canoe that we now know as the Peterborough canoe had emerged.

It was a rush to have it patented because local competitors were anxious to copy it, along with the Americans, who would be flooding in for the A.C.A. regatta at nearby Stoney Lake in a few months. The patent was obtained on July 17, 1883, processed in Ottawa on August 9, and filed in Washington on August 13 of the same year.

By then, Stephenson's wife was terminally ill. He was a designer, not a businessman, so he decided to sell out to Rogers, including the Canadian and American patents he had recently obtained. While Stephenson continued to work for Rogers on a contractual basis, Rogers became the owner of the then named Ontario Canoe Company after the 1883 A.C.A. regatta.

After his wife died, Stephenson left Peterborough for a while and worked in Ottawa for Algonquin logging baron J. R. Booth. He returned in the mid-1890s anxious to tinker again. He married a woman twenty-nine years his junior. In 1899, at the age of sixty-nine, he fathered a son, and suddenly had a family to support with little means to do it. He worked independently on ideas for mechanizing paddle making, and he built a new canoe form at the age of eighty-one. In 1920 the final Stephenson shop was dismantled, and two months later, the "Father of the Peterborough Canoe" passed away at the age of ninety.

The Ontario Canoe Company

These "Open Canadian" canoes being built in Peterborough were not at once a hit. An American camp song jibed that a canoe without a sail was like "a monkey without a tail." The *Peterborough Examiner* countered that Peterborough was the "birthplace of the form of canoe which may be excused for ranking as the best of the many varieties in vogue."

In 1887 the American magazine *Forest and Stream* published a comment on the Canadian canoe that emphasized its lack of decks, a misnomer for indeed it had decks and they were essential for the construction of the craft; however, they appeared virtually nonexistent when compared to the kayaklike canoes popular elsewhere:

> *The typical Canadian Canoe, such a craft as may be found on nearly every sheet of water in Canada, is a craft of about 30 in. of beam and 12 in. of depth for 16 ft. of length. She has a flat floor with a quick turn at the bilge and her topsides generally fall in a little. Her lines are, while long, full enough to give her great carrying capacity, and she will rise to a choppy sea without waiting to be expostulated with. Decks she has none, except a pretence thereat, at bow and stern, which is purely ornamental, and her stem is peculiar to herself alone, as are the peculiar curves of her stem and stern piece. Her internal fittings are of the simplest description. If she is a rib and batten, floorboards are buttoned to her bottom. If she has a smooth interior, there is nothing but thwarts, solid pieces of timber that not only keep the whole craft from spreading, but that serve as kneeling rests. Her outfit consists of a pair of leeboards, that can be strapped to a thwart when in use and when idle fold into small compass, a lateen mainsail, occasionally a jigger, and a couple of single-bladed paddles.*

By 1883 a "preliminary" catalogue of the Rogers' Ontario Canoe Company showed that all the canoes at that time were the Open Canadian style, similar in shape to the birchbarks. But Rogers was eager to capitalize on every market possible, and that included styles in vogue with the A.C.A. members. Rogers planned to add stock "as fast as possible ... to supply anything our patrons may require in the shape of canoes...." By 1892 Rogers also included smooth skin and lapstrake skiffs and steam launches from twenty to fifty feet in length.

Throughout the history of canoe building, every challenge was met. In 1883 Rushton produced his eleven-pound "Sairy Gamp" made famous by the tiny writer for *Forest and Stream* magazine, George

Washington Sears, "Nessmuk." Not to be outdone, Rogers' Ontario Canoe Company responded to the competition with a new one-man canoe claimed to be far superior in strength. Unlike the Sairy Gamp, Rogers' canoe included thwarts, decks, and floorboards. Perhaps tongue in cheek, Rogers later said that unlike the Sairy Gamp that was paddled by "one small person," his were paddled by "almost two hundred canoeists."

As the nineteenth century neared its end, major changes were afoot in the canoe market, which led directly to Chestnut's pre-eminence in the world of canoe building. Chestnut, as well as Old Town and others, owe their success to those turbulent times. Canoeing had been dominated by the affluent who were dedicated to emulating the pioneer/Indian spirit, but in European style and elegance. As more and more immigrants with little money to spend were achieving leisure time, they needed a less expensive canoe. As well, those involved in surveying, resource development, hunting, and fishing required the new, more practical Open Canadian canoes.

The all-wood builders—those in Peterborough and Rushton south of the border who just a few years earlier could barely keep up with the burgeoning demand—found themselves for the first time with unsold stock and heightening competition due to an economic downslide and a drop in the A.C.A. membership. Then came the final blow to nearly half a century of the prominence of canoeing as an elegant activity: Americans took on a new recreational pastime. By the 1890s the construction of good roads brought a new sport: pedalling the penny-farthing. The future of canoeing now clearly lay in a practical craft, leaving the hallmark Victorian elegance a thing of the past. Even Rushton switched to the Open Canadian canoes, relying on a stiff American import duty for a competitive edge.

The Peterborough Canoe Company

Almost every canoe builder in history has been devastated, at one time or another, by a fire. Rogers' Ontario Canoe Company was no exception. On May 9, 1892, fire struck. Everything except the office and one storehouse burned to the ground. The setback was devastating. Insurance, at a rate of 9 per cent, had been out of the question.

The fire resulted in unemployment for many skilled canoe builders, and spurred a flurry of new activities in the Peterborough area. Immediately, competitors began to capture Rogers' market, and his craftsmen. A few months after the fire, the Canadian Canoe Company was organized with some of Rogers' builders. The firm's name capitalized on the then ubiquitous term "Canadian canoe." In the same year Robert Strickland, son of Samuel Strickland, started up again in Lakefield, setting up his son who had been working with Thomas Gordon.

Meanwhile, Rogers struggled to rebuild a small portion of his operations, but he was extremely short of funds. Before the year was out, four Peterborough investors, with $10,000 in capital, built a brick factory on a former mill site in a blatant attempt to put him out of business. The front sign read "The Peterborough Canoe Company, We have succeeded to the business of the original builder of the Peterborough Canoe." An 1896 business directory indicates the Peterborough Canoe Company boasted of the high standards of the canoes but also attested to manufacturing camping goods, furniture, and office fittings. Rather than fight, Rogers came on board as manager, bringing with him his experience and the original Stephenson patents. He later became a major shareholder in the company.

Rogers was in his element as a large-scale manager. The capitalization on the Peterborough name proved extremely successful. He took the demarcation "Peterborough" off the original wide-board basswood, and put it first on the cedar rib canoe, then on what was to become the most popular model, the Cedarstrip. He wasn't shy with the name: The metallic label on the canoe decks read "The Peter-borough Canoe, The Peterborough Canoe Company, Peterborough Canada." (All three models originated with Stephenson.)

In January 1918 the Peterborough Canoe Company burned to the ground. This time it was immediately rebuilt on the same site. During the inter-war years, it was managed by Rogers' son, Claude H. Rogers, and William Richard-son, who played a prominent role in the later merger with Chestnut. They acquired the troubled English Canoe Company in 1923. An unexpected event in that same year led to the Peterborough Canoe Company and the Canadian Canoe Company—thus encompassing almost all of the major Peterborough builders—moving via a merger under the name of Canadian Watercraft Limited east to New Brunswick, where the Chestnut Company had been, for the last quarter century, their principal competitor.

The Chestnut Canoe Company

The Chestnut Family

One of the many myths surrounding the Chestnut canoe is that the name has something to do with chestnut wood. In fact, the Chestnut story has nothing to do with *Castanea dentata,* the North American chestnut tree. It has a great deal to do with the Chestnut family.

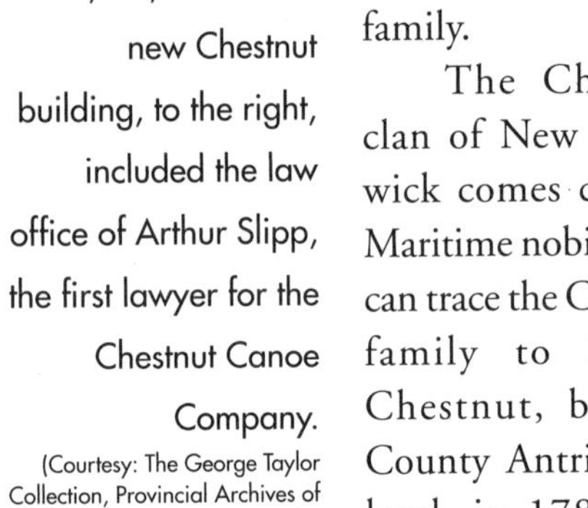

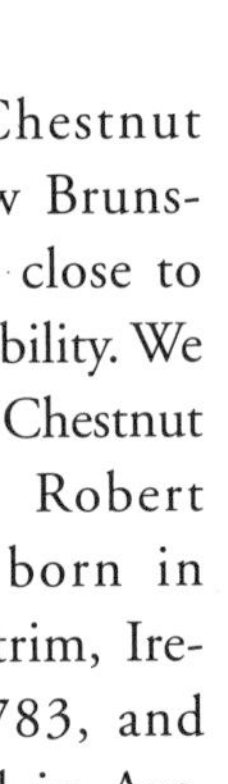

R. Chestnut & Sons store, left, 1900. The new Chestnut building, to the right, included the law office of Arthur Slipp, the first lawyer for the Chestnut Canoe Company.
(Courtesy: The George Taylor Collection, Provincial Archives of New Brunswick.)

The Chestnut clan of New Brunswick comes close to Maritime nobility. We can trace the Chestnut family to Robert Chestnut, born in County Antrim, Ireland, in 1783, and who settled in Ayr, Scotland, nineteen years later. His son, also named Robert, was born in Scotland and arrived in Saint John in 1834, after surviving a near fatal shipwreck at sea. Details of the disaster are not fully known, but the junior Robert Chestnut was awarded the key to the city of Saint John for bravery in rescuing victims of the wreck.

He must have quickly immersed himself in Canadian life. Robert Chestnut soon married a Saint John girl, Margaret Anthony, who gave birth to their son named Henry in 1835. The following year, Robert opened a hardware store on Fredericton's Phoenix Square. That year a second son, Enoch, was born. In 1858 the family business was incorporated as R. Chestnut & Sons. The hardware enterprise became the backbone of the Chestnut family's financial interests and lasted almost one hundred years.

The business of R. Chestnut & Sons prospered and expanded its market in "frontier" Fredericton. It became to Fredericton what Sears Roebuck, Eaton's, or Simpsons was to modern cities by expanding to carry everything from clothing to appliances to sporting goods. The latter captured the family's fancy and became the heart of the operation that would ultimately lead to the Chestnut canoe. Chestnut departed, though, from almost every other canoe builder in history. Where most canoe innovations came from the tinkering of craftsmen and backwoodsmen, the original Chestnut was the product of rich sporting gents employing skilled craftsmen to build both "stolen" (or borrowed) designs and new designs, especially those inspired by their sporting lifestyle. The company gradually made many innovations and built a fleet of canoes that were exported around the world.

The formative years of the young Chestnuts,

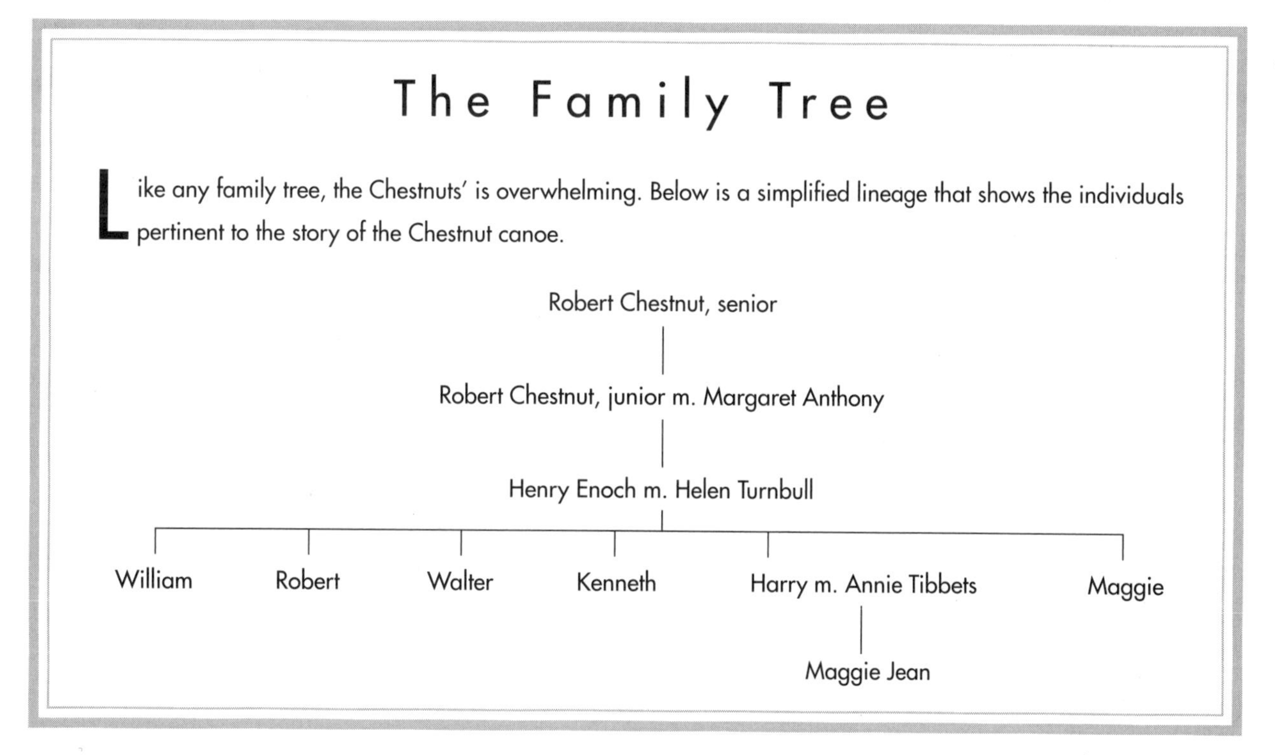

The Family Tree

Like any family tree, the Chestnuts' is overwhelming. Below is a simplified lineage that shows the individuals pertinent to the story of the Chestnut canoe.

especially Harry and William, primed them to be the future operators of the Chestnut Canoe Company. They acquainted themselves, both professionally and personally, with the backwoods sporting life of the new "frontier" country. Harry and William grew up paddling birchbarks, and knew them well. They had learned paddling from the same Malecite whose birchbark canoes they owned. By the time Robert Chestnut's sons were teenagers, canoe travel had become a way of life for them.

They journeyed up and down the St. John River, the Oromocto, the Washademoak, and the Jemseg. They explored Grand Lake. They even took their Malecite birchbark on an adventurous journey—half by rail and half by water—all the way to Florida. They spent most of that winter nudging from one coastal island to another. In spring they sold their canoe and returned to New Brunswick as Pullman passengers.

So when these newfangled wood-and-canvas canoes began to find their way into New Brunswick, Harry and William could easily appreciate the importance of what they were seeing. These canoes were prohibitive to import because of stiff duty rates. No one was producing them in Canada, so why shouldn't they? By then the Chestnut family had both the facilities and the market at their fingertips.

Robert Chestnut

As one of the major Fredericton merchants and a force in the commercial life of Central New Brunswick, Robert Chestnut had wide interests. Besides running R. Chestnut & Sons, which sold every conceivable item required for nineteenth-century life, he operated a lumber mill down river; became an agent for the Albion Metal Works and a director of the Bank of Fredericton; he also tried to remain active in civic affairs. He was especially interested in the city's heritage, assuring the upkeep of the monuments in the Old Burial Grounds.

Henry Chestnut

Robert's oldest son Henry headed the local merchant's association that lobbied on tax and other commercial matters and also was involved in town projects, such as the installing of a town clock in the new city hall tower. Henry Chestnut also became principal stockholder in Joseph Risteen's window and door factory on King Street, which was instrumental in opening the Chestnut Canoe Company.

In 1865, six years after his father's death, twenty-year-old Henry Chestnut married Helen Turnbull from Bear River, Nova Scotia, and over the next ten years, they had six children: William, Robert, Walter, Kenneth, Harry, and Maggie. The Chestnut children were educated during an era in which hard work and a keen appreciation of the value of a dollar were considered essential assets. Victorian Fredericton possessed dozens of small manufacturing and commercial operations engaged in trade throughout the Saint John River valley, as well as with other provinces and the United States. Fredericton was often called the Elm or Celestial City, for its tranquil beauty and its predominance in commercial life of the Upper St. John River valley, though it competed with Saint John for influence along the lower sixty miles of the river between the two cities.

William Chestnut

William Turnbull Chestnut is one of the two Chestnut brothers who started the Chestnut Canoe Company. He, along with his eventual business partner, Harry, enjoyed the outdoors, hunting and fishing with some of New Brunswick's famous guides. Though he shared Harry's adeptness at wilderness sports, he didn't possess the business skills or interest of his younger brother. William was instrumental in organizing a New Brunswick sportsman's booth at the 1901 Chicago Sportsman's Show that featured animal trophies and a log cabin. Members of the Association of New Brunswick Guides were also present and eager to arrange hunting and fishing trips for Americans.

If not an avid businessman, his people skills were impressive. His friendly manner enabled him to get inside the rival Old Town Canoe factory in 1904 and convince ten skilled workers to move from Maine to Fredericton to build canoes for Chestnut. Enraged by the raid, Old Town launched a lawsuit against R. Chestnut & Sons, although it seemed to have little effect on the Chestnut business.

William had equal equity with his brother in the fledgling Chestnut Canoe Company, but he drifted out of the operation as Harry dominated business matters. By the 1920s, William spent much of his time elsewhere, often hunting and fishing throughout northern New Brunswick. He died in 1936.

A group of Fredericton businessmen stop for lunch while on a snowshoe tramp. William Chestnut is third from right and Harry Chestnut is fourth from right.
(Courtesy: The George Taylor Collection, The Provincial Archives of New Brunswick.)

Harry Chestnut

A prominent real estate owner, Harry was an active member of Fredericton's recreational clubs, including the Automobile and Boating Club and the Tennis Club. Harry was also a natural athlete and excelled at all sports. An outstanding skater as well as a bit of a showman, he and his friends would often stage impromptu skating displays at the Arctic Rink while the Fredericton Brass Band accompanied their feats. In an historical commentary of the times he is referred to as "the celebrated Harry Chestnut." Among his claims to fame, Harry Chestnut owned one of Fredericton's first automobiles and according to the *Daily Gleaner,* had one of New Brunswick's first auto accidents in 1904.

Harry Chestnut (in light suit) at Camp Comfort, early autumn 1886.
(Courtesy: The George Taylor Collection, The Provincial Archives of New Brunswick.)

Harry and his older brother William were the two most outgoing of the Chestnut boys and both loved the outdoors. Their passion for hunting and fishing became legendary as they befriended some of New Brunswick's famous guides, including the Ogilvy brothers. Harry hunted and fished throughout North America but especially loved the waters of the Miramichi and Restigouche. He always employed his trusted guide, Albert Goodine, when salmon fishing in New Brunswick.

These two brothers were the instigators of the canoe business, although Harry Chestnut became the best known and the mastermind behind the Chestnut Canoe Company's rapid success. Besides founding and running the canoe plant, Harry assumed his father's role in the hardware business after Henry's death in 1909. Harry ran the retail business until financial pressures and his responsibilities with the canoe company led him to sell R. Chestnut & Sons to hardware competitor James S. Neill & Sons in 1924.

Consistent with his appreciation of the wilderness, Harry was concerned about the growing foreign control of New Brunswick's salmon rivers. He was able to convince the Provincial Minister of Lands and Mines to reserve a section of the Restigouche River called the Soldier's Run for provincial anglers. Beginning about 1918, this practice of reserving portions of the crown salmon waters for resident licences was expanded to other rivers to ensure New Brunswickers access to angling waters. (The practice is still in effect today.)

Harry Chestnut married Annie Tibbets of Fredericton who later, along with their daughter, Maggie Jean, assumed an important role in managing the Chestnut Canoe Company in the 1940s. Harry Chestnut died at age sixty-nine in 1941.

Kenneth Chestnut

The youngest brother, Kenneth, lived much of his life in Victoria, British Columbia He remained close enough to the family business that when asked by the Fredericton Historical Society to write a history of the Chestnut Canoe Company, he was able to piece together a short but accurate account of the company's first fifty years.

Annie Chestnut (née Tibbets)

Miss Annie Tibbets was the eldest daughter of Deputy Provincial Secretary R. W. Tibbets. In 1902 she married Harry Chestnut in a large Methodist church wedding in downtown Fredericton. After a three-week honeymoon in Upper Canada, the couple settled into married life and Annie began working earnestly for charitable organizations in the growing provincial capital.

In 1911 she became the first president of the University Alumnae Society and inspired her daughter, Maggie Jean, to continue her university work. In 1939, when Harry's health was failing, Annie was appointed to the Chestnut Canoe Company's board and along with her daughter, was given a single share of the company's stock. She worked with the company over the next fifteen years. After her husband Harry and her daughter Maggie Jean had died, Annie was the last Chestnut involved in the Chestnut Canoe Company.

She worked closely with the Chestnut manager and secretary-treasurer, Harold Smith, as well as the then present Peterborough partners. Annie attended her last meeting of the Chestnut shareholders on October 14, 1954. Probably more by coincidence than design the peak years in the Chestnut company and the onset of its gradual decline coincided with the end of the Chestnut family involvement in the company.

Maggie Jean

Like the Chestnuts before her, Maggie Jean was keenly interested in sports and the outdoors, as well as being committed to community affairs. A local golf champion, she graduated from the University of New Brunswick in 1927 and two years later, received her Master's degree from the University of Toronto. After graduating, Maggie Jean worked with her father, learning the canoe business and sharpening her business skills.

As her father's health began to deteriorate in the late 1930s, she had begun to dominate in the Chestnut office, and acquired a reputation as an astute business woman. In the 1939 reorganization, Maggie Jean had been appointed secretary-treasurer. After her father's death in 1941, Maggie Jean became much more involved in the canoe business. In 1943, after assuming the managing director position, she became president.

Unmarried and able to devote her full attention to her outside interests, Maggie Jean became devoted to university affairs and fund-raising activities. She served as president of the University Alumnae Society, and she became a member of the University Senate. Her work with the Red Cross during World War II in raising awareness about the need for blood donations was well known throughout New Brunswick.

With the help of Lord Beaverbrook among others, the Maggie Jean Chestnut Residence opened in 1949. In the same year, at age forty-four, Maggie Jean passed away, after eight years of running the family's canoe business. As one of Fredericton's best-known citizens, her funeral, at her home on Waterloo Row, was well attended. Her grave is located in the family plot at the Old Burial Ground on Brunswick Street.

Fishing on the St. John River. This is a picture of part of the Chestnut family likely taken before the start of the Chestnut Canoe Company. The canoe is an all-wood Peterborough style. (Courtesy: Donald Fraser.)

Evolution of the Chestnut Canoe Company

While the history of the Chestnut Canoe Company is inexorably linked with that of the Peterborough builders, both as predecessor and later as partners, Chestnut is a company devoted almost entirely to the wood-and-canvas design. In examining the wood-and-canvas development, our story takes a detour, south of the New Brunswick border, to Maine. As stated earlier, Gerrish is the builder generally attributed with "inventing" the wood-and-canvas canoe.

The canoes William and Harry Chestnut purchased at the shores of the St. John River would have been from the second tier of Maine builders. Three companies quickly sprang up in the area surrounding Bangor, Maine, after Gerrish—E. M. White, B. N. Morris, and the Old Town Canoe Company. White and Morris catered to the professional market, with big, flat-bottomed canoes, ideal for extended journeys on the east coast's large and abundant rivers because they were quick to respond to paddle or pole when travelling up and down rapids. Old Town catered more to the recreational market, and successfully making the transition to synthetic canoes, is still in business today.

The hunters who travelled the length of the St. John River to Fredericton were professionals, and it is most likely that the canoes the Chestnut brothers were becoming familiar with were built by White or Morris. These canoes were not Pleasure models, and one intention of the Chestnut brothers was to produce a line of canoes suitable for the crowds that swarmed the St. John River at Fredericton on summer days. These designs were entirely the conception of the Chestnut brothers—adopting the lines of the local Malecite bark canoes—and were the first in a long line of Chestnut designs that would make the company famous.

The history of canvas canoe construction in Canada begins in 1897 or 1898 at Fredericton when, probably a Morris canoe was on exhibit at R. Chestnut & Sons hardware store. Across the street at Jack J. Moore's boatbuilding shop, Moore had noticed that the Morris canoe was being admired by enthusiastic canoeists. Of all the Maine builders, the B. N. Morris Canoe Company of Veazie, Maine, was considered the leading canvas canoe builder during the 1890s, and these canoes were beginning to appear in New

Brunswick. It is not known how the Morris canoe on display was acquired by William Chestnut.

Jack Moore had been building all kinds of boats, including lapstrake wooden canoes for hunting and fishing parties at his Phoenix Square shop on Queen Street. While they were much in demand by guides, the arrival of the new canvas canoe almost immediately changed people's appetites, especially when William Chestnut, returning from trying the canvas canoe at his Pine Bluff camp, pronounced the Morris canoe superior in every way.

Jack Moore, especially, knew the needs of hunting and fishing parties in the New Brunswick wilderness at the turn of the nineteenth century. He and his famous brother, champion bear killer Adam Moore had fished and hunted in New Brunswick all their lives. Adam Moore was the most renowned sporting guide in the province. In the late 1800s, when wealthy Americans began to flock to the region to tap the rich bounty of unexploited woods and waters, Adam Moore had built two sporting lodges for non-resident sportsmen. He was also vice-president of the newly formed New Brunswick Guides Association and began to attend displays at sportsmen's exhibits in the States to attract clientele. Moore was quite successful in luring sportsmen to the New Brunswick wilderness, but he encountered a shortage of wilderness vehicles to transport his visiting "sports" and turned to his brother the boatbuilder for help.

The first canvas canoe was a copy of that Morris on display, built by Moore and his assistant Allan Meads. Undoubtedly, the Chestnut brothers had a hand in it, too.

Within two years, Adam Moore and the other outfitters were receiving regular deliveries of his brother's hunting and fishing canoes. They cost thirty-five dollars each, which amounted to about a ten-dollar savings over importing the Maine canoes. Over the next fifty years, the New Brunswick outfitters would play an important part in the development of the Chestnut Canoe Company. Guides and their canoeing needs would inspire the company to design new models, including their famous salmon fishing canoes, the Ogilvies.

Men of Camp Comfort Island are just one example of the popular "sports" camps that cropped up in New Brunswick. Canoes were used for travel and sport. (Courtesy: The George Taylor Collection, The Provincial Archives of New Brunswick.)

When Jack Moore's first canvas canoe was finished, William and Harry Chestnut praised the eighteen-footer as equal in all respects to the Morris canoe. They offered to sell at R. Chestnut & Sons any canoe Moore could make and offered to help market his canoes. Jack Moore's experiment was over; he was ready to start building canvas canoes in larger quantities.

The Chestnut brothers soon hired Jack Moore to work full time for them building canoes. The following season, Jack Moore and Allan Meads continued to build custom boats and canoes at their cramped quarters next to city hall. A steam yacht was built for Fredericton businessman Alfred Branscombe; while for the Chestnut brothers, canvas canoes were built. As the canvas canoe continued to gain popularity the small, two-man operation struggled to meet the demand.

In 1904, the *Daily Gleaner* reported that the Chestnut brothers, William and Harry, had begun building canoes in the upstairs section of the J. C. Risteen sash and door company while an addition to their factory was in progress. The newspaper reported that Allan Meads was the foreman in charge of production, but the work was only being undertaken on a small scale as no experienced workmen could be located. The *Daily Gleaner* also predicted that the next season would see the company able to finally supply the heavy demand for canoes in three lengths: sixteen, eighteen, and nineteen feet.

By February of the following year, the *Daily Gleaner*'s prediction came to pass. With a full modern building, installed with electric lighting and a gas engine, R. Chestnut & Sons owned the only canoe factory in Canada building the wood-and-canvas canoe. On a sales trip throughout the Maritmes, Montreal, and Ottawa, Harry Chestnut had secured orders for seventy-five canoes, including a five hundred dollar order from the Grand Trunk Pacific Railway for canoes to be used in surveying work. The little canoe business was beginning to look good. Canoe orders were pouring in. William Chestnut had solved their skilled manpower problem by inviting Old Town's experienced workers to move to Fredericton. Old Town not only filed a lawsuit but threatened to set up a canoe factory in Canada to counter the hostile raid. A small business of building a few canoes was one thing, but the Chestnut brothers were becoming competitive with their new factory and other canoe builders were becoming concerned!

Chestnut's charter in 1907 shows that it was conceived with ambition by the following officers: Henry Chestnut, president; Willard Kitchen, vice-president; Harry Chestnut, secretary-treasurer and managing director. Thus the seeds were sown for a family empire.

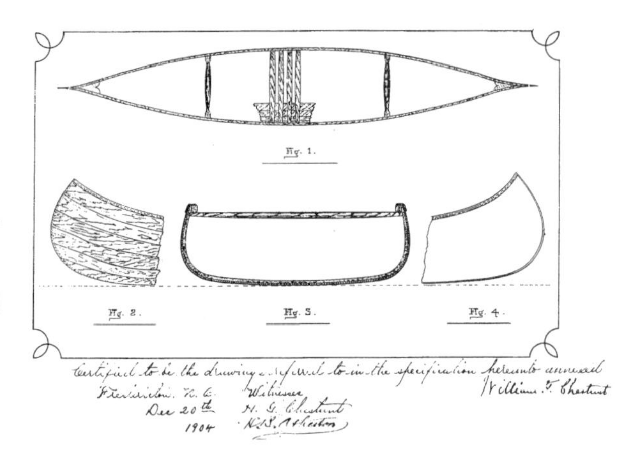

William Chestnut's patent of 1905 (filed December 1904) gives a generalized account of wood-and-canvas construction: "It is to be understood that in carrying out my invention certain changes might be made in the details of construction without materially departing from the spirit of the invention. I, therefore, do not limit myself to the exact details of construction shown and described herein." (Courtesy: Canada Patent Office.)

Chestnut Patents its Canoe

In his Queen Street office, next door to the Chestnuts, company lawyer Arthur Slipp helped Harry Chestnut develop a strategy to secure a Canadian patent on the wood-and-canvas canoe construction technique that Jack Moore had copied for them from a Morris canoe. These letters of patent would create a protected monopoly. Thus, on February 28, 1905, a remarkable event took place that was to shake the world of Canadian canoe builders for years to come: Combining business sense, and a good deal of luck, R. Chestnut & Sons obtained a Canadian patent on the wood-and-canvas construction technique. As a 1908 catalogue cautioned: "We hereby warn anyone in Canada against using our construction."

One wonders how such a broadly defined technology as the wood-and-canvas canoe, evolved by so many different people over hundreds of years, could ever have been patented. However, acquiring a patent in Canada at the turn of the century was fairly easy: one petitioned the provincial government—in this case New Brunswick—to grant a patent licence on the basis that yours was the only company engaged in the procedure, and the other provinces would recognize it as long as no one could prove to have superseded your request. Patents lasted an incredibly short time—the original Chestnut patent lasted six years.

Maintaining and defending a patent was another matter, especially as Chestnut began to sell canvas canoes to customers of the Peterborough Canoe Company, primarily the Hudson's Bay Company. To this point, the Peterborough canoe had been used almost exclusively in Canada. But within a year, Chestnut would be running a sixteen-man work force year-round and shipping its first carload of canoes to Vancouver, establishing a Canada-wide presence. The wood-and-canvas canoe was taking over the entire canoe market in North America, and Chestnut, on paper at any rate, held exclusive rights in Canada.

Not content to watch its business decline, the Peterborough company challenged the Chestnut patent in the marketplace and in the courts. The patent was certainly a thorn in the sides of Chestnut's competitors, although its power seemed to be based more on fear than legal action. Other companies continued to build wood-and-canvas canoes, though not many models. It appears the patent was not completely enforceable. It was more likely Chestnut's specialty in and high number of different wood-and-canvas models, combined with their highly publicized fear mongering, that kept the patent convincing in the public eye. Undoubtedly, the patent, even if out of date, had some weight in encouraging the later merger of the great companies. Peterborough tried to keep their wood-and-canvas market, which was all-important to the survival of the large company. By contrast, the Chestnut Canoe Company was a small family business and seemed to be always swamped by the orders it was receiving, especially in its new role as monopoly holder.

Incorporating Chestnut

It was not until 1907 that Harry Chestnut decided to obtain a company charter and incorporate his fledgling canoe company. That summer marked the tenth year R. Chestnut & Sons had been dealing in canoes, and the construction of their third factory, located on York Street. With orders coming in from around the world, it was time to reorganize and officially launch a separate canoe business, which they called the Chestnut Canoe Company.

Like most entrepreneurs, the Chestnut brothers were concerned about losing control if they incorporated, but Arthur Slipp, their lawyer, made sure that Harry, William, and their father, Henry, were named as the provisional company directors. With forty-eight thousand dollars in capital stock at one hundred dollars per share, the Chestnuts also retained the majority ownership. Only two non-family members had a sizable stake in the new company: Kingsclear merchant and railway contractor Willard Kitchen was issued one hundred shares, and Saint John lumberman Ned Murchie was given fifty. To recognize Jack Moore's importance to the emerging enterprise as its pioneer builder, five shares were given to his wife, Amelia Moore. Five also went to Arthur Slipp. William and Harry each retained one hundred twenty-five shares of the four hundred eighty units offered.

Chestnut Canoe Factory on York Street under construction in 1907.
(Courtesy: The George Taylor Collection, Provincial Archives of New Brunswick.)

Together they had twenty-five thousand dollars of the capital stock. Bylaw No. 5 of the new company clearly stated that all business transactions required a quorum of not less than three shareholders, with not less than twenty-five thousand dollars of the company's capital stock—family control was ensured.

On August 27, 1907, Harry Chestnut and Arthur Slipp obtained the incorporation papers signed by New Brunswick's Lieutenant-Governor, the Honourable L. John Tweedie, and the Chestnut Canoe Company was incorporated. In November 1907 the Chestnut brothers gathered at Willard Kitchen's office and celebrated their new operation. They had bigger plans than selling guns at their father's hardware business and more ambitious dreams than the entire St. John River valley could deliver—they had set their sights on the entire Canadian canoe market.

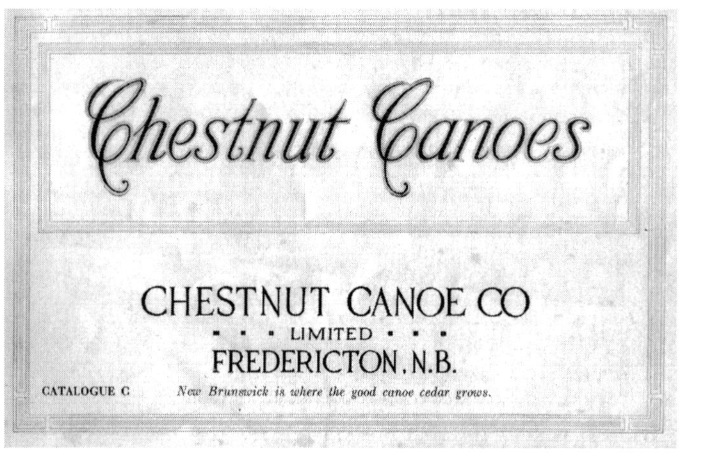

Chestnut Canoes
CHESTNUT CANOE CO
LIMITED
FREDERICTON, N.B.
CATALOGUE C
New Brunswick is where the good canoe cedar grows.

The Chestnut Canoe Company's catalogues captured the interest of a wide audience. The title page of a series C catalogue, shown here, is an early example in the A to H series published. (Courtesy: Jill Dean.)

The new company's first year ended successfully. While no dividend was declared for stockholders, the managing director and secretary-treasurer, Harry Chestnut, was voted a salary of eighteen hundred dollars, a sizable sum for what was effectively a part-time business for the Chestnuts, who also ran their father's hardware store among other interests. While their full attention may not have been on building canoes, the business was beginning to flourish and to demand more capital investment. Their first year inventory revealed a stock on hand value of almost eighteen thousand dollars. This inventory was comprised of canoes in various stages of construction, different strengths of duck canvas, and plenty of uncut wood.

Over the next four years, capital demands for financing the young company grew. Year end 1911 marked the first payment of a dividend, set at 5 per cent of the issued stock. The following year, a 6 per cent dividend was paid and the managing director's salary was increased to twenty-five hundred dollars. A five hundred dollar bonus was paid the year after. By 1912 the shareholders had agreed to authorize the borrowing of up to twenty-five thousand dollars from the Royal Bank for day-to-day operations. These were years of excellent growth for Chestnut. Canoes were shipped throughout North

America. At the start of World War I, the company began shipping canoes to Europe.

After the war, the Chestnut Canoe Company continued to prosper. In 1920 additional letters of patent were granted by the province to try to reinforce its exclusive hold on the Canadian canvas canoe market. At the same time, the company's capital stock was increased to nine hundred seventy shares at one hundred dollars each, in order to increase its total capital stock to ninety-seven thousand dollars. Two years later it doubled again.

∞

Chestnut's future was inexorably altered during the winter of 1921 when the main York Street factory burned to the ground. Considering that wooden factories maintained round-the-clock furnace stoking and were stocked with such combustibles as cedar shavings, linseed oil, varnishes, and paints, what is really more surprising is that there were not more fires. (There were some, though, who suspected that the York factory fire was no accident.)

The loss of canoes and valuable wood was indeed a setback, but the major problem centred around rebuilding, in particular the cash requirement the now sizable business needed to get started again. Harry was now in his early fifties, and while he was still a keen sportsman and businessman, rebuilding from scratch would take considerable energy and a lot more money than the fire insurance would provide.

With strong demand for product but no inventory to sell, rebuilding would have to be done quickly before another canoe builder could step in to supply Chestnut's customers. The Peterborough Canoe Company's fire had already shown that such an event was a perfect opportunity for a new player to enter the business. The money for construction came from the Royal Bank, which had been loaning the company money for its daily operations. The bank agreed to guarantee sixty thousand dollars towards reconstruction, but for a price. Within two years, the bank would play an instrumental role in the restructuring that would result in a quiet merger between the two major Canadian canoe manufacturers, resulting in a firm that was the culmination

The new York Street factory built after the 1921 fire.

(Courtesy: Harvey Studios ©1985.)

The Snowshoe Catalogue

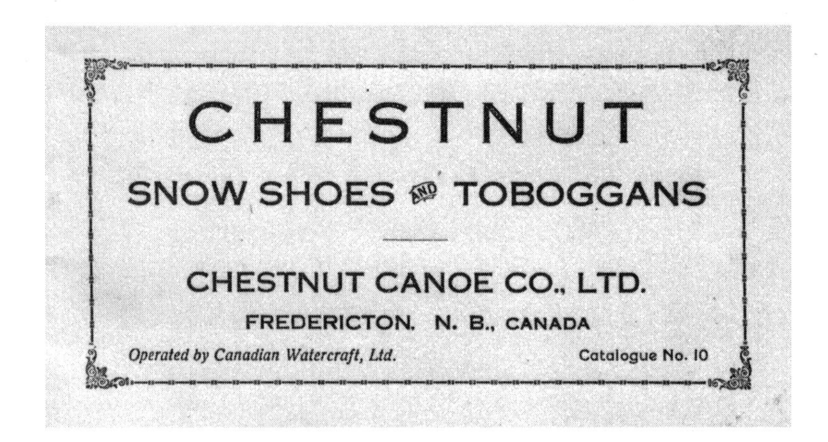
CHESTNUT

SNOW SHOES AND TOBOGGANS

CHESTNUT CANOE CO., LTD.

FREDERICTON. N. B., CANADA

Operated by Canadian Watercraft, Ltd.

Catalogue No. 10

Chestnut Snowshoe Catalogue.
(Courtesy: The Author.)

Chestnut diversified into a number of wooden articles, but none were as important as the snowshoe line. Many swore by Chestnut snowshoes as the best in the world.

The Snow Shoes & Toboggans Catalogue No. 10 is unique not only for its products, but because it is the only advertising literature I have found that openly reveals the Peterborough/Chestnut "merger" under Canadian Watercraft Limited. The cover clearly states "Operated by Canadian Watercraft Ltd." In the back two pages there is reference to the "Peterborough line" of winter sports equipment, including skis, and the "Peterborough HBC Model Dog Sleigh." The pamphlet suggests obtaining the entire Peterborough "Winter Sports Equipment" catalogue either from Peterborough or Chestnut.

of Canadian canoe building enterprises, all the way back to Stephenson.

While the new factory was under construction, two crucial decisions were made which would affect the future of the Chestnut Canoe Company. First, to balance out the seasonal nature of canoe production, Chestnut decided to diversify its business into building snowshoes and toboggans. (Cash flow was always a problem in operating a canoe company because salaries, operating expenses, and material purchases are paid year-round; however, the income comes principally in the spring.) Over time, this move contributed handsomely to Chestnut's financial picture as tens of thousands of snowshoes were produced. Prime Minister Mackenzie King declared the Chestnut Canoe Company an essential war industry, which allowed it to remain open and acquire wood that would otherwise have been rationed.

Second, Harry Chestnut dropped his role as office manager of R. Chestnut & Sons to devote his full attention to managing the canoe company. The family's hardware store was losing steam as canoe building took priority. Within two years, it was sold to the O'Neill sporting and hardware business that exists today. The sale of the hardware business provided the much needed cash for the rebuilding of the York Street factory. Payments to the bank were still due, and Harry and William had been personally liable for the accumulating debt of their canoe company as they gradually bought out their former partners. If anything was twisting Chestnut's "arm" for a conciliatory gesture towards the competition, this was it.

At the same time, the Peterborough Canoe Company had problems of its own. It was not particularly known for or good at wood-and-canvas design and construction. Furthermore, Chestnut's patent was consistently returning to haunt the company. It was a good time for something to give.

Eighty thousand pairs of snowshoes were shipped during World War II.

(Courtesy: The Provincial Archives of New Brunswick.)

The Rise and Fall of Canoe Corporations

The first Chestnut canoe factory, c. 1904, was located on King Street in Fredericton.
(Courtesy: The George Taylor Collection, The Provincial Archives of New Brunswick.)

No one kept an accurate account of the merger between the Chestnut and Peterborough canoe companies, but legend has it that Harry Chestnut and W. A. Richardson met at some point riding the rails westward on the sportsmen show circuit. They realized they could help each other more by joining forces than continuing to compete: Chestnut had the patent for the most popular design and Peterborough had a great distribution network. Imagine, two great canoe companies in competition, except that the canoes were all the same. But customers didn't need to know about the merger. The competition would serve to increase sales. Chestnut could concentrate on building wood-and-canvas canoes. By labelling many of them Peterborough, they would sell the larger numbers of canoes they needed to ensure the success of the rebuilt York Street plant. Peterborough could concentrate on what they did best—all-wood canoes and boats—obtaining most of their wood-and-canvas canoes from Chestnut. Together, the Peterborough and the Chestnut canoe companies perpetrated one of the greatest shell games in Canadian business. Only at the end of the Fredericton assembly line did a wood-and-canvas canoe receive a brand-name.

At the time of the merger, the story of the Chestnut and the Peterborough canoe companies becomes the story of a new entity called Canadian Watercraft Limited. By the 1920s all the Peterborough builders had migrated to the Peterborough Canoe Company. Peterborough had just bought the remains of the William English Canoe Company. Within Canadian Watercraft Limited, Chestnut became the minority shareholder, although within the new structure it still retained complete control over its own operations. In just a few years Canadian Watercraft Limited would buy the Canadian Canoe Company, supplying it, too, with Chestnut canoes. From 1923 the history of the Chestnut and the Peterborough canoe companies becomes intertwined. For

From 1918 to World War II, Chestnut's catalogue format remained unchanged. They were demarcated through the years by a letter on the first page—Catalogue A through H. Each edition can be given an approximate date by examining the "testimonials" which appear throughout the text.
(Courtesy: Jill Dean.)

decades, paddlers would argue around campfires over the relative merits of Chestnut, Peterborough, and Canadian canoes. Few canoeists ever knew that they were all one and the same.

Considering all the parties involved in the merger, not just the canoe companies but the banks to which Chestnut was in debt, the transformation into Canadian Watercraft Limited was complicated. The Royal Bank's managers, George Taylor and J. M. Carleton, were issued five hundred Chestnut shares "in trust" on March 20, 1923, in order to secure Chestnut's debt. This was a "stay of execution" for Chestnut, which was still recovering from the fire. That summer, the Chestnut directors passed By-law No. 32A, and agreed to surrender all assets, including whatever remained of the canvas construction patent, to Canadian Watercraft Limited for a price of not less than $125,000, which would be paid in the form of capital stock of the new company.

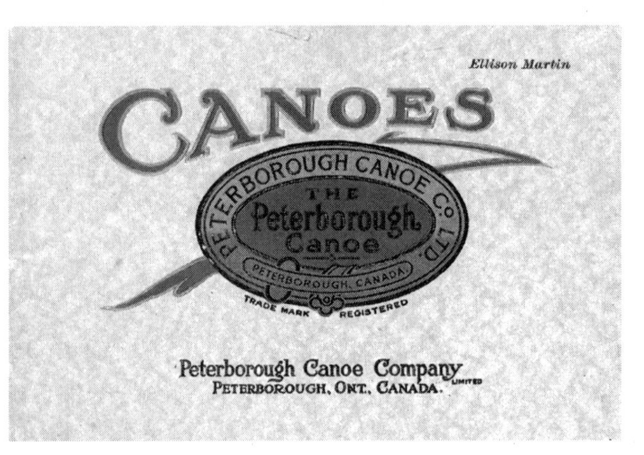

Peterborough Canoe Company's catalogue cover of 1918 features an embossed stamp of the logo. (Courtesy: Jill Dean.)

The effect of this by-law is questionable for two reasons. First, it is doubtful the patent still carried any legal weight. Second, after the by-law, nothing much changed: Peterborough did not significantly increase its construction of wood-and-canvas canoes. Instead, it bought those canoes from Chestnut imprinted with the Peterborough logo.

The Canadian Appraisal Company had been hired to prepare an appraisal and submitted an estimated value of the Chestnut company at $138,395, including $90,000 for the new factory. Machinery and equipment were valued at $31,872 while the then twenty-nine classic Chestnut canoe forms and patterns—the heart of the Chestnut Canoe Company—were valued at a mere $4899.50. (Interestingly, the next appraisal was not done for almost forty years and would assess the company's market value at below the 1923 appraised value. Chestnut's then forty-five canoe forms were judged by the appraisers as virtually worthless in terms of re-sale.)

However, Chestnut did not get a particularly rosy deal in the merger. Canadian Watercraft Limited would not accept Chestnut's bank debt, only its assets—including its new factory and machinery. Harry Chestnut was forced to assume the liability for all outstanding company debts. In the fall of 1923, an agreement with the bank was reached. (Payment terms must have been satisfactory because on December 6, 1923, the five hundred Royal Bank shares were marked "cancelled.") The same fall, the three remaining Chestnut company directors agreed unanimously that due to Harry Chestnut's "assumption of the outstanding liabilities," all remaining assets of the Chestnut Canoe Company would "be transferred to and become the property of Harry Chestnut," making Harry the sole owner, in name, of the Chestnut Canoe Company. However the company's assets had been passed onto the new enterprise—Canadian Watercraft Limited—with headquarters in Peterborough.

The new holding company issued stock of 4,922 shares split evenly between Peterborough and Fredericton and valued at $492,200. In 1927 Canadian Watercraft Limited purchased the Canadian Canoe Company, finalizing the greatest takeover in the world of canoes. Prior to 1923, the Peterborough Canoe Company catalogues highlighted their wooden canoes and runabouts, with few of the new, more utilitarian wood-and-canvas models. After the merger both the Peterborough and Canadian canoe companies issued new, expanded catalogues that included a list of canoes identical to those sold by Chestnut, but with new names. In terms of canoe building, Fredericton had taken over as the canoe capital of the world, though few canoeists knew it.

Between 1923 and 1938 the combined companies made a total profit of $302,972. Because communication across the country was difficult, in 1938 further reorganization was undertaken "... to simplify the operation, inasmuch as the Canadian Watercraft Limited was a separate Capital organization, and as business with the public was done under the names of 'Peterborough Canoe Company' and 'Chestnut Canoe Company' respectively, and as the Charters of each of these Companies had been kept in force, it was decided to transfer the Assets back to each Company, so that there would be three distinct organizations or Capital structures, the shares of which would be held by Canadian Watercraft Limited." The result was that after the closing of the 1938 accounting period, Canadian Watercraft Limited became a holding company with no fixed assets, instead of an operating company.

This reorganization seemed to work. From 1938 to 1950 Peterborough made an operating profit of $588,387; Chestnut made $418,977 in profit. The post World War II boom created new markets for recreational crafts, and in 1952 Peterborough listed a net operating profit of $246,595. As manager Jack Richardson stated: "The shorter work week, the boom in our economy, and the improved roads into Canadian hinterlands have made and will make boating popular and more a part of our way of life."

Also, at this point, Peterborough was making a lot of paddles—probably it was more successful in this area than Chestnut—and Richardson went on to say that the "demand for paddles is so great we … can't keep up with production," even though production averaged between twelve and fifteen thousand paddles a year.

In 1941 Harry Chestnut died. Management of the Chestnut Canoe Company was passed on to his daughter, Maggie Jean, who had been his assistant for many years. Maggie Jean had no children, so when she died in 1949, her shares went to her mother, Annie. At this point Annie owned all the Chestnut shares, having received them bit by bit from other members of the family.

In 1954 she succumbed to the persistent pressure that had begun in 1923. She sold all her shares of Chestnut to Harold Richardson, a son of W. A. Richardson of the Peterborough company (W. A. Richardson died in 1952.) Peterborough then owned and controlled the Chestnut Canoe Company. The principal step Peterborough took was in 1955 to put one of their own men, George Birch, in the position of manager for Chestnut's operations. Birch later became Chestnut's principal owner.

George Birch

Originally trained as a funeral director/embalmer, he gave up the work due to a health problem. In 1947 George Birch started working on the Peterborough shop floor. After six months he took a position in sales, moving quickly up the management ranks. In 1953 he was given one share of Peterborough "in trust." In 1955 he was sent by the Peterborough head office to manage the Chestnut operations in Fredericton.

Birch brought with him many ideas for expansion: in 1956 the first canvas-covered outboard boats; in 1957 the first molded mahogany outboards and all the fibreglass developments. He noted a difficulty in marketing after the eventual Peterborough Canoe Company closure because Peterborough had marketed up to 80 per cent of Chestnut's production.

In 1958 the Industrial Development Bank (IDB) began loaning money to Peterborough, and the Chestnut shares, owned by Harold Richardson, were used as collateral, falling into the bank's control. Birch bought his first 1414 shares from the bank. (R. E. Whicket, a longstanding plant worker was also given some shares. He's the man pictured holding with one hand the Featherweight above his head in all the catalogues.) In 1965 George Birch arranged the purchase from the IDB of the rest of the Chestnut shares. He bought 52 per cent. Together, his brother John and the company's accountant, Peter Haines, purchased the other 48 per cent.

What George Birch has to say about his years with Chestnut is even more significant when one realizes that when he started working for Peterborough in 1947 the Canadian Watercraft Limited partnership was in full swing. He attests that from his first days with Peterborough, the canoes being sold as Peterboroughs were Chestnuts and that they made up about 90 per cent of the total canoe inventory.

It is also clear that George Birch did not get along with the eventual Lock-Wood management. He was forced to sell his controlling interest to Lock-Wood, and thus he was out of a job. He is one of the few interviewees who is of the opinion that Chestnut could have held on if Lock-Wood had not entered the picture. He supported the piecework contract that Lock-Wood eliminated because of how much more quickly canoes were built. In his example, however, he used fibreglass canoes. Perhaps if George had had his way, he would have been able to modernize Chestnut and bring it successfully into the age of plastics, as Old Town did to the south.

George Birch retired quietly from the canoe scene. He went into real estate sales, where he continues working today.

The Chestnut Canoe Company Under Peterborough Control

The 1950s were good years for the newly owned Chestnut Canoe Company, despite the Chestnut family fading out of the picture. In Chestnut's first full year with George Birch acting as vice-president and managing director, sales had increased to about $350,000 with a pre-tax profit of $23,373 and a declared dividend of $6 for each of 1414 shares.

The Chestnut Canoe success was due also to the large number of experienced and knowledgeable factory workers and veteran supervisors like foreman Merle Burse or canvasser Bob Logan. Merle Burse received an $800 bonus that year. "The world's most experienced canoe builder" was a particularly apt advertising slogan used during the fifties. Average employment was sixty men with an eight-hour day and pay for Good Friday and statutory holidays. Wages rose considerably throughout the fifties.

Three years later, Chestnut racked up sales of $555,000 and showed a profit of $37,000. In 1958 the company celebrated its most prosperous year to date and future earnings promised to be even better. The sixty-five employees were working full time; George Birch, who now owned one-quarter of the company, was paid $7,550 per year in salary; and a dividend of $10 per share was declared.

As optimistic as things seemed in the late fifties, disaster for both the Chestnut and Peterborough canoe companies was waiting in the wings that would bring to an end the era of great canoe companies in Canada. In both instances, demise followed an unmanageable expansion. Also, both companies failed to keep up with technology, which was, for better or worse, changing the canoe industry. Indeed, the changes permeated all manufacturing in the twentieth century since Henry Ford: production line efficiency and modern materials and technologies were designed to eliminate labour hours.

Much of this technology was borrowed from other, larger industries. For example, World War II aircraft designers first developed the molded plywood construction to build early bomber aircraft. Later this was adapted by the Plycraft company for canoe construction. The postwar era saw an abundance of aluminum "scraps" that were quickly converted for outboard motorboat construction and canoes. Leading the way was the Grumman company, which began building canoes in 1953. To its credit, it made a canoe of excellent shape. Many thought it was stolen from Chestnut's designs. Canoe liveries and camps were unable to resist a canoe that was so inexpensive and considered almost "bombproof." (It is interesting to note that in the next phase of technology even aluminum canoes proved too labour intensive.

Grumman was purchased in 1990 by the Outboard Marine Company, and in 1996 the canoe operations were closed.).

The final blow to the canoe companies was hastened by the petrochemical onslaught of cheap plastics that were quick and easy to mold into a boat. The rate of developments in the canoe world was overwhelming, almost addictive, to the public. First came fibreglass, later Kevlar, ABS, and dozens of others. Boats of these materials could be built, especially the low end "chopper-gun" or injection molded PVC construction, with astounding speed.

The prices of canoes continue to vary widely. For example, the 1997 Canadian Tire Catalogue offers a fifteen-foot Coleman polyethylene canoe for $519.99. In contrast, our current Chestnut Canoe Company's catalogue offers the fifteen-foot Pleasure model (Chum) wood-and-canvas canoe—with hand-carved decks and thwarts, hand-caned seats, built with basically nineteenth-century technology—for $2,725. It has been, and will continue to be, difficult to compete.

Demise of the Peterborough Canoe Company

How easily the mighty fall. The Peterborough Canoe Company became overconfident with record profits after enjoying decades of successful cooperation with Chestnut. The decision was made to construct a new facility and vacate the shops used since 1891. What Peterborough planned to do with the move led to the company's soon to follow downfall.

In 1958 Peterborough obtained a $350,000 loan from the IDB to build a large new cedarstrip runabout plant in Ontario. The loan was secured by hypothecating to the bank of all of Chestnut's original shares. The bank also required Chestnut's guarantee to repay the loan, using, if necessary, all the assets in Fredericton. In 1956 Peterborough employed over 206 people, sold over 8,000 boats and canoes worth more than $1.5 million; it was the largest boatbuilder in Canada. But by 1961 Peterborough's gamble on a new factory had failed.

Instead of capitalizing on changing technologies, Peterborough tripped on the doorstep to the future. The problem was timing. The old factory on Water Street had three thousand square feet. The new factory was a modern building with forty-five hundred square feet. The emphasis in production was outboard motorboat runabouts. The Canadian Canoe Company was moved into the Water Street site but Peterborough's troubles forced it, too, to close soon thereafter in 1960.

Unforeseen problems soon emerged. Technology was on the threshold of major change. Peterborough had designed their new plant towards wooden lapstrake runabouts, but the heyday of these craft was over. The future was in fibreglass, even more so in motorboats than in canoes. The Peterborough Canoe Company attempted to enter the synthetics market in 1961, but their seasoned woodworkers were not particularly good at this new method of construction, and other manufacturers, dedicated to plastics from the start, had this market cornered.

With a $2 million debt, on October 24, 1962, the Peterborough Canoe Company closed. The IDB in Fredericton stepped in to prevent Canadian Watercraft Limited from further draining the Chestnut Canoe Company. The bank split Chestnut away from Canadian Watercraft Limited and became the Fredericton company's new owner. If not for the reorganization in 1936, when Canadian Watercraft Limited was made a holding company, Chestnut would surely have gone down with Peterborough.

It was nonetheless a battle to salvage Chestnut from the ashes of Canadian Watercraft Limited because the Peterborough company had marketed the majority of the Chestnut canoes. More importantly, with the loss of its parent company, Chestnut lost $350,000 in working capital, which was badly needed in the seasonal business.

By the sixties, Chestnut Canoe Company was an integral part of New Brunswick's heritage, and the source of up to one hundred jobs in Fredericton. Inevitably, provincial politics became a major force in keeping the company afloat. The government began by guaranteeing working capital loans from the Bank of Nova Scotia, and soon provided direct governmental loans as well.

It seems that Chestnut learned little from the Peterborough company's experience, for Chestnut duplicated the same error juct one decade later.

Demise of the Chestnut Canoe Company

In retrospect, it was that fateful meeting on July 31, 1958, that was the beginning of the end for the Chestnut Canoe Company. To assist the Peterborough expansion, in 1958 the Chestnut directors voted unanimously to pass By-law No. 87. It committed the Chestnut Canoe Company "to guarantee repayment of a loan to be made to the Peterborough Canoe Company by the Industrial Development Bank of $240,000." The by-law also set the repayment schedule for Chestnut at $2,500 per month plus 6 per cent interest, and pledged all land, buildings, machinery, and equipment to the IDB.

Chestnut began to receive some of the obsolete Peterborough canoe forms and other equipment from Peterborough, but at considerable expense. By the end of their first year alone, 1963, Chestnut was facing a net loss of $30,000—its first loss in many years. To alleviate the seasonal nature of the canoe business, Chestnut attempted to diversify its products into lacrosse and hockey sticks, winter skis, even some furniture. The problem then became where to find badly need working capital for inventory. The Province of New Brunswick stepped in as guarantors of a new operating loan. The principal loan operator, the Bank of Nova Scotia, showed an interest, and the two parties were fighting over ownership of the original Chestnut shares.

Warning signs should have been heeded. The Chestnut factory was starting to show its age. A 1962 appraisal by the Dominion Appraisal Company reported a replacement value for the business at $549,465 but a market value of only $135,491. Little or no value was assigned to the classic Chestnut canoe forms that had shaped the famous canoe models since the early 1900s.

However, in 1965 George Birch obtained all the shares of the Chestnut Canoe Company, and it seemed to everyone involved that the company had survived. It was a fresh start, and few would have guessed that the Fredericton company would soon be forced to close its doors. In the same year, Chestnut commissioned a report on its operations from the Research and Productivity Council of New Brunswick. The report states: "It is recommended that the company aim at a drastic reduction in overhead expenses and reduce the size of the operation to about twenty-five direct employees...." This notion of consolidation is a theme throughout the report. Yet, the direction Chestnut followed was quite the opposite.

The cause of Chestnut's final decline is the subject of radically different and emotionally charged opinions. Some facts are generally agreed upon, such as the decision to move to a new plant designed for modern manufacturing processes. A grant was obtained from the Department of Regional Economic Expansion (DREE) for relocation. In 1974 Chestnut moved to a brand new 77,000 square foot factory in the neighbouring town of Oromocto. Though opinions differ, one fact is consistent—the new plant was a disaster. The building carried an enormous overhead that required $100,000 a year in mortgages, heat, and insurance alone. The move also halted production for half a year. The new plant was an albatross. As one plant visitor commented, "Imagine the incongruity of entering a massive structure of steel and concrete with thirty-foot ceilings, only to see an Indian woman sitting on the floor filling snowshoes."

Aside from costing so much that Chestnut would have had to produce just about every canoe sold in North America to make the move succeed, nothing about the building seemed suitable. Its drying room held less than the old building, and there was less storage space, so any benefit of increased production space was lost. The old building was serviced by both CP and CN railways, yet for the new one $10,000 had to be spent to put in siding—and that was only serviced by CN. Continuing testimony to the impracticality of the building is that from the end of Chestnut until the present day it has been vacant. Once it was temporarily in service to store beer for the local Canadian Armed Forces base.

By contrast, the former factory on York Street has been renovated into a successful office complex. The former boiler room has been transformed into a popular watering hole known as the "Chestnut Pub." The factory sits on high-priced downtown property.

Chestnut lost favour with the New Brunswick Government. Four years later Chestnut was refused any further funds or guarantee of bank loans. The company had to find new money or face receivership.

By necessity, the company was for sale, although it was difficult to find a buyer. When a reasonable offer—backed by the New Brunswick Government—was made by a major local window manufacturer, Lock-Wood Limited, the offer was quickly accepted. Lock-Wood took over in December 1977, buying George Birch's shares at that time.

Michael Mallory was appointed as manager. He knew nothing about canoes but was a shrewd businessman assigned the job of revitalizing the Chestnut Canoe Company. Mallory learned the canoe business quickly and produced a new Chestnut catalogue, which was much improved over previous ones. He had a badly needed new twenty-four-foot Freighter form built. Although he presented to Lock-Wood proposals for rejuvenating the company, realistically, he could not see eliminating losses for at least three years. Neither could he guarantee a profit. Lock-Wood decided to shut down Chestnut's production. In September 1978 the closure of Chestnut was announced.

However, Lock-Wood wanted the company to close with a clear record. A last batch of orders was to be filled and as many bills as possible were to be paid. But the New Brunswick Government forgave over $500,000 in loans, and the Bank of Nova Scotia lost an undisclosed amount—at least $300,000. One by one, employees left the factory for the last time and historic canoe forms were sold. The last Chestnut canoe was built in May 1979.

Lock-Wood attempted to find a buyer for the Chestnut name and the canoe forms for what seems to have been an incredibly low price—$35,000—considering the hundreds of thousands of dollars in debts from which a new owner would have been released. Chestnut did not go into bankruptcy, but its factory doors were closed indefinitely.

It is easy to point a finger at fibreglass, aluminum, Kevlar, and ABS canoes and argue that the age of the wood-and-canvas canoe had come to an end. Yet that is surely an oversimplification. Chestnut had difficulty adapting to change, whether technical innovations or financial downturns. The company was using nineteenth-century manufacturing in the last quarter of the twentieth century. The Chestnut canoes had been designed for cheap labour. They took a great deal of time to build and were not well suited to assembly line manufacturing. Furthermore, the building materials were no longer available in the quantities required. Technical change was attempted but more time for research and development would have been necessary to make the transition successful. Chestnut did not capitalize on the uniqueness of their canoe shapes with the new materials because the intricacies in the shape of a hand-built wooden canoe simply couldn't be copied: split mold technology that would have enabled Chestnut's "tumble home" to be copied in plastic was still years down the line. And after all these years, no plastic boat has proven capable of replacing the famous Chestnut Freighter. Chestnut made a crude entry into the world of synthetic canoes. The company made fibreglass canoes and had aluminum canoes made for them, but these canoes didn't account for a significant portion of Chestnut's income.

Few people saw the final catalogue that Lock-Wood published. The text emphasizes quality of craftsmanship in the Chestnut legacy, pointing to a sincere attempt to turn Chestnut around. (Courtesy: The Author.)

If Chestnut had consolidated operations and sold the product on the basis of quality to the market

Roy Green

Building "real wood" canoes was the heart of the craft to Green. When the economy forced changes to the industry—wood-and-canvas in particular—it seemed time to quit. "I went back to it later on but was disgusted at what I saw! The art was gone. I had nothing in common with the people who worked in the canoe 'factories.' Everything had changed."

Green's two canoes are a sight to behold. In all my years of searching, I have never seen two better examples for both perfection of construction and preservation. I suspected they took months to build. "That canoe there … three hours to set up your mold with keelson, stem, and ribs. Six hours to sheath. Six to eight to finish. We worked fast. Bang, bang, bang! Wap, wap, wap! No slowing down for the easy parts. But with the fine work there was never any question as to how long it would take. You do a good job regardless of the time. Nobody's going to ask you any questions.… The wood sheathing is cut to patterns, but the final fitting is done when you put the boat together. You take a sliver here, a sliver and a half there. You can't see what will be the inside of the canoe. You go by feel. Then came the time cards. Peterborough started it. You had one good day, got more work done than usual, and you were always expected to keep up that pace. Quality went right to hell." (from Kenneth Solway's "Roy Green's Legacy," in *Canoe* June 1986) size that was realistic, it may have weathered the seventies better. However, downsizing was a foreign concept in a decade preoccupied with steady commercial expansion. As Gerry McMullen of Lock-Wood stated, "They [Chestnut] should have moved their operations to a low-rent barn on the outskirts of the city." Instead, Chestnut continued to diversify its products, in the mistaken belief that the dealers who sold canoes also wanted runabouts, rowboats, sailboats, and that they wanted them all from the same manufacturer.

Further damage to the Chestnut business was a decline in construction quality. Anyone who had bought Chestnut canoes in the 1960s and 1970s recalls them with disdain. The quality of the once fine Chestnut canoes disappeared at a crucial time when city-raised purchasers were buying their canoes as much to look at as to use. The decline can be mostly attributed to the piecework contract established in 1955, which was more than welcomed by the union, for as long as workers did their jobs quickly they stood to earn much more per hour. All Chestnut employees had to be taught was to perform one process quickly in the assembly line. Wood-and-canvas canoes can be built quickly, but the craftsmanship suffers.

The result of the piecework contract was disastrous for the durability of canoes. For example, I know of one children's camp that purchased a fair number of these late Chestnut canoes. Apparently, Chestnut had either run out of the brass or silicon bronze ring nails ordinarily used to hold the ribs to the inwales or they were "economizing." Straight nails were used instead. There is a fair amount of stress there, as the ribs' natural tendency is to want to spring back away from the inwale. Within days of the purchase, all the canoes were showing evidence of the ribs letting go. Even the screws used to hold the outwales on were steel instead of brass and were too short. Within a couple of years everything was popping apart. To its credit, Lock-Wood eliminated piecework contracts as soon as it took over, and quality was immediately on the rise.

Perhaps most important, Chestnut wasn't listening to its customers in the way the Peterborough Canoe Company had done for them during the Canadian Watercraft Limited relationship. This particularly damaged their rapport with the Hudson's Bay Company, whose business accounted for one-third of Chestnut's output. The Canadian North was dependent upon the Chestnut Freight canoes. To accommodate larger outboard motors, Hudson's Bay Company customers wanted a new twenty-four-foot model to accommodate larger horsepower motors. Chestnut responded by building canoes on the twenty-two-foot form and extending the canoes two feet. This was hardly what the Hudson's Bay Company wanted. Meanwhile, a competing new canoe company in Quebec called Nor-west Canoes saw the opportunity and responded with a Freighter that was not only twenty-four feet, but was wider and deeper as well, strengthened with a two-by-four keelson and custom forged metal braces. Nor-west thrives on, and this is the Freight canoe one sees most often in the North today.

Marketing presented a particular problem for the Chestnut Canoe Company. Mass production requires mass sales, achieved by placing the canoes in stores around the world. While Chestnut was losing money, its representatives were not. In most cases, at the end of a season any unsold canoes could be sent back to the manufacturer for a refund. It has been said that mark-ups were sometimes enormous. The Hudson's Bay Company, for example, is said to have marked up canoes 300 per cent. It was a no lose situation for the stores, and often a no win situation for the manufacturer.

Lock-Wood's unsuccessful attempts to rescue the Chestnut Canoe Company in the seventies resulted in a significant financial loss to the window company. The perception at Lock-Wood was that it had been "led on" by the New Brunswick Government. At the time of the sale it understood that Chestnut's problems were due to manufacturing difficulties—something Lock-Wood thought it could rectify—but it quickly learned that the major difficulties were in management and marketing.

Lock-Wood even tried to revive the company in another form. According to Gerry McMullen at Lock-Wood: "We tried to revive the company in a different location. We wanted Carl Jones, Don Fraser, and possibly others to run the company at the old Dorchester Chemical Plant (some distance away) to see if it could work on a reduced scale. We would pay room and board and transportation on the weekend to their homes. All the woodworking would be done at Lock-Wood and the assembly would be done at the Dorchester plant. This would reduce the overhead." Not surprisingly, this offer wasn't popular.

Lock-Wood then offered to give all the forms to Carl Jones in return for a percentage of a new company that he would set up. Carl refused and bought his forms separately. In the end, Chestnut was formally merged with Lock-Wood for tax reasons. A single buyer could not be found, so the Chestnut name and the canoe forms were sold separately.

Canoe Company Catalogues 1903–1936

R. Chestnut & Sons Catalogue, 1905

The Chestnut Canoe Company is without a doubt the most influential canoe building company in the history of the Canadian canoe. With over sixty models under the Chestnut name—from eleven-foot Featherweights to motorized Freighters—the goal to cater to as wide a market as possible on an international level was achieved. Yet, there were no revolutionary inventions. Founded in Fredericton, New Brunswick, by William and Harry Chestnut, the company was incorporated in 1907 at the same time as they patented their wood-and-canvas design. Chestnut's initial design was derived from the sporting lifestyle, of which William and Harry were very much a part. Quality craftsmanship in wood-and-canvas canoes, aimed at both recreational and professional canoeists, was the trademark of the Chestnut Canoe Company for many years. In 1978, Chestnut announced its closure after attempts to salvage it failed.

High Grade Canvas Canoes
MANUFACTURED BY
R. CHESTNUT & SONS
FREDERICTON, N.B. CANADA
1905

The first Chestnut canoe catalogue, 1905, depicts drawings and dimensions that illuminate many mysteries about the earliest days of these canoes. Note the capped (closed) gunwales in the line drawings.

A WORD ABOUT OUR LOCATION.

Fredericton is nicely situated on a beautiful stretch of the St. John River, and has long been the canoeing centre of the Province. It is touched by the I. C. R., C. P. R. and Star Line Steamers, so has ample shipping facilities. Millions of lumber are handled annually, giving us a splendid stock from which to select our material.

CONSTRUCTION.

The canvas on each canoe is one entire piece, consequently there is no seam to leak, and the ends are fully protected with brass which makes a neat and durable finish. As the canvas is not affected by extremes of heat or cold, the canoes are always absolutely tight in any climate. The frame work is strongly constructed. The ribs are New Brunswick cedar covered with a thin planking of the same material. All fastenings are brass or copper. Over all is the canvas, fitting perfectly, and so smooth and even that the canoe slips through the water with the minimum of resistance. Not a seam, joint, wrinkle or lump to impede the headway.

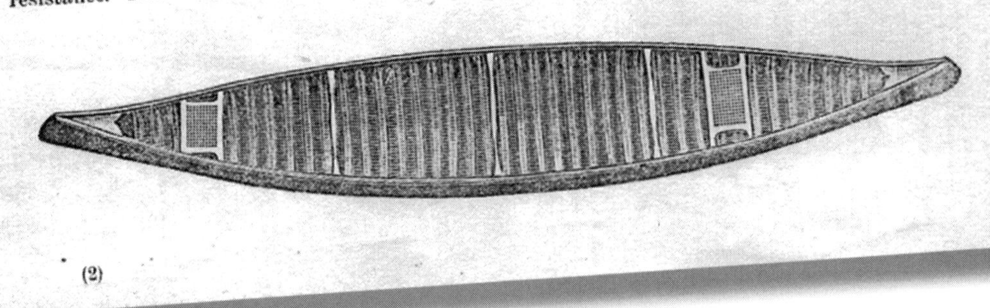

(2)

OUR canoes, although light in weight, will stand a wonderful amount of wear and tear, and will outlast a wooden canoe by many years. The outline is most graceful and symmetrical, and very pleasing to the eye. They are unexcelled as a pleasure craft and a marvel of steadiness.

PLEASURE MODEL.

Made in one grade only — The best.

Telegraph Code	Length	Width	Depth	Approximate Weight	Price
AJAX,	16 ft.	31 in.	11 in.	65 lbs.	$48 00
ASTER,	17 "	31 "	11½ "	70 "	49 00
ALPHA,	18 "	32 "	12½ "	75 "	50 00

THIS is the highest grade canoe possible to build, and is guaranteed first class in every respect. Bars and decks are best maple, gunwales of selected spruce. Has two cane seats which will be found very durable, as well as cool and comfortable for summer use. The canvas is filled with a special composition which conceals all trace of the grain, making a highly polished and perfectly smooth surface, which is finished in colour and varnish.

Standard colours are red and green, but they can be finished in any shade to suit purchaser if order is placed in time. The ribs and planking are perfectly clear cedar, natural finish, making a very handsome appearing canoe. This model is light, roomy, and very safe. It is one of the tastiest crafts afloat, and as its name implies is particularly adapted for pleasure purposes.

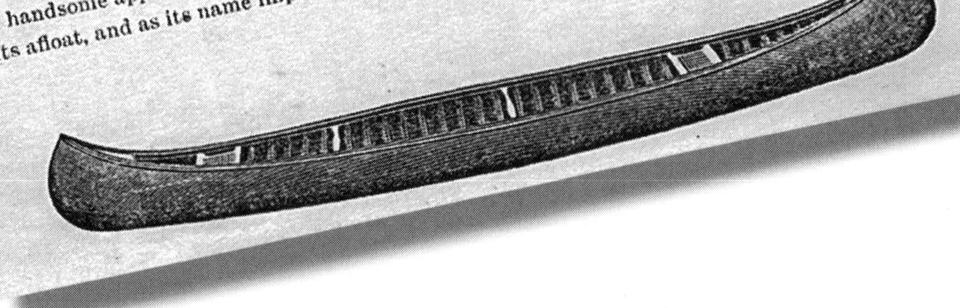

CRUISING MODEL—Made in Two Grades.

Telegraph Code. 1st Grade.	Telegraph Code. 2nd Grade.	Length	Width	Depth	Approximate Weight	Price 1st Grade	Price 2nd Grade
PREMIER .	KRUGER. .	16 ft.	32 in.	11½ in.	65 lbs.	$43 00	33 00
PRIMUS .	CRONJE .	17 "	33 "	11½ "	70 "	44 00	34 00
LEADER .	STOESSEL	18 "	34 "	12 "	75 "	45 00	35 00

THIS is a larger canoe than our pleasure model, higher towards the ends, and designed to stand rougher water. The first grade contains first class material only, and has the same finish on the canvas as the pleasure model, but on account of slight differences in shape, construction, etc., can be produced somewhat cheaper. It has two cane seats and natural finish and is a remarkably fine canoe for the money.

The second grade has the same construction as the first grade, but the cedar is not selected with the same care, and knotty stock is often used provided it has the required strength. This grade has not the special highly polished finish used on the canvas of the first grade, but is finished with a special waterproof composition designed for very hard usage, and is most serviceable for fishing, hunting, exploring trips, etc. The inside is natural finish, and the outside a dull slate colour. Has one cane seat in the stern, and bar forward, instead of two cane seats as used in the higher priced canoes. Anticipating that these canoes may see very rough service, we are using heavier canvas than on the first grades.

SPECIAL GUIDES' CANOE.

Telegraph Code.	Length	Width	Depth	Approximate Weight	Price
BOONE, ...	16 ft.	32 in.	11½ in.	70 lbs.	$38 00
CROCKET, ...	17 "	33 "	11½ "	75 "	39 00
MOSES, ...	18 "	34 "	12 "	80 "	40.00

Realizing that on rough, rocky streams there is need of a canoe practically indestructible, we build a 2nd grade canoe with half or "short" ribs between the long ribs, placing them throughout the entire length of the canoe. This so stiffens and strengthens the bottom that the canoe will stand almost any amount of hard usage, and is essentially the craft for canoeing on rocky streams in low water.

PACKING AND TERMS.

All canoes are packed in hay or straw and covered with burlap ... harge. If crated, a reasonable charge will be made for same. Our terms to parti... ts with us are cash with order.

EXTRAS.

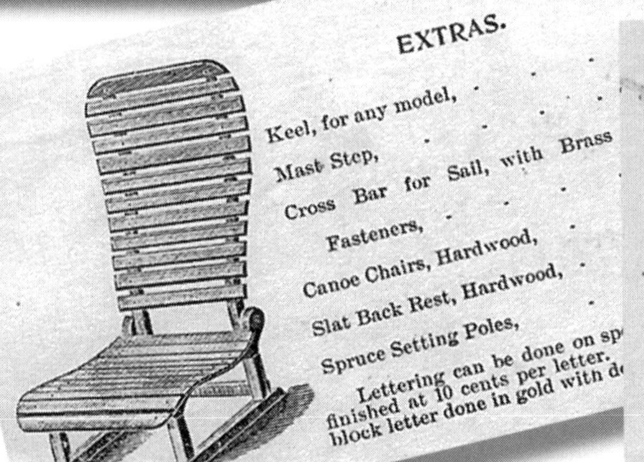

Keel, for any model, .

Mast Step, .

Cross Bar for Sail, with Brass Fasteners, .

Canoe Chairs, Hardwood, .

Slat Back Rest, Hardwood, .

Spruce Setting Poles, .

Lettering can be done on sp... finished at 10 cents per letter. ... block letter done in gold with d...

Maple Paddles, lengths from 5 to 6 feet.

Style A or B, First Quality, $1.75 each. Second Quality, $1.50 each.
Birds Eye Maple, $2.00 to $3.00.

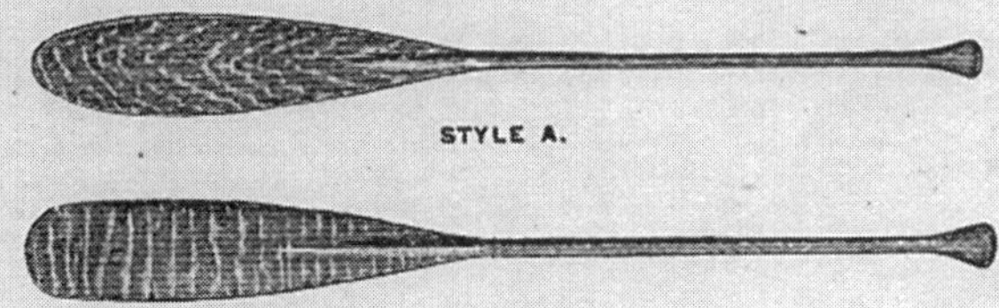

STYLE A.

STYLE B.

All paddles are filled and varnished ready for use. The first grade are the best obtainable, the second are good sound paddles.

WE give below memo of freight rates from Fredericton to different points on I. C. R. and C. P. R. Canoes 19 feet and under carry the following freight classification.

Single canoes are billed at 600 lbs.

Two canoes crated together are billed at 700 lbs.

Three " " " " " 800 "

Via I. C. R.

To	Rate per 100 lbs.	One Canoe	2 Crated Together	3 Crated Together
Dorchester	36	$2 16	$2 52	$2 88
Moncton	36	2 16	2 52	2 88
Amherst	38	2 28	2 66	3 04
Truro	40	2 40	2 80	3 20
Halifax	42	2 52	2 9[illegible]	
Digby	44			
Windsor				

(10)

Via C. P. R.

To	Rate per 100 lbs.	One Canoe	2 Crated Together	3 Crated Together
St. John	$0 28	$1 68	$1 96	$2 24
Quebec	42	2 52	2 94	3 36
Sherbrooke	48	2 88	3 36	3 84
Montreal	48	2 88	3 36	3 84
Ottawa	52	3 12	3 64	4 16
Toronto	64	3 84	4 48	5 12
Winnipeg	2 14	12 84	14 98	17 12
Vancouver	3 35	20 10	23 45	26 80

Carload to Montreal, $44.00.—To Ottawa, $52.00.—To Toronto, $64.00.

Chestnut Canoe Company Catalogues, 1934

From 1918 to World War II, Chestnut's catalogue format did not change. The editions were distinguished through the years by a letter on the first page—A through H. Each edition in the letter series can be assigned an approximate date by examining the dates of "testimonials" printed in each catalogue. The copy that is pictured here is catalogue C, chosen because it contains the most information. No other canoe catalogue in history offered such a broad range of canoe designs, yet unlike other builders, the Chestnut catalogue is almost exclusively devoted to canoes, and canoes of wood-and-canvas construction.

Chestnut Canoes
CHESTNUT CANOE CO
LIMITED
FREDERICTON, N.B.
New Brunswick is where the good canoe cedar grows.
CATALOGUE C

Chestnut Canoes

LOOKING BACKWARD

Since we first put canvas canoes on the Canadian market and since our last catalogue was issued, this type of watercraft has come into such universal use that it hardly seems necessary now to describe or explain the construction.

Our earnest desire to constantly improve our goods together with the careful selection of materials, coupled with the best of workmanship has enabled us to retain our lead as manufacturers of canvas covered canoes, and we believe our line of models is larger than that of any other maker either in North America or elsewhere. Many of our models are made in two grades designated as first and second.

The **No. 1** or first grade is made of perfectly clear cedar finished natural and except in the special light weight canoes, canvas is No. 8. The filler in this canvas is brought to a very smooth surface and finished in varnish with bright colors, stock shades being red and green.

The **No. 2** or second grade is made from perfectly sound and good cedar but is not always clear. The finish inside is natural on the smaller canoes as well as on the Prospector models, but the Nestable, Freight and other large models have a painted finish inside.

October 26th, 1926

The Chestnut Canoe Co., Ltd.
Fredericton, N.B.

Dear Sirs:
Would you please send me your catalogue on your canoes. I have used Chestnut canoes during the gold strike at Red Lake, and found they were the only canoe for hardship.
Please send me freight rates to Northern Quebec.

Yours truly,
(Signed) CHARLIE GRO[illegible]

c/o Amulet Gold Mine,
Rouyn, P.Q.

Chestnut Canoe Company Limited, Fredericton. N.B., Canada

Chestnut Canoes

Chestnut Featherweight

The acme of perfection has been reached in the construction of our featherweight canoe.

By eliminating every ounce of weight that can possibly be done away with and by using extra light wood, carefully selected as to strength, we are able to produce a strong, sturdy canoe that will carry two men and a load, the weight with light shoe keel being only 34½ to 35 lbs. This weight is a mere nothing on a portage and this craft can easily be taken in to almost inaccessible lakes where the big fish hide and where it is quite necessary to have an easily handled craft to get them.

Built in the first grade only with our standard varnished finish, but can be supplied in dull finish to order at the same price. Has one cane seat in stern, centre bar and bar in bow.

Code Word	Length, Ft.	Width, Ins.	Depth, Ins.	Weight, Lbs.	Price Without Paddles
Featherweight..........	11	34	11¾	34½	$66.00

We will build any of our canoes except the above and our 50-lb. canoe, specially light to order, reducing the weight about 10 lbs. for an extra charge of $5.

...noes

Our 12-Foot Canoe

Originally designed for one man and his pack the width and depth are such that it is often used for larger loads. Its shortness is a great advantage in navigating crooked streams and in portaging through heavy brush.

A prime favorite with muskrat hunters. Carried in stock in two grades, both grades having bow and stern cane seats.

Telegraph Code 1st Grade	Telegraph Code 2nd Grade	Length Ft.	Width In.	Depth In.	Weight Lbs.	Price Without Paddles 1st Grade	Price Without Paddles 2nd Grade
Teddy............	....Trapper..............	12	34	14	55	$66.00	$60.00

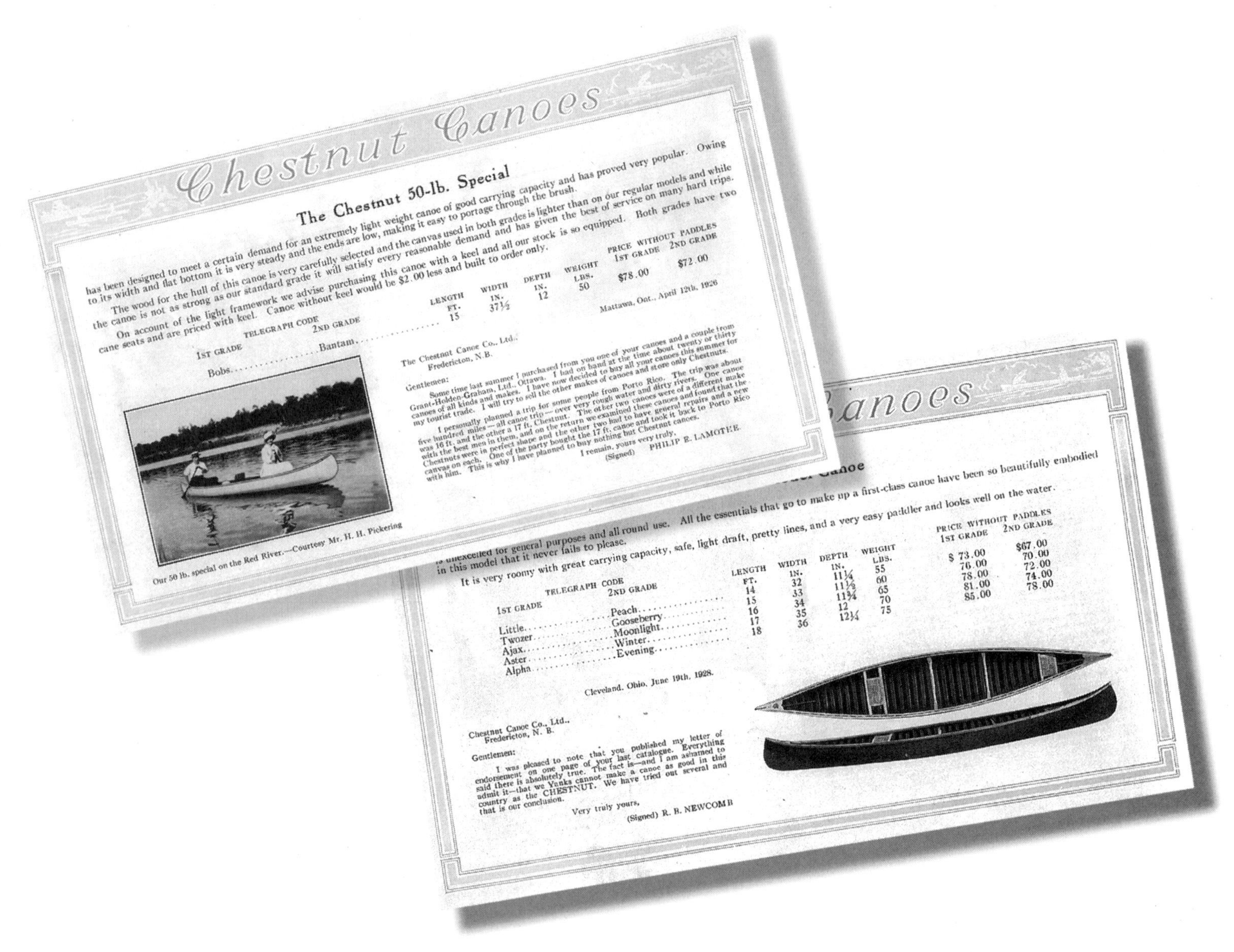

Chestnut Canoes

The Chestnut 50-lb. Special

has been designed to meet a certain demand for an extremely light weight canoe of good carrying capacity and has proved very popular. Owing to its width and flat bottom it is very steady and the ends are low, making it easy to portage through the brush.

The wood for the hull of this canoe is very carefully selected and the canvas used in both grades is lighter than on our regular models and while the canoe is not as strong as our standard grade it will satisfy every reasonable demand and has given the best of service on many hard trips.

On account of the light framework we advise purchasing this canoe with a keel and all our stock is so equipped. Both grades have two cane seats and are priced with keel. Canoe without keel would be $2.00 less and built to order only.

Telegraph Code 1st Grade	Telegraph Code 2nd Grade	Length Ft.	Width In.	Depth In.	Weight Lbs.	Price without Paddles 1st Grade	Price without Paddles 2nd Grade
Bobs	Bantam	15	37½	12	50	$78.00	$72.00

Mattawa, Ont., April 12th, 1926

The Chestnut Canoe Co., Ltd.,
Fredericton, N.B.

Gentlemen:

Some time last summer I purchased from you one of your canoes and a couple from Grant-Holden-Graham, Ltd., Ottawa. I had on hand at the time about twenty or thirty canoes of all kinds and makes. I have now decided to buy all your canoes this summer for my tourist trade. I will try to sell the other makes of canoes and store only Chestnuts.

I personally planned a trip for some people from Porto Rico. The trip was about five hundred miles—all canoe trip—over very rough water and dirty rivers. One canoe was 16 ft. and the other a 17 ft. Chestnut. The other two canoes were of a different make with the best men in them, and on the return we examined these canoes and found that the Chestnuts were in perfect shape and the other two had to have general repairs and a new canvas on each. One of the party bought the 17 ft. canoe and took it back to Porto Rico with him. This is why I have planned to buy nothing but Chestnut canoes.

I remain, yours very truly,
(Signed) PHILIP E. LAMOTHE.

Our 50 lb. special on the Red River.—Courtesy Mr. H. H. Pickering

...anoes

...el Canoe

is unexcelled for general purposes and all round use. All the essentials that go to make up a first-class canoe have been so beautifully embodied in this model that it never fails to please.

It is very roomy with great carrying capacity, safe, light draft, pretty lines, and a very easy paddler and looks well on the water.

Telegraph Code 1st Grade	Telegraph Code 2nd Grade	Length Ft.	Width In.	Depth In.	Weight Lbs.	Price without Paddles 1st Grade	Price without Paddles 2nd Grade
Little	Peach	14	32	11¼	55	$ 73.00	$67.00
Twozer	Gooseberry	15	33	11½	60	76.00	70.00
Ajax	Moonlight	16	34	11¾	65	78.00	72.00
Aster	Winter	17	35	12	70	81.00	74.00
Alpha	Evening	18	36	12¼	75	85.00	78.00

Cleveland, Ohio, June 19th, 1928.

Chestnut Canoe Co., Ltd.,
Fredericton, N. B.

Gentlemen:

I was pleased to note that you published my letter of endorsement on one page of your last catalogue. Everything said there is absolutely true. The fact is—and I am ashamed to admit it—that we Yanks cannot make a canoe as good in this country as the CHESTNUT. We have tried out several and that is our conclusion.

Very truly yours,
(Signed) R. B. NEWCOMB

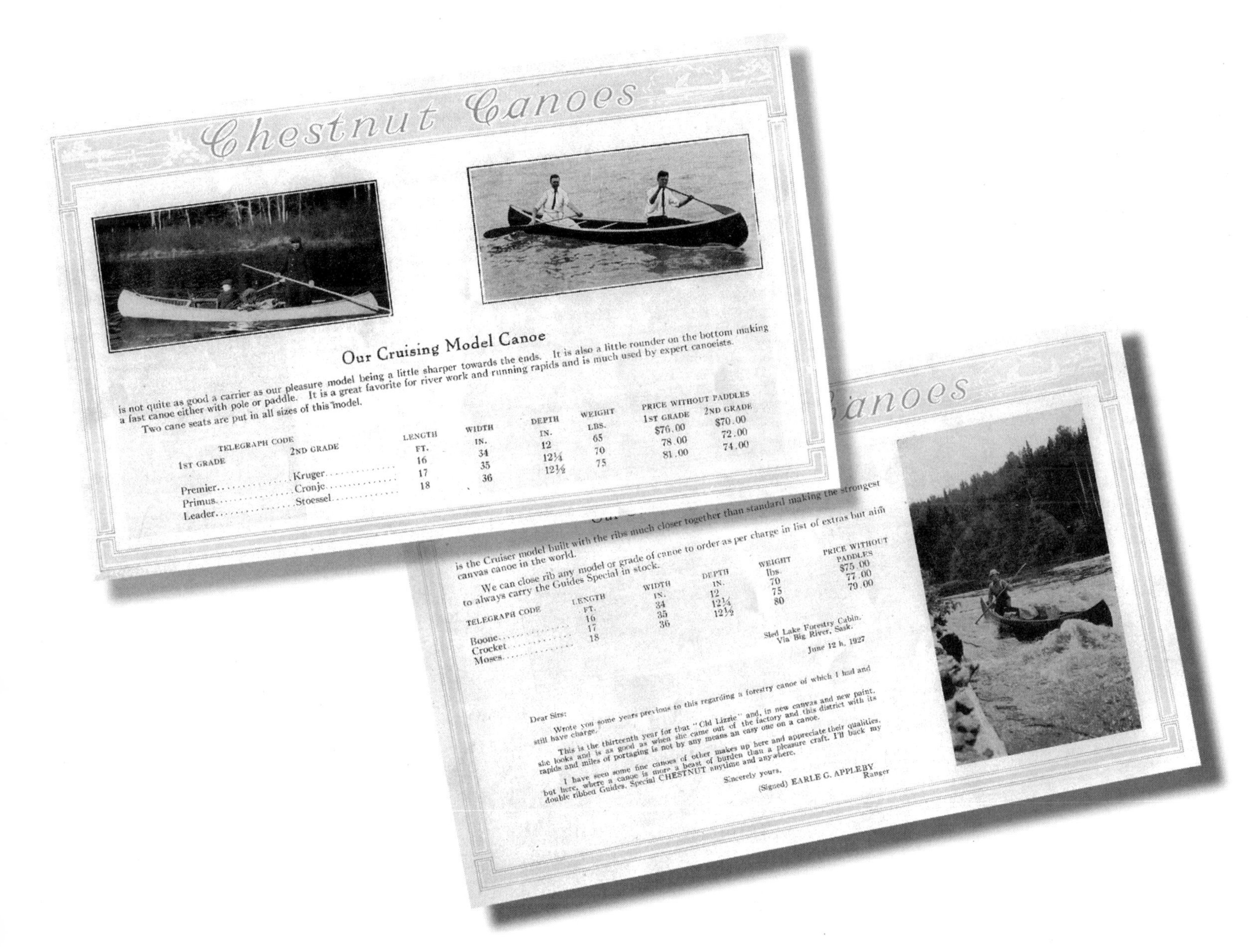

Chestnut Canoes

Our Cruising Model Canoe

is not quite as good a carrier as our pleasure model being a little sharper towards the ends. It is also a little rounder on the bottom making a fast canoe either with pole or paddle. It is a great favorite for river work and running rapids and is much used by expert canoeists.

Two cane seats are put in all sizes of this model.

Telegraph Code 1st Grade	Telegraph Code 2nd Grade	Length Ft.	Width In.	Depth In.	Weight Lbs.	Price Without Paddles 1st Grade	Price Without Paddles 2nd Grade
Premier	Kruger	16	34	12	65	$76.00	$70.00
Primus	Cronje	17	35	12¼	70	78.00	72.00
Leader	Stoessel	18	36	12½	75	81.00	74.00

…anoes

is the Cruiser model built with the ribs much closer together than standard making the strongest canvas canoe in the world.

We can close rib any model or grade of canoe to order as per charge in list of extras but aim to always carry the Guides Special in stock.

Telegraph Code	Length Ft.	Width In.	Depth In.	Weight lbs.	Price Without Paddles
Boone	16	34	12	70	$75.00
Crocket	17	35	12¼	75	77.00
Moses	18	36	12½	80	79.00

Sled Lake Forestry Cabin,
Via Big River, Sask.

June 12 h, 1927

Dear Sirs:

Wrote you some years previous to this regarding a forestry canoe of which I had and still have charge.

This is the thirteenth year for that "Old Lizzie" and, in new canvas and new paint, she looks and is as good as when she came out of the factory and this district with its rapids and miles of portaging is not by any means an easy one on a canoe.

I have seen some fine canoes of other makes up here and appreciate their qualities, but here, where a canoe is more a beast of burden than a pleasure craft. I'll back my double ribbed Guides. Special CHESTNUT anytime and anywhere.

Sincerely yours,

(Signed) EARLE G. APPLEBY
Ranger

Chestnut Canoes

Winners of ladies doubles at Westfield, N. B. August 1922.
Miss Babbitt (bow) Miss Chestnut (stern)

The above canoe known as the **Indian Maiden** is primarily a craft for two for use at Summer Camps, Pleasure Resorts, etc. and is designed for those wishing a jaunty looking distinctive model. Stock canoes are attractively finished in bright colors. Special orders will be striped or finished or lettered according to instructions. This canoe has no centre bar, the whole space amidships being devoted to the comfort of the passenger. Owing to the excessive turn up at bow and stern the method of making the ends is a departure from our regular custom. In this canoe the inside gunwales are set into the decks for a distance of several inches and the outside gunwales are not soft wood for the entire length of the canoe being finished out in hardwood where the heavy curve comes. This arrangement makes an exceedingly strong canoe.

The Indian Maiden is only made in the first grade but is put up in two finishes, the code word Maiden designating spruce gunwales, cedar decks, hardwood bars, etc., and the code word Indian designating gunwales, bars, seat frames, decks, etc., of mahogany. Canoes with mahogany trim made to order only.

Telegraph Code	Length	Width	Depth	Weight	Price without Paddles.
Indian	16 ft.	33	12	75 lbs.	$100.00
Maiden	16 ft.	33	12	70 lbs.	88.00

Canoes

Prospe... Model

This is now one of our most popular lines, supplying a demand for canoes larger than our Pleasure or Cruiser models but not quite as large as our Freight cances.

This model is now made in six sizes offering a most complete range that embodies the good points of both our Pleasure and Cruiser models. These canoes have large carrying capacity but are of light weight considering their size and are built with the second grade finish only, except to order. Canoes both close ribbed and with standard ribbing are carried in stock in all lengths. Each canoe has two cane seats hung well below the gunwales.

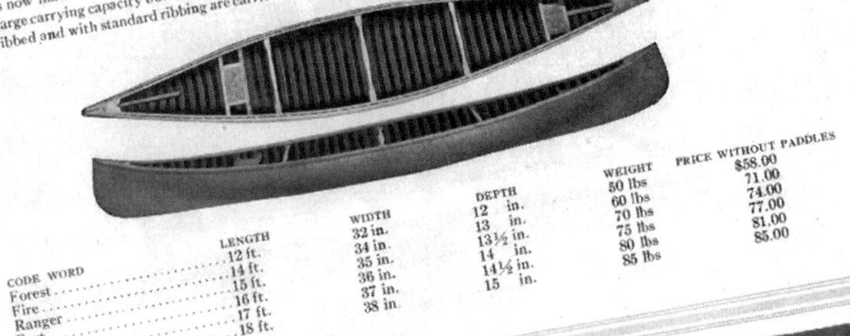

CODE WORD	LENGTH	WIDTH	DEPTH	WEIGHT	PRICE WITHOUT PADDLES
Forest	12 ft.	32 in.	12 in.	50 lbs	$58.00
Fire	14 ft.	34 in.	13 in.	60 lbs	71.00
Ranger	15 ft.	35 in.	13½ in.	70 lbs	74.00
Fort	16 ft.	36 in.	14 in.	75 lbs	77.00
Garry	17 ft.	37 in.	14½ in.	80 lbs	81.00
Voyageur	18 ft.	38 in.	15 in.	85 lbs	85.00

Extra for close ribbing $5.00, for keel $2.00.

Chestnut Canoes

Ogilvy Special

In collaboration with that dean of New Brunswick guides, Mr. David Ogilvy, we produced in the late autumn of 1931 a new 18 foot canoe which we tried out thoroughly and after changing the model slightly four different times through 1932 we find it now approaches in both looks and performance the perfection insisted upon by our manager. Ogilvy Bros. and other guides who have used it say it is "just right" and the "best yet". This model will be known as the Ogilvy Special and the illustrations herewith are designed to show up the special features of this craft.

It is so straight on the bottom and so flat from side to side that it skims over the top of the water rather than through it and has therefore a very light draft. It can be poled through the heaviest rapids with the minimum of effort and the flat floor makes it very comfortable for the feet of the poler on an all day's trip. The shape is such that it is probably the steadiest canoe of its size ever built, as indicated by the photo of a 200 pound man standing well into the bilge without upsetting or even getting the gunwale down near the water.

Ogilvy Special

We can trim it any special way to order but for fishing or general guides use have arranged it as shown in the cuts, a fixed cane seat in the stern and a removable slat seat in the bow. The angler uses this seat when fishing and then when the guide so desires he removes the seat and sits on the bottom using the seat, against the bow bar, as a back rest.

During 1933 we will work on the 20 foot length and after trying it out thoroughly and getting it just as we want it we will build a number for stock and expect to be able eventually to supply this model in lengths of 22 and 24 feet and possibly in shorter lengths. It is so very hard to upset that in the 16 foot length it would make an excellent pleasure canoe and particularly for tyros.

Telegraph Code	Length	Width	Depth	Weight	Price without Paddles.
Dave	18 ft.	36″	13″	85 lbs.	$80.00

Canoes

Ogilvy Special

Chestnut Canoes

Our 22 foot Fishing Model

Taken at Indian House on the famous Restigouche River.

The canoe shown in the illustration is our 22 ft. Poling and Fishing model brought out by us in 1918. It is an easy running canoe with the paddle in quiet waters, and for poling up rapids, for anchoring and fishing in rapid waters, has proven so popular that we are enlarging the line and building in four sizes as per list below.

The 18 and 20 ft. lengths have bow and stern cane seat. Shoe keel and deep keel supplied to order $2.00 extra.

The 22 and 24 ft. lengths have shoe keel and bow and stern seats of wood. These seats are easily removable when the guides stand up for poling, and are hung low so that when the guides are sitting down and the sportsman standing up to fish the canoe is safe and steady.

The thwarts in the 24 ft. length are very wide and hung several inches below the gunwales. The 22 ft. length is carried in stock with square stern for outboard motor. On other lengths this will be supplied to order. Extra for square stern is $8.00

If canoe is to be used for fishing in rapid waters we supply open top anchor rope pulley, either bow or stern, right or left side as specified. Extra for same $1.00. The finish on all four canoes for stock is our regular No. 2 in grey.

Telegraph Code	Length	Width	Depth	Weight	Price without Paddles.
Trout	18 ft.	33 in.	13 in.	80 lbs.	$ 70.00
Grilse	20 ft.	36 "	14 "	95 "	85.00
Salmo	22 ft.	38 "	14½ "	140 "	100.00
Salar	24 ft.	41 "	15 "	160 "	120.00

Canoes

Canoes

We have achieved such success with our freight canoes that the transport men in the far North, where most of them are used, will buy no other if they can possibly obtain a Chestnut. These sturdy canoes are made with wide thick ribs, heavier planking than on the smaller canoes, have wood seat, hardwood bars and decks, and sail bar and mast step forward. As per list below we now make six lengths, the first five being made up for stock and the 25 ft. made to order only. Canvas on the first three lengths is No. 6, and on the others No. 4. All lengths are equipped with keel and the 22 ft. has three bilge keels on each side.

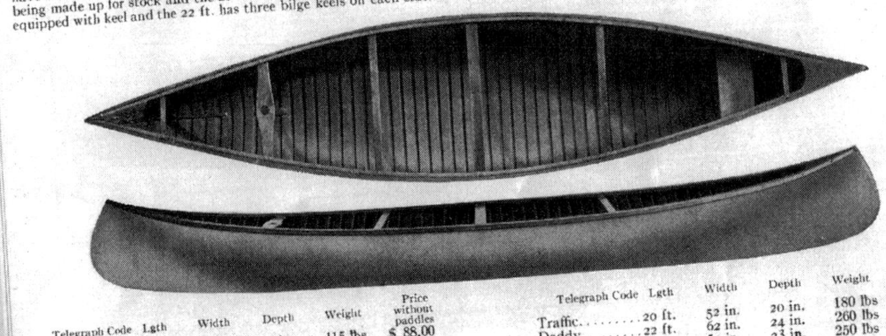

Telegraph Code	Lgth	Width	Depth	Weight	Price without paddles
Hudson	17 ft.	45 in.	17 in.	115 lbs	$ 88.00
Bay	18 ft.	46 in.	18 in.	130 lbs	100.00
Company	19 ft.	51 in.	19 in.	150 lbs	120.00

Telegraph Code	Lgth	Width	Depth	Weight	Price without paddles
Traffic	20 ft.	52 in.	20 in.	180 lbs	$160.00
Daddy	22 ft.	62 in.	24 in.	260 lbs	250.00
Rupert	25 ft.	50 in.	23 in.	250 lbs	250.00

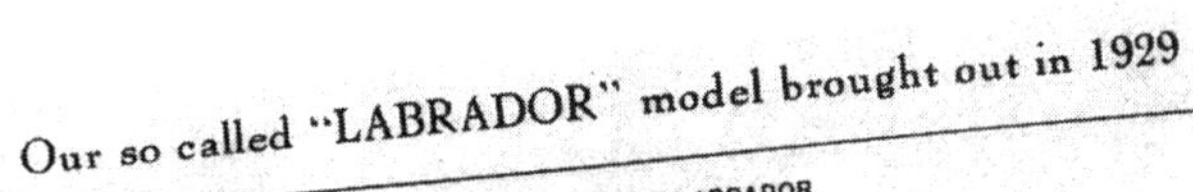
Our so called "LABRADOR" model brought out in 1929

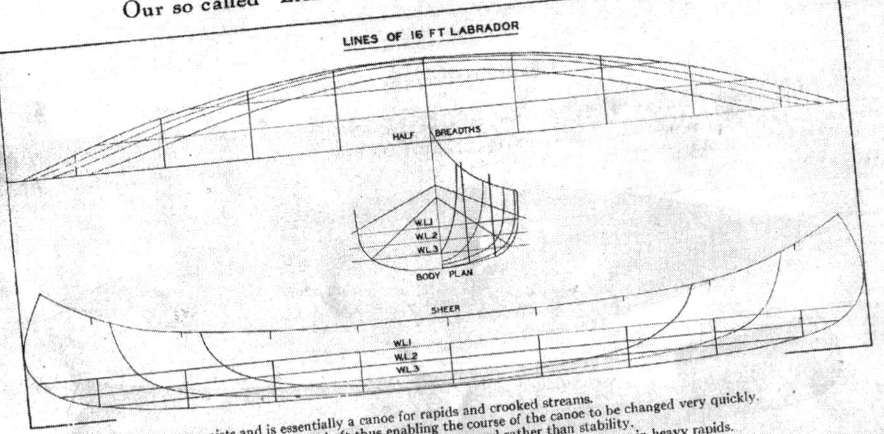

This model is for expert canoeists and is essentially a canoe for rapids and crooked streams.
The bottom lines have considerable rise fore and aft thus enabling the course of the canoe to be changed very quickly.
A cross section of the center shows a rounding bottom that makes for speed rather than stability.
There is no tumble home at any point, and the flaring sides towards the ends throw off the waves in heavy rapids.
Sizes come between our Prospector model and Freighter models.
The 15 and 16 ft. Lengths have two cane seats, with the stern seat placed as far aft as possible. The 18 ft. length has hardwood thwarts only. Standard finish is a smooth green outside, varnished inside. No. 8 canvas on all lengths, and no keel unless to special order.

Telegraph Code Word	Length	Width	Depth	Weight	Prices without Paddles
Manitou..............................	15 ft.	34 in.	15 in.	65 lbs.	$74.00
Mingan..............................	16 "	38 "	16 "	75 "	80.00
Moisie..............................	18 "	40 "	17 "	95 "	88.00

Canoes

For 1930 we have been asked to built our 18 ft. Labrador with straight top so it will lash snugly to the underbody of the Fairchild hydroplane, cabin type. The illustrations show this canoe, also the removable ends or hoods. These ends are shipped securely fastened inside the hull and upon arrival at destination may be quickly and easily attached both bow and stern, converting the straight top canoe into the original shape of the Labrador with considerable rise both forward and aft.

No special instructions are necessary either to attach or remove the ends. Anyone looking at the outfit will see how the job is to be done, and with the use of a screw driver and a small monkey wrench the work may be accomplished in a very few minutes.

The canvas of the hood laps over the canoe canvas under the straight, outside gunwales, making a watertight and satisfactory joint hidden from the eye. The idea is not so much to provide a canoe for daily transport by air as to supply a craft that may easily be carried to destination by hydroplane, and then in a few minutes be converted to the original model with more or less permanent ends for riding waves, running rapids, etc. This same construction may be supplied on any of our models at an extra charge of $24.00.

Page Nineteen

Chestnut Canoes

Nestable Canoes

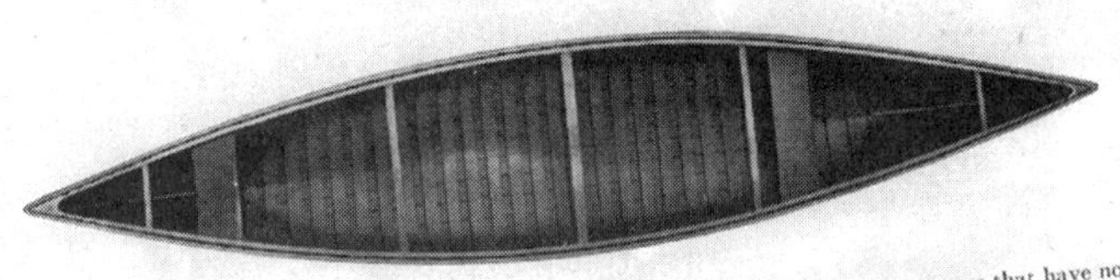

For shipment to remote points where the freight is a great consideration, we have designed a line of canoes that have no tumble home and will therefore, nest one within the other.

They are built with our standard grade of materials, the finish being a painted one, both inside and out. They have double open gunwales and can be nested without removing the decks. To take out or replace the seats and bars is only the matter of a few minutes' work and after the arrival of a shipment the canoes are soon ready for the water.

The lowest classification under which canoes not nested can be shipped by rail freight, is three and one half times first-class rate but, nested canoes, when crated, may be shipped at one and a half times the first-class rate or when boxed, at the first-class rate, the minimum weight, when so shipped, being figured at 800 lbs. On long hauls it is easy to see the great saving in favor of the Nestable Model, provided several canoes are shipped in one nest.

For stock, we only build these canoes in the Second Grade, but will build them in the First Grade on special orders.

Canoes

Nestable Canoes—*Continued*

Owing to the flaring bows and lack of tumble home, the Nestable model is very desirable for use with motor or for towing behind boat equipped with motor. The several lengths have almost the carrying capacity of our regu ar Chestnut models of equal size, and the Egg and Nest make admirable freight canoes and for stock are equipped with keel, the shorter lengths being supplied without keel unless otherwise ordered. We now build the White, Egg, and Nest for stock with square stern and keel.

Telegraph Code	Length	Width	Depth	Weight	Price without Paddles.
Chicken	14 ft.	32 in.	12 in.	55 lbs	$ 68.00
Yolk	15 ft. 3 in.	36½ in.	13½ in.	75 lbs	75.00
White	16 ft. 6 in.	41 in.	15 in.	95 lbs	82.00
Egg	17 ft. 9 in.	46 in.	17 in.	125 lbs	95.00
Nest	19 ft.	51 in.	19 in.	150 lbs	120.00

Swastika, Ont., April 11th, 1927

Chestnut Canoe Co., Ltd.
Fredericton, N.B.

Gentlemen;

At your earliest convenience please send me your canoe catalogue with price list for 1927.

I might add that I have used your canoes all over Northern Ontario for the last twenty years as a prospector and find that for an all around canoe they can't be beat. Yes I have handled a lot of makes too but give me a Chestnut every time.

Yours repectfully,
(Signed) THOS. ELLISON

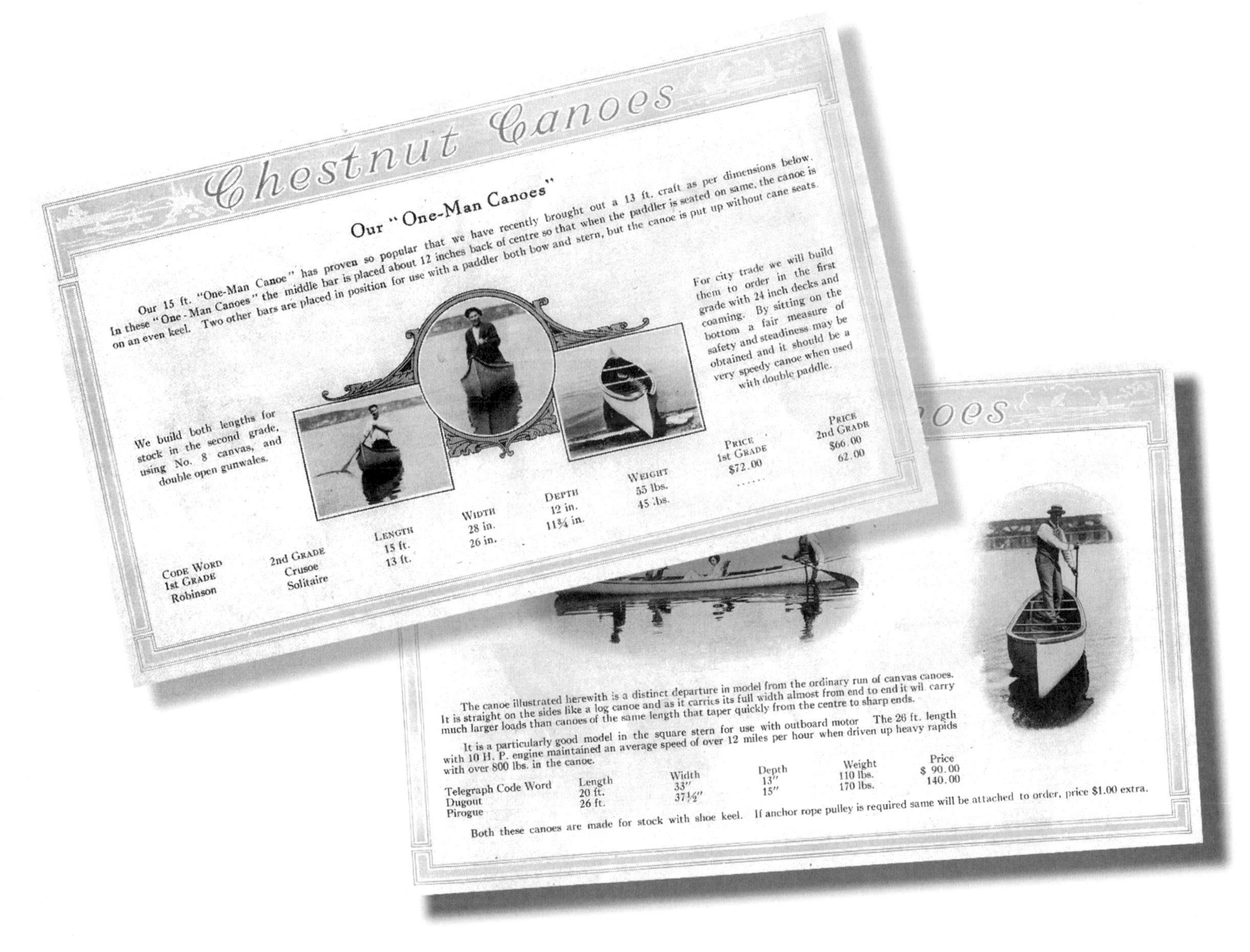

Chestnut Canoes

Our "One-Man Canoes"

Our 15 ft. "One-Man Canoe" has proven so popular that we have recently brought out a 13 ft. craft as per dimensions below. In these "One-Man Canoes" the middle bar is placed about 12 inches back of centre so that when the paddler is seated on same, the canoe is on an even keel. Two other bars are placed in position for use with a paddler both bow and stern, but the canoe is put up without cane seats.

For city trade we will build them to order in the first grade with 24 inch decks and coaming. By sitting on the bottom a fair measure of safety and steadiness may be obtained and it should be a very speedy canoe when used with double paddle.

We build both lengths for stock in the second grade, using No. 8 canvas, and double open gunwales.

Code Word 1st Grade	2nd Grade	Length	Width	Depth	Weight	Price 1st Grade	Price 2nd Grade
Robinson	Crusoe	15 ft.	28 in.	12 in.	55 lbs.	$72.00	$66.00
	Solitaire	13 ft.	26 in.	11¾ in.	45 lbs.	......	62.00

oes

The canoe illustrated herewith is a distinct departure in model from the ordinary run of canvas canoes. It is straight on the sides like a log canoe and as it carries its full width almost from end to end it wil. carry much larger loads than canoes of the same length that taper quickly from the centre to sharp ends.

It is a particularly good model in the square stern for use with outboard motor The 26 ft. length with 10 H. P. engine maintained an average speed of over 12 miles per hour when driven up heavy rapids with over 800 lbs. in the canoe.

Telegraph Code Word	Length	Width	Depth	Weight	Price
Dugout	20 ft.	33"	13"	110 lbs.	$ 90.00
Pirogue	26 ft.	37½"	15"	170 lbs.	140.00

Both these canoes are made for stock with shoe keel. If anchor rope pulley is required same will be attached to order, price $1.00 extra.

Keels

We put keels on any canoe to order, also outside stems of hardwood. A keel can be attached to a canoe at any time, but a canoe for outside stems should be built accordingly from the very start.

...f canoe is ordered with "keel" we supply a narrow hardwood keel, about one inch in depth. This stiffens the bottom very much, and we ...ly recommend it for livery canoes as well as large sponson canoes.

..."shoe keel" is ordered what we supply is ½ inch thick, 3 inches wide at the centre, and tapering towards the ends. This is a great pro... in rocky waters, and unquestionably lengthens the life of a canoe very materially.

...r price for outside stems is $2.50 per pair, for either style of keel, $2.00, if attached to the canoe when it is being built. When keels are ...d to canoes that have been warehoused, the charge will be $3 as we have to cart the canoes back to the Factory, unpack same, attach ...int and re-pack canoe and re-cart to the Warehouse.

Style A

Style B

Maple and Spruce Paddles from 4½ to 6 Feet

... A or B, first quality $2.00 each, 2nd quality $1.50 each. Selected birdseye maple from $3.00 to $4.00 each. Ontario pattern paddles ...ecial style supplied to order.

...addles are filled and varnished in first-class shape. The first grade are the best obtainable, and the second grade are good, sound paddles.

...iling we furnish mast steps and screws all ready to attach to the ribs, and a detachable cross bar to hold mast. This is quickly fastened ...wales with thumb screws, and can be removed in a few seconds.

...wing sponson canoes we supply oars and detachable rowlocks. These rowlocks fit on plates and are screwed into hardwood blocks that ...d on the tops of the sponsons. For prices see list of extras.

Chestnut Canoes

Square Stern Canoes

The wonderful development and improvement in outboard motors has created a great demand for square stern canoes. We have experimented with different styles of square stern and are now making all of these canoes with the type of stern illustrated herewith.

The advantage of this stern is that while it will handle any standard outboard motor, the canoe below the waterline is just the same as a sharp stern canoe and handles the same with either pole or paddle.

We can build any of our models to order with square stern but are stocking them in all lengths of Freights canoes and in the Prospector model in lengths of 16, 17 and 18 ft. The extra charge for square stern on any model is $8.00.

Canoe Chairs

Our Canoe Chair has a folding back that in use is rested against a thwart. It and our slat back rest are both made of hardwood and will be found strong, comfortable and serviceable.

All our canoes have ring in bow deck for tying purposes. Towing rings placed nearer the water line will be attached to order.

All canoes are properly packed for shipment, free of charge. If crating is required in addition to hay or straw and burlap the crate will be charged for according to size, the average price being $5.00.

Extras

Sponsons, on Pleasure model canoes	$20.00
" " Prospector model canoes	25.00
" " Freight model canoes	30.00
Close ribbing, any grade or model	5.00
Removable cross bar for sail, with brass fasteners	2.00
Mast step and screws	.80
Oars, brass rowlocks and blocks for Sponson Canoes	14.00
Medium or long decks	$8.00-10.00
Building deeper than standard, per in. Prospector model or smaller	2.00
Building deeper than standard, per in. larger than Prospecter models	4.00
Rowing Seat, adjustable	3.00
Sails, lateen or sprit	14.00
Spruce canoe poles	2.00
" " " with steel socket	3.00

Price $3.00

Cedar Neck Yoke $4.00

Price $1.00

English Canoe Company Catalogue, 1903

William English of Peterborough, Ontario, founded the English Canoe Company shop in 1861. His beautifully combined aboriginal design and European carpentry made the company known for its basswood plank canoes. Wood joinery innovations developed rapidly, at this time in canoe building history, culminating in the eventual shiplapped cedarstrip canoe. The English Canoe Company was bought out in 1923 by the Peterborough Canoe Company.

Of Ourselves

We have pleasure in placing before our friends and customers our Catalogue for the season of 1903. We have endeavored to condense into as handy a shape as possible information about the Canoes and Boats we build and the Fittings we can supply.

In our list it will be found that a number of New Models have been catalogued, as well as Canoes of Standard sizes and approved Models. We will be pleased to furnish further descriptions in regard to those wanting them. Our aim has been to be as concise as possible. We have a number of other Models suited for special purposes only and it will be to your interest to ask us for what you do not see catalogued.

Hoping to have the pleasure of hearing from you, we are,

Yours respectfully,

THE WILLIAM ENGLISH CANOE CO.

PETERBOROUGH, ONT.

—2—

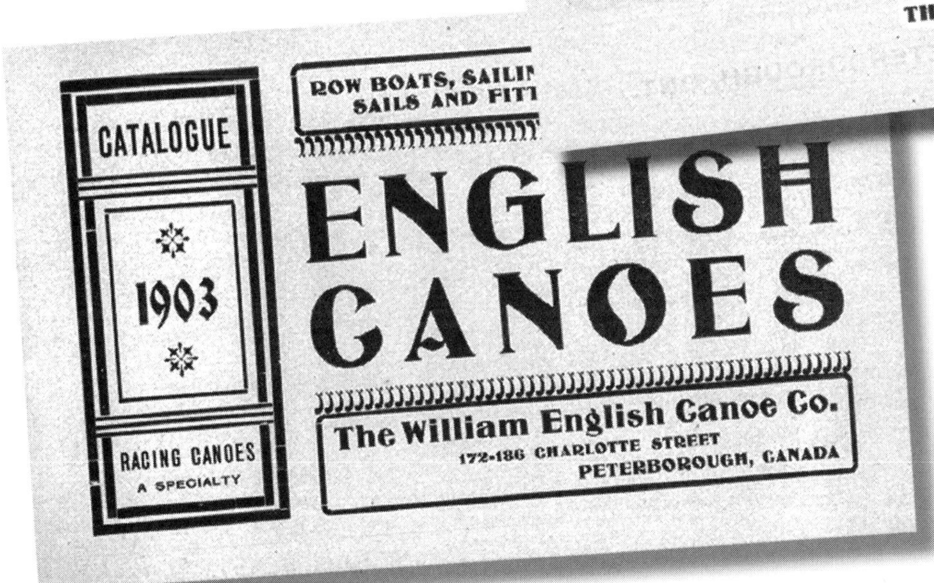

CATALOGUE
1903
RACING CANOES
A SPECIALTY
ROW BOATS, SAILI
SAILS AND FITT
ENGLISH
CANOES
The William English Canoe Co.
172-186 CHARLOTTE STREET
PETERBOROUGH, CANADA

Price List of Canoes

THE price list of Canoes which we give is of our general purpose and Club Canoes. It does not apply to Sailing Canoes or Canoes for other special purposes.

Model I. DIMENSIONS: length 18 ft., beam 37 inches, depth 13 inches.

This Canoe is specially adapted for a hunter's or trapper's canoe where a fair burthen capacity is required. It is exceedingly popular with Hunt Clubs.

PRICES

No. 1—Painted Basswood	$33 00	No. 120—Painted Cedar	$40 00
" 40—Varnished Basswood	40 00	Longitudinal Cedar Strip	56 00
" 80—Varnished Cedar	46 00	Cedar Rib	80 00

—3—

Model XXI. DIMENSIONS: length 16 ft., beam 31 inches, depth 13 inches.

This is a very easy running Canoe, and is between the No. 20 and No. 5 as far as the lines are concerned. It is a beautiful Canoe for rough weather and will carry a fairly good load. It was designed in 1898 and became popular at once.

PRICES

No. 21—Painted Basswood	$25 00	No 140—Painted Cedar	$32 00
" 60—Varnished Basswood.	32 00	Longitudinal Cedar Strip	45 00
" 100—Varnished Cedar	38 00	Cedar Rib	55 00

Model XXII. DIMENSIONS: length 16 ft., beam 31 inches, depth 12 inches.

This is the Rice Lake model. It is very flat on the bottom and turns very quickly at the bilge. It is all right for use on rivers or calm lakes as a good, dry Canoe on a rough sea.

PRICES

No. 22—Painted Basswood	$25 00	No. 141—Painted Cedar	$32 00
" 61—Varnished Basswood.	32 00	Longitudinal Cedar Strip	45 00
" 101—Varnished Cedar	38 00	Cedar Rib	55 00

—13—

War Canoes

The greatest event in Canoeing history took place at the A. C. A. camp when nine huge War Canoes, each representing different clubs, came through the water a mile straight away as fast as 15 men in a canoe could carry it along. Just think 135 men in one race. The sport is bound to become popular. Our new model is safe as well as speedy. Write the Toronto Canoe Club or the O. C. C. or Britannia Boating Club of Ottawa, Ont. They will tell you all about them. The popular dimensions are 30 ft. long, 48 inch beam and 20 to 22 inches deep. ☞ Prices are as follows, including large steering paddle.

Painted Basswood	$90 00
Varnished Basswood	120 00
Painted Cedar	$120 00
Varnished Cedar or Butternut . . .	160 00

—18—

Pleasure Boats and Skiffs

THERE is still a demand for our popular Skiffs and Pleasure Boats. We are always endeavoring to improve them in every way in order to guarantee satisfaction to their users. Our planking is all selected Basswood or Cedar, and is built either smooth or laystreak. The ribbing is of selected elm or oak, with the regular finish to the decks, gunwales and seats.

No.	Length	Beam	Depth	Seating Capacity	Price: Cedar Smooth	Basswood	Cedar Lapstreak
A	16	42	13	4	$55 00	$35 00	$45 00
B	17	40	13	5	58 00	38 00	48 00
C	17' 6	42	14	5	60 00	40 00	50 00
D	18	45	14	6	65 00	45 00	55 00
E	19			7	70 00	50 00	60 00

These Skiffs and Boats can be made of narrow, longitudinal strips, at an increased cost of 30 per cent. on Cedar price.

—19—

Paddles

The diagram on outside back page of cover shows a few of the different styles of Paddles in use. It is utterly impossible to show them all. We have every shape of Paddle imaginable for those who want them, and specials can be turned out on the shortest notice.

SINGLE PADDLES

No. 1—	5 ft. 10 inches long	No 4—	5 ft. 5 inches long
" 2—	5 " 5 " "	" 5—	5 " 5 " "
" 3—	5 " 10 " "	" 6—	4 " 11 " "

DOUBLE PADDLES

Double Blade Paddles, jointed, 7 to 9 ft. $3 50
Double Blade Paddles, jointed, spoon blade 4 50

Club and Racing CANOES

It is our pleasure to boast of our success in supplying the wants of numerous Clubs in Canada, United States and England. This has, no doubt, been occasioned by our having so many "Club" Models that a class can be picked suitable for the waters at any place. We take pleasure in furnishing designs at any time required

As has always been the case we are to the fore in building racing Canoes. We have several new single and tandem designs. Write us before you order.

—23—

Lakefield Canoe Company Catalogue, 1915

The Lakefield Canoe Company emerged from the amalgamation between the Gordon Canoe Company (owned by Thomas Gordon) and Strickland & Company (owned by George Strickland). Gordon was the first to commercialize plank canoe construction and establish the world's first canoe shop. Canoe racing became popular in Lakefield, a small community near Peterborough, from 1835, when George Strickland's "Lakefield dugout" named *Shooting Star* won the race and attention for its all-wood design. From 1918–1942 Lakefield Canoe Company underwent at least four ownership and structure changes. In 1942 the plant burned, but the Gordon forms were safe, perhaps because they were in storage elsewhere. The classic Gordon forms are used today by the company Peel Marine, in Lakefield.

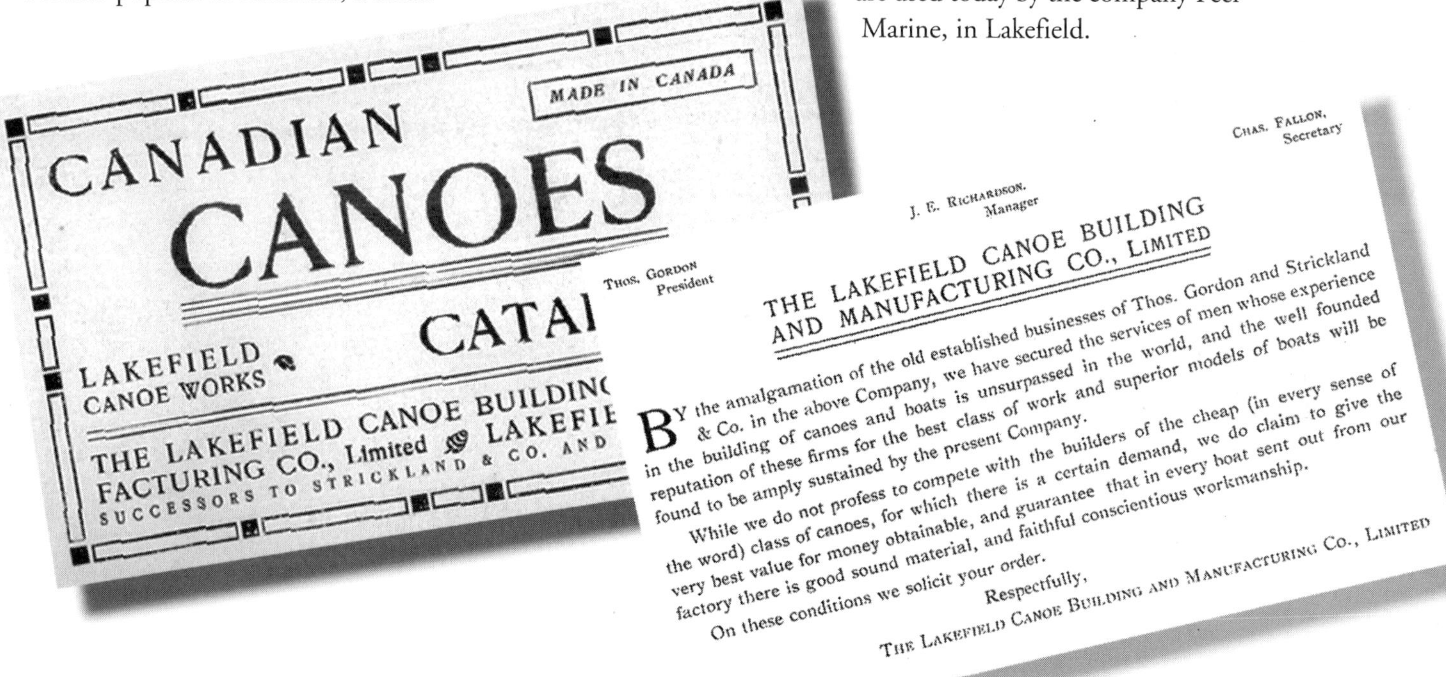

CHAS. FALLON,
Secretary

J. E. RICHARDSON,
Manager

THOS. GORDON
President

THE LAKEFIELD CANOE BUILDING
AND MANUFACTURING CO., LIMITED

BY the amalgamation of the old established businesses of Thos. Gordon and Strickland & Co. in the above Company, we have secured the services of men whose experience in the building of canoes and boats is unsurpassed in the world, and the well founded reputation of these firms for the best class of work and superior models of boats will be found to be amply sustained by the present Company.

While we do not profess to compete with the builders of the cheap (in every sense of the word) class of canoes, for which there is a certain demand, we do claim to give the very best value for money obtainable, and guarantee that in every boat sent out from our factory there is good sound material, and faithful conscientious workmanship.

On these conditions we solicit your order.

Respectfully,

THE LAKEFIELD CANOE BUILDING AND MANUFACTURING CO., LIMITED

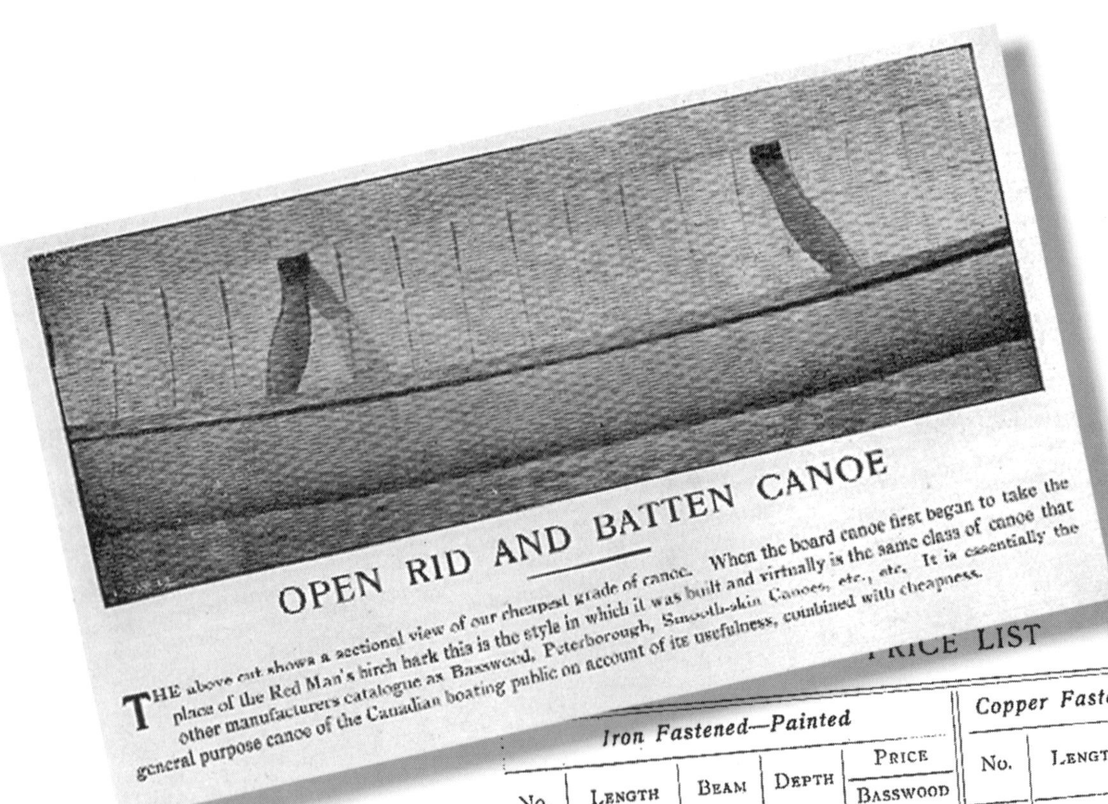

OPEN RID AND BATTEN CANOE

THE above cut shows a sectional view of our cheapest grade of canoe. When the board canoe first began to take the place of the Red Man's birch bark this is the style in which it was built and virtually is the same class of canoe that other manufacturers catalogue as Basswood, Peterborough, Smooth-skin Canoes, etc., etc. It is essentially the general purpose canoe of the Canadian boating public on account of its usefulness, combined with cheapness.

CANOES

PRICE LIST

Iron Fastened—Painted

No.	Length	Beam	Depth	Price Basswood
0	14 ft. 6 in.	28 in.	11 in.	$25 00
1	15 0	29	11	26 00
2	15 6	30	11½	28 00
3	16 0	31	12	29 00
4	16 6	32	12	31 00
5	17 0	33	12½	33 00

Copper Fastened—Varnished or Painted

No.	Length	Beam	Depth	Price Basswood
20	14 ft. 6 in.	28 in.	11 in.	$32 00
21	15 0	29	11	33 00
22	15 6	30	11½	35 00
23	16 0	31	12	37 00
24	16 6	32	12	39 00
25	17 0	33	12½	40 00

Price includes Two Paddles—Larger sizes, if required, at proportionate prices

—3—

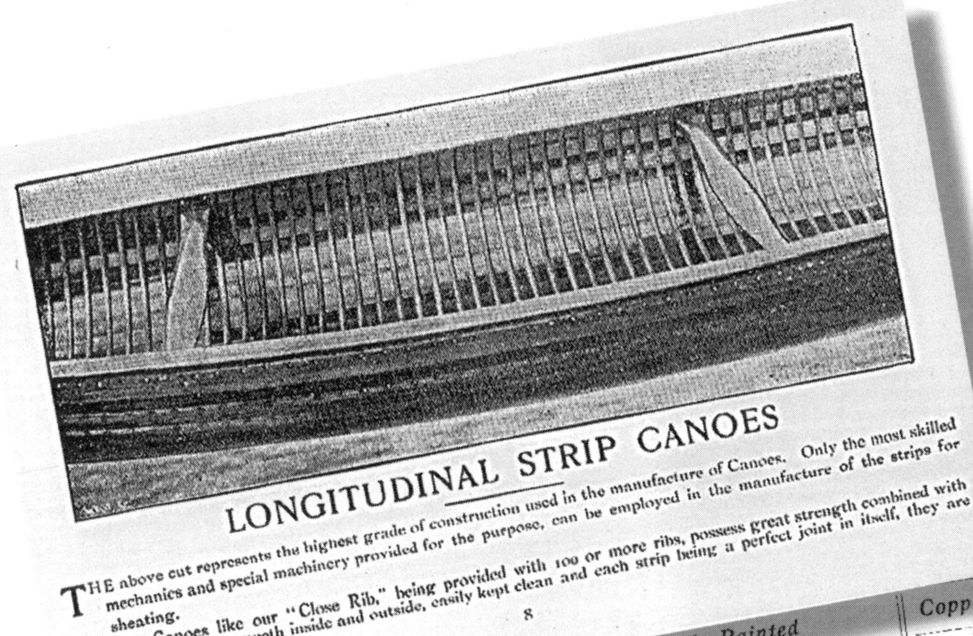

LONGITUDINAL STRIP CANOES

THE above cut represents the highest grade of construction used in the manufacture of Canoes. Only the most skilled mechanics and special machinery provided for the purpose, can be employed in the manufacture of the strips for sheating.

These Canoes like our "Close Rib," being provided with 100 or more ribs, possess great strength combined with lightness. They are smooth inside and outside, easily kept clean and each strip being a perfect joint in itself, they are absolutely watertight.

8

P CANOES

Iron Fastened—Painted					Copper Fastened—Varnished or Painted				
No.	Length	Beam	Depth	Price Basswood	No.	Length	Beam	Depth	Price Cedar or Butternut
120	14 ft. 6 in.	28 in.	11 in.	$30 00	140	14 ft. 6 in.	28 in.	11 in.	$43 00
121	15 0	29	11	31 00	141	15 0	29	11	45 00
122	15 6	30	11½	32 00	142	15 6	30	11½	47 00
123	16 0	31	12	33 00	143	16 0	31	12	50 00
124	16 6	32	12	35 00	144	16 6	32	12	53 00
125	17 0	33	12½	37 00	145	17 0	33	12½	56 00

Price includes Two Paddles—Larger sizes, if required, at proportionate prices Copper Fastened, Varnished or Painted Basswood, add $7.00, to Iron Fastened, Painted Basswood Prices.

— 9 —

PADDLES AND OARS

PRICE LIST

SINGLE PADDLES

Hard and Soft Maple or Butternut, common grade, varnished............	$1 25
Hard and Soft Maple or Butternut, selected grade, varnished............	1 50
Bird-eye Maple, Walnut or Cherry...	2 00

DOUBLE PADDLES

Double Paddles...............from $3 00 to 5 00

OARS

Made of Spr

LEATHERED

Straight Blade..........

Spoon Blade..........

White Ash

SAILING CANOES

WE build full and half-decked Sailing Canoes on any of our moulds and fit them with centreboard, drop rudder, steering gear ,sails, seat, mast tubes, etc.

PRICE—$50.00 to $250.00

According to size, style of construction, sail plan and finish desired.

Our factory being equipped with the best modern machinery and having an efficient staff of skilled workmen, we are prepared to build Canoes from private designs and faithfully carry out the instructions of our customers.

AILS and all GEAR Made to Order

ORDERING

INTENDING purchasers should place their order for Boats or Canoes some weeks in advance of the date they require them, as it takes time to finish a Canoe properly and we may not happen to have in stock the size or build wanted.

SHIPPING AND PACKING

FOR foreign shipment or long journey by rail, the first six canoes on our list of sizes are so arranged that they can be nested and put in one case, and the thwarts and decks numbered so that they can be easily placed in position again on arrival at destination.

Crates for single Canoes..	$1 50 to $3 00
Crates for Canoes nested..	5 00 to 10 00
Canvas Covers, each..	1 50

TERMS

NET cash must accompany order, or else a deposit of 25% made and article sent C. O. D. for the balance.

THE LAKEFIELD CANOE BUILDING AND MANUFACTURING CO., LIMITED
LAKEFIELD, ONTARIO, CANADA

N. B.—All previous Price Lists cancelled.

Rice Lake Canoe Company Catalogue, 1918

Daniel Herald's canoe company, Herald & Hutchinson, was founded in 1862 and called Herald Brothers in 1892, before Herald's sons renamed it the Rice Lake Canoe Company. Herald is best known for his 1871 patented cedar double rib canoe design, the predecessor of the molded plywood concept. His design involved an in between layer of fabric made rot resistant by two coats of white lead, a precursor to wood-and-canvas. Rice Lake Canoe Company closed its Montreal-based doors in 1928.

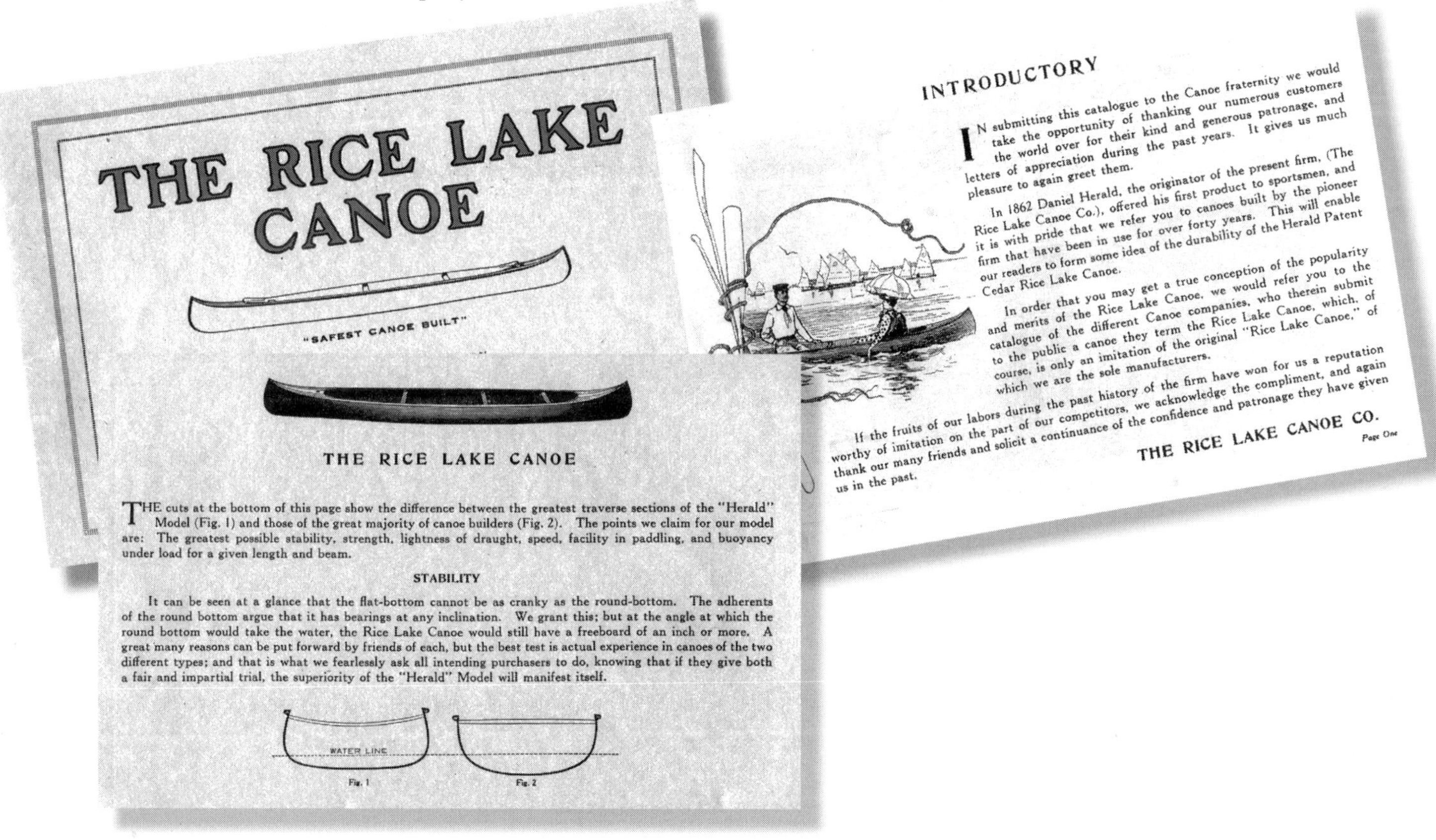

THE RICE LAKE CANOE

"SAFEST CANOE BUILT"

THE RICE LAKE CANOE

THE cuts at the bottom of this page show the difference between the greatest traverse sections of the "Herald" Model (Fig. 1) and those of the great majority of canoe builders (Fig. 2). The points we claim for our model are: The greatest possible stability, strength, lightness of draught, speed, facility in paddling, and buoyancy under load for a given length and beam.

STABILITY

It can be seen at a glance that the flat-bottom cannot be as cranky as the round-bottom. The adherents of the round bottom argue that it has bearings at any inclination. We grant this; but at the angle at which the round bottom would take the water, the Rice Lake Canoe would still have a freeboard of an inch or more. A great many reasons can be put forward by friends of each, but the best test is actual experience in canoes of the two different types; and that is what we fearlessly ask all intending purchasers to do, knowing that if they give both a fair and impartial trial, the superiority of the "Herald" Model will manifest itself.

INTRODUCTORY

IN submitting this catalogue to the Canoe fraternity we would take the opportunity of thanking our numerous customers the world over for their kind and generous patronage, and letters of appreciation during the past years. It gives us much pleasure to again greet them.

In 1862 Daniel Herald, the originator of the present firm, (The Rice Lake Canoe Co.), offered his first product to sportsmen, and it is with pride that we refer you to canoes built by the pioneer firm that have been in use for over forty years. This will enable our readers to form some idea of the durability of the Herald Patent Cedar Rice Lake Canoe.

In order that you may get a true conception of the popularity and merits of the Rice Lake Canoe, we would refer you to the catalogue of the different Canoe companies, who therein submit to the public a canoe they term the Rice Lake Canoe, which, of course, is only an imitation of the original "Rice Lake Canoe," of which we are the sole manufacturers.

If the fruits of our labors during the past history of the firm have won for us a reputation worthy of imitation on the part of our competitors, we acknowledge the compliment, and again thank our many friends and solicit a continuance of the confidence and patronage they have given us in the past.

THE RICE LAKE CANOE CO.

Page One

THE RICE LAKE CANOE

THE OPEN BASSWOOD CANOE

THE Open Basswood Canoe is the style of canoe that is in the most use among canoeists in this country. It possesses the recommendation of lightness, cheapness, and almost unlimited capacity for storage in hunting excursions. As a pleasure canoe, the extraordinary demand for them from the various Canoe Clubs speaks volumes for the estimation in which they are held.

The Canoes we keep in stock of this style, are finished with short decks about two feet long, with three thwarts, mast-ring and step. We can make the decks longer if wished, though the shorter the decks are, the more handsome and rakish the canoe looks. These canoes can be built light or heavy as required, though we think the weights on the next page are as light as is consistent with strength. They are planked with basswood a quarter of an inch thick; the ribs are 3/4 x 5/16 and spaced 6 inches apart. The joints of the planks are battened on the inside, making a perfectly smooth-skinned canoe on the outside. The Varnished Basswood is made of clear White Basswood, with Brass and Copper finishing throughout. We use only the best quality varnish and finish in the natural wood. There is no shellac to turn white and spoil beauty of finish. The Painted Basswood is built with iron nails, and painted any color to suit, and the outside is varnished over paint. This season we are making all the fittings of Brass, which greatly enhance the beauty of the painted canoe. The decks and thwarts are oiled and varnished. We sometimes receive an order for a Painted Basswood Canoe to be planked with copper nails; this we do at an additional cost of $1.50. We build three special sizes to pack inside one another for long distance shipments to save freight. The sizes are 15½x28x11½; 16x30 x12; 17x32x12. The decks and thwarts are taken out and, with the paddles, are packed inside the canoe. The whole outfit is securely packed in a strong crate at a cost of $5.00. We do not build cedar canoes in this style. Basswood is the only wood that will stand without checking. Upon application, we can make a cheaper painted canoe for hunting only.

NOE

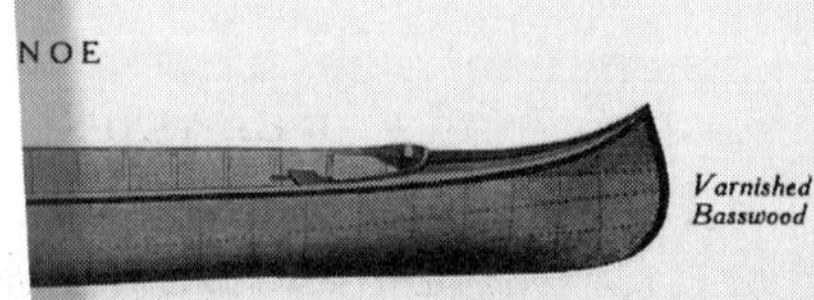

Varnished Basswood

D CANOES

No.	Length	Beam	Depth	Weight Approximate	Varnished	Painted
1	13 feet	28 inches	11 inches	40 lbs.	$32.00	$25.00
2	15½ "	28 "	11¼ "	45 "	34.00	27.00
2½	14 "	31 "	12 "	55 "	36.00	28.00
3	**16 "**	**31 "**	**12 "**	**60 "**	**37.00**	**29.00**
4	17 "	32½ "	12 "	70 "	43.00	33.00
5	16 "	30 "	12 "	60 "	37.00	29.00
6	19 "	42 "	16 "	135 "	58.00	48.00
7	16½ "	37 "	15 "	90 "	45.00	37.00
A	16 "	30 "	12 "	60 "	37.00	29.00
B	17½ "	33 "	13 "	75 "	45.00	36.00
C	20 "	32 "	12 "	85 "	56.00	46.00

Price includes 2 paddles.
Use air tanks (see page 14).
Names or Stripes painted, $1.00 extra.
Painted Canoes copper nailed, $1.50 extra.
Canoes painted White, $1.00 extra.
Extra depth, $1.00 per inch.
Numbers 5 and A are the regular A. C. A. racing size. Greatest beam of A. B. C. at water line is 16 in. aft of centre.

Painted Basswood

Page Five

THE RICE LAKE CANOE

HERALD'S PATENT CEDAR CANOE

OUR Open Cedar Canoe, "Herald's" Patent, is the strongest, most durable and lasting canoe that has ever been invented. These canoes are built with two thicknesses of cedar, with water-proof canvas between, fastened with iron or copper nails, smooth inside and out, and require no ribs or linings, the grain of the inside thickness running transversely to that of the outside, which is fore and aft. Owing to this peculiar construction it is not liable to leak or get damaged; so we claim that it is the most serviceable hunting canoe that a sportsman can buy. The lasting qualities are such that we know of many canoes that were built fifteen or twenty years ago, and are as sound to-day as the day they were built. An impression has gone abroad that these canoes rot when water gets in between the two thicknesses. When they were first introduced the top plank was put in of bass-wood, thinking because it was above the water-line it would stand. This was found to be a mistake, as in the course of a few years the basswood rotted, but the cedar was as sound as ever. After that experience they were built of cedar only, and we will give a guarantee, when requested, that they will remain perfectly sound. Every canoe gets two coats of white lead paint between the two thicknesses. The varnished cedar is finished with brass and copper throughout. The painted cedar is planked with iron nails; the decks, gunwales and thwarts are oiled and varnished. The thwarts are cedar, the decks butternut, and the gunwales are oak. When a painted cedar canoe is ordered copper fastened, we make an extra charge of $2.50. Upon special orders we can make alterations in sheer, length of decks, finish, etc. Each additional inch in depth, $2.00 extra. Canoes painted White and stripes on Canoes are also extra. For Canoes required Varnished inside and Painted outside, the price will be the mean between the varnished and painted prices.

Varnished Cedar

... CEDAR CANOES—HERALD'S PATENT

No.	Length	Beam	Depth	Weight	Varnished	Painted
1	13 feet	28 inches	11 inches	40 lbs.	$52.00	$45.00
2	15½ "	28 "	11½ "	50 "	55.00	48.00
2½	14 "	31 "	12 "	60 "	60.00	51.00
3	**16** "	**31** "	**12** "	**65** "	**65.00**	**55.00**
4	17 "	32½ "	12 "	75 "	68.00	58.00
5	16 "	30 "	12 "	60 "	65.00	55.00
A	16 "	30 "	12 "	60 "	65.00	55.00
C	20 "	33 "	12 "	85 "	85.00	75.00

2 paddles go with each canoe.
Painted Canoe, copper nailed, $2.50 extra.
Centre Keel and Bilge Keels, $3.00 per set.
Cane seats, $1.00 each.
Extra depth, $2.00 per inch.

The models are the same shape as those upon which our Basswood Canoes are built. A and C built for speed.
Greatest beam of A and C at the water line is 16 inches, aft of centre.

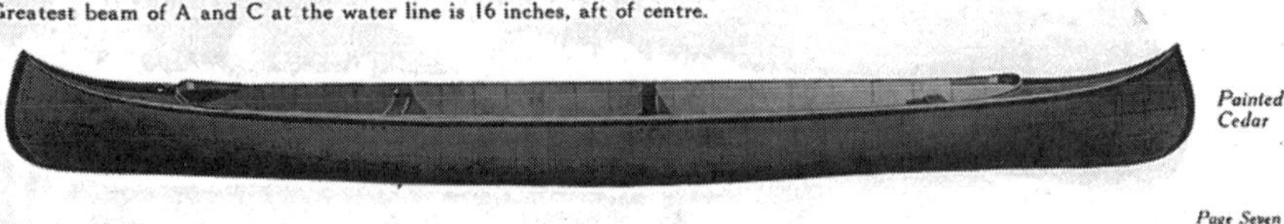

Painted Cedar

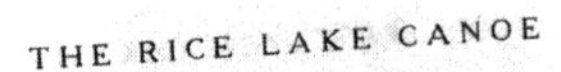

THE RICE LAKE CANOE

SAILING CANOES

THE original Canadian canoe was essentially a paddling canoe. It is yet the favorite among the canoeists in this country, but there is a gradually increasing class who go in for sailing alone; at a small cost they can get a craft that can beat the average small yacht that costs ten times the money. In addition, the sailing canoeist gets a boat of fine finish, fittings and appointments, that he takes a pride in keeping trim and neat, and inventing fixtures where he sees improvements can be made. We only build sailing canoes to order, as no two parties desire the same style, some want a shorter cockpit than others, others want more or less sheer, and still others want special material and finish.

We generally make the decks of butternut, as experience has taught us that it will stand more hard work than most wood, besides being a handsome wood. Decks of Mahogany, Spanish Cedar, Black Walnut, Cherry, Alternate Strips and Birch Bark, $2.00 to $6.00 extra. The combings are made of rock elm. We would strongly advise intending purchasers to have moveable airtight tanks instead of airtight bulkheads; the bulkhead in such a light built craft as a canoe, though put in perfectly watertight at the beginning, is sure to get strained at some time and leak.

In ordering a sailing canoe be sure and give correct plans at the start, as there is an expense when alterations are required when the canoe is well under way.

KE CANOE

PRICE LIST OF SAILING CANOES

No.	Length	Beam	Depth	Varnished Cedar	Painted Cedar	Varnished Basswood	Painted Basswood
1	13 feet	28 inches	10 inches	$62.00	$55.00	$42.00	$35.00
2	15 "	28 "	11 "	65.00	58.00	44.00	37.00
2½	14 "	31 "	12 "	70.00	61.00	46.00	38.00
3	**16** "	**31** "	**12** "	**75.00**	**65.00**	**47 00**	**39.00**
4	17 "	32½ "	12 "	78.00	68.00	53.00	43.00
5	16 "	30 "	12 "	75.00	65.00	47.00	39.00
A	16 "	30 "	12 "	75.00	65.00	47.00	39.00
C	20 "	33 "	12 "	97.00	87.00	68.00	58.00

Nos. 2, 5 and A are racing canoes. Prices include trunk for centre board, two bulkheads or air tanks, and mast tubes.

CANVAS COVERED CANOES Built to Order. Model and Sizes same as Basswood Canoes described on Page Five.

ROW BOATS, all sizes, Painted or Varnished Built to Order.

THE RICE LAKE CANOE

HALF-DECKED CANOES

THESE canoes possess, only in a lesser degree, the combined good qualities of both the sailing and paddling canoes. The fore and after decks are from 2 feet to 2½ feet long, and are extended the entire length of canoe at the sides to a width of 3 or 4 inches. A combing 1 inch deep is run around the cockpit.

The side decking and the combing brace the canoe so strongly that we are able to dispense with fixed thwarts and have them moveable. This is a great advantage to parties out on trips of a few days' duration, as by putting up a short mast at each end and drawing a cord tightly from one to the other, a blanket may be utilized as a tent by throwing it over the cord ridge pole and no thwarts in the way. A proper canoe tent if wished, can be constructed for them at a small cost. It makes a first-class paddling canoe and by the addition of a canvas or rubber apron on forward part of cockpit it becomes an excellent sailing canoe. They can be constructed on either the Herald's Patent principle, of cedar, or of basswood rib and batten.

The varnished style is copper fastened throughout. The painted style is planked with iron nails and painted any color and varnished over paint, the fittings are all of brass, and decking is oiled and varnished. If wished, any style of centre-board can be fitted in.

E CANOE

…e is on same principle, and planked on same models …cked as per illustration above.

…D CANOES

No.	Length	Beam	Depth	Varnished Cedar	Painted Cedar	Varnished Basswood	Painted Basswood
1	13 feet	28 inches	9½ inches	$60.00	$53.00	$40.00	$33.00
2	15 "	28 "	10 "	63.00	56.00	42.00	35.00
2½	14 "	31 "	11 "	68.00	59.00	44.00	63.00
3	**16** "	**31** "	**11** "	**73.00**	**63.00**	**45.00**	**37.00**
4	17 "	32½ "	11½ "	76.00	66.00	51.00	41.00
5	16 "	30 "	11 "	73.00	63.00	45.00	37.00
A	16 "	30 "	11 "	73.00	63.00	45.00	37.00
B	17½ "	33 "	11½ "	78.00	68.00	63.00	53.00
C	20 "	32 "	11½	95.00	85.00	65.00	56.00

Thwarts are moveable.

Fitted with 2 mast tubes.

Air tanks extra.

SAILS

Lateen Sails

No.	Area	Complete with Mast, Yard, and Boom	Complete to Hoist with Halyards
1	15 feet	$4.50	$6.75
2	25 "	5.00	7.75
3	35 "	6.00	8.25
4	50 "	8.00	10.00
5	75 "	10.00	12.00
6	85 "	12.00	14.00

Mohican Sails

No.	Area	Sail only	Complete with Reefing Gear to Hoist with Halyards
7	15 feet	$2.75	$8.50
8	25 "	3.25	10.00
9	35 "	3.75	11.00
10	45 "	4.25	12.25
11	55 "	5.25	13.75
12	65 "	6.25	15.25

Prices for special sizes and shapes furnished on application.

Our sails are made by a practical sailmaker of reputation, therefore patrons are guaranteed in having a well-fitting sail. The above sails are made out of the best bleached steamloom. Can make a good strong working Lateen sail also, to hook on mast; made of strong cotton from $3.25 for a 25 ft. sail to $5.00 for a 50 ft. sail.

PRICE LIST OF PADDLES

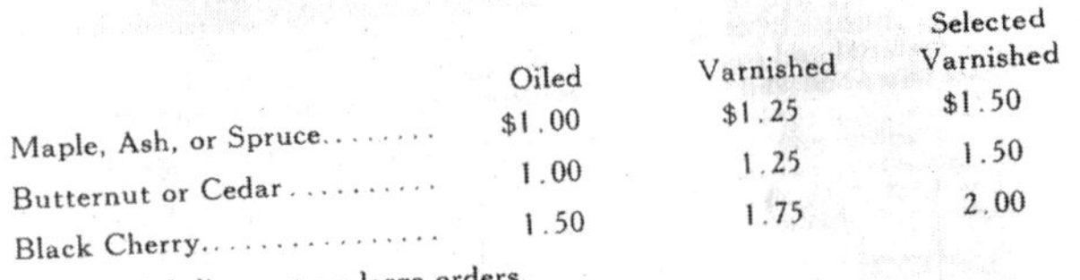

	Oiled	Varnished	Selected Varnished
Maple, Ash, or Spruce	$1.00	$1.25	$1.50
Butternut or Cedar	1.00	1.25	1.50
Black Cherry	1.50	1.75	2.00

Special discount on large orders.

DOUBLE BLADE PADDLES

8-9 ft. long, spruce, flat blade, jointed	$3.50
8-9 ft. long, spruce, spoon blade, jointed	4.00
Handle to make single blade	.75

FITTINGS, EXTRAS, Etc.

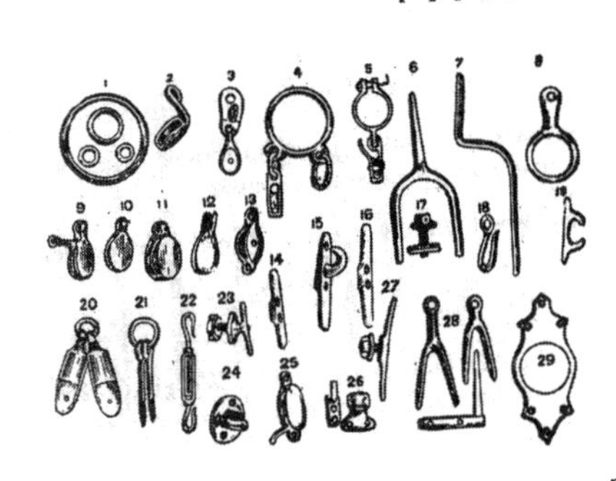

No.	Description	Price
1	Rings, 2 to 2½ in	$0.20
2	Block for Mast Head	.60
3	" "	1.00
4	" Mast Foot Gear	1.00
5	" for Sail Yard	1.00
6	Jaws, double	.60
7	" half-round	.50
8	Mast Ring	.50
9	Block, clutch	.70
10	" small	.40
11	Block, double	.90
12	" snatch	.60
13	" main sheet	.50
14	Cleats, jamb 2 in.	.20

No.	Description	Price
15	Cleats, Blanche	$ .40
16	" jamb 4 in.	.40
17	Bolt, Steering Gear Wheel	.25
18	Hooks, spring, small	.10
19	Cleat, Chock from	.40 to .80
20	Connecting Socket	.60
21	" Links	.40
22	Tighters for Rudder, per pair	.80
23	Cleat with nut	.40
24	" Cam	.60
25	" Clutch	.70
26	" Clutch and Fairleader	.75
27	" with nut	.50
28	Rudder Braces, per pair	.75
29	Mast Plates	.50
	Cord Braided for Halyards, per yard	.04
	" " reefing	.03
	" " lashing	.02
	Chain, safety, per foot	.10
	Combing Braces	.15
	Friction Paddle Joints, 1⅛ to 1¼	.75 to .95
	Keel fitted to Canoe	2.00
	Iron on bottom	1.00
	Brass "	1.00
	Lee Boards	2.50 to 3.50
	Outriggers, per pair	5.00
	Masts, per foot	.10
	Yard and Boom, per foot	.08
	Steering Gear, Deck	2.50
	Back-board	.50
	Folding back-board	1.50
	" " cushioned	3.00
	Rudders	2.50 to 7.50
	Crates for Shipping	3.00 to 5.00
	Canvas packing for Canoe	1.50

Peterborough Canoe Company Catalogue, 1918

This classic Peterborough catalogue with a coloured embossed cover, shows the grandiose scale of production from the company, which included all methods of canoes, rowing, sailing, and motorized boats and accessories. Wood-and-canvas canoes are included in spite of Chestnut's patent.

Note the all-wood freight canoes with an "optional" canvas covering. It is possible that some of the "canvas" canoes were built on the all-wood forms as builders were extremely handy at all types of manipulations. While here wood-and-canvas seems to be an aside, in just a few years (after the 1923 merger) the Peterborough line of wood canvas suddenly jumped to completely duplicate the Chestnut line—after all, that's exactly what they were. Later, few models of these canoes appeared from Peterborough.

THE PETERBOROUGH CANOE COMPANY, Limited

WHAT WE MANUFACTURE

CANOES

Methods of Construction.

RIB AND BATTEN, planked with wide boards, with the edges of the boards held together with a batten the same size as the ribs.

FLUSH BATTEN, planked with wide boards, the edges of the boards being held together with a batten which is halved into planking to cover the joint. This batten runs the full length of the canoe, and leaves the inside of the canoe perfectly smooth between the ribs.

METALLIC JOINT, built the same as the above, using a thin copper batten in place of the wooden batten.

CANVAS COVERED CANOES, constructed of Cedar and covered with tough canvas, treated with paint and oil.

SPONSON CANOES. Canvas covered canoes with an air chamber built over the outside of the boat, along each gunwale. Absolutely unsinkable.

LONGITUDINAL CEDAR STRIP CANOE. Built of strips running longitudinally and grooved together.

CEDAR RIB CANOES. Built of Cedar strips supplied out of stright grain lumber, tongued and grooved, strips 1 inch wide running from gunwale to gunwale. The strongest canoe in the world.

RACING CANOES. Built on lines and of lightness to sacrifice everything to speed. Our models are always successful.

DECKED CANOES. Any of our canoes can be decked in "Solid Comfort," "Juniper," "Ontario," or "Torpedo" Decking.

These several styles are referred to at length under separate classification.

ROWBOATS

CEDAR LAPSTREAK SKIFFS. Planked with Cedar, about 4 inches wide with the edges lapped. The most popular form of construction.

CANOE SKIFFS, or smooth skin row boats are built the same as the canoes above mentioned, but on row boat models.

We build a large number of special skiffs with square sterns suitable for use with outboard motors.

SAILING BOATS

LAPSTREAK SAILING DINGHYS. Narrow planking of Cedar with the edges lapped.

SMOOTH SKIN OR RIB AND BATTEN DINGHYS. Built of the same construction as "rib and batten" canoes, smooth outside.

Sails can be used on all our canoes and skiffs.

SPECIALTIES

We manufacture a large number of different kinds of special boats described in this and other catalogues, also full line of accessories.

MOTOR BOATS

We manufacture and describe in another catalogue a complete line of motor boats.

We also equip to order any of the small boats above mentioned with motors of suitable power.

THE PETERBOROUGH CANOE COMPANY, Limited

EVOLUTION OF THE CANOE.

THE functions of the Canoe are many and varied. No other water craft may take its place or supplant it in popular esteem. As a means of transportation and travel it easily holds a first place on this continent. Explorer, voyager, surveyor and trapper have all proved its usefulness. The great enterprises carried on by the fur trading companies were only made possible and certainly made profitable by means of the canoe. To its ever ready service in the early past and in the later present the country at large is indebted. As the birch bark canoe served the needs of the Indian tribes for centuries or as the "dug out" made from the trunk of a tree, it met the wants of the early settlers, and as the refined product of the skill and experience of the last thirty years we have, as we build them, the board canoe. Constructed of light, but strong materials and giving a maximum of strength combined with lightness, graceful outlines, large carrying capacity, easily propelled, water-tight and safe.

In the canoe, as in other lines of manufacture, the specialist is the one whose work is sought after and whose product is esteemed. Specializing makes for concentration to attain a definite object, to improve methods of construction, to combine with skill and appreciation materials best suited for a purpose into a perfect whole. We are specialists of many years experience. That kind of experience which throws aside that which is, and has ceased to be absolutely up-to-date, and seizes new methods and principles, and retaining these only after they have been proved true and desirable.

THE PETERBOROUGH CANOE COMPANY, Limited

THE PERFECT PETERBOROUGH.

PETERBOROUGH is the home of the Perfect Canoe. Why so? Because in the city originated and was built the first "Board Canoe," as distinguished from the birch bark or log models. The form of construction was not an inspiration but an evolution. Abundant materials, absolutely perfect for strong and durable construction. It was fitting that these should be made use of.

The original and first product from our factory was the "Open Basswood." Why the name? Open for the full length except the bow and stern decks, inserted to strengthen the canoe at the ends. Basswood, because this wood had suprising qualities of toughness and lightness, and could be bent and coaxed to follow the lines of a model. This desirable wood, when painted and kept painted at intervals, made a canoe unsurpassed for burthen carrying capacity, resistance to hard usage, medium in weight and of graceful lines. It is the canoe of the great Hudson Bay Co., and for other enterprises. In it the prospector, miner and explorer have done, and are doing their work.

Then the demand for canoes of appearance and beauty. Appearance is typified in graceful lines, buoyant, yet safe models. Woods finished to bring out the beauty of grain and color, in which many of our native woods are favored. These are the canoes used for pleasure purposes and for utility as well, for they combine with handsome appearance the results of skilled construction and inspection. These canoes we build in many styles and of many models. On following page we enumerate a number of lines, each having its desirable points.

PETERBOROUGH CANOE CO LTD
THE
Peterborough
Canoe
REGISTERED
TRADE MARK
The Stamp of Quality
Always look for this Trade Mark in the Bow of Canoe.

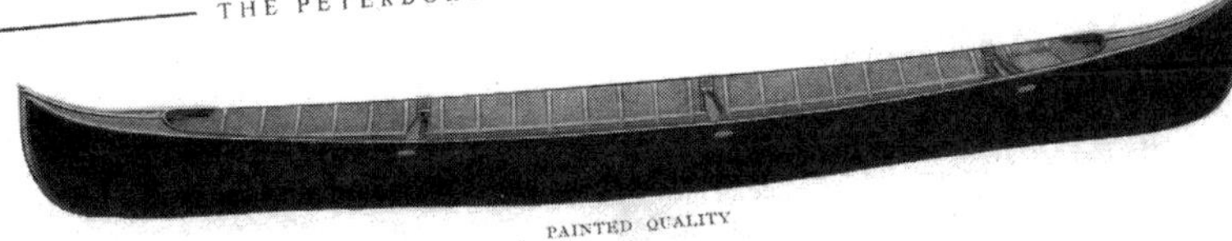

PAINTED QUALITY

RIB AND BATTEN CANOES.

THE term "RIB AND BATTEN" used in describing a canoe refers to the peculiar construction of the frame work and the method of fastening together the edges of the boards which form the planking. The ribs are ¾" and ⅞" half round made of rock elm running in one continuous piece from one edge of the canoe or gunwale to the other. Over the edges of the planking, where the boards meet, is fitted a strip of the same material as the ribs called a "batten." This "batten" is carefully curved on the ends to fit over the ribs. When nailed and clinched this fitting draws the edge of the planking up tight against the batten and the batten in turn drawn tight against the ribs making the whole frame of the canoe very rigid. This coving of the ends of each batten while requiring a lot of extra work in the building is one of the points that go to make up the superior construction of a PETERBOROUGH RIB AND BATTEN CANOE over all other makes of this kind of canoe. The general practice in inferior makes of this class of canoe is to cut the batten off square at the ends and not bother fitting it into the ribs as we do. This allows all the strain caused by knocking against anything when the boat is in use to be taken up by the planking of the boat instead of the ribs. This shortens the life of the boat and after a season or so it is bound to cause the canoe to leak.

The frame as above mentioned is covered with a planking of the finest grade of selected basswood, cedar or mahogany ¼" thick. The edges of this planking are held together by the batten as above described. The gunwales, thwarts and decks are of oak and butternut finished in the natural wood.

ATTEN" AND "FLUSH BATTEN" CANOES.

PAINTED QUALITY

Number	Length	Beam	Depth	Weight About	Capacity with 6 inch Draft	Painted Basswood	Painted Cedar	Painted Basswood Flush Batten
	Feet	Inches	Inches	Pounds	Pounds			
61	14½	26½	11	60	395	$30.00	$39.00	
62	15	28	12	65	425	30.00	39.00	$36.00
63	15½	29½	12	70	460	31.00	40.00	38.00
64	**16**	**31**	**12**	**75**	**480**	**32.00**	**42.00**	**39.00**
65	16½	33	12½	80	550	34.00	44.00	41.00
66	17	35	13	85	600	36.00	47.00	
67	17½	36	13¾	90	750	39.00	51.00	
68	18	37	14	95	820	42.00	54.00	
68½	18½	38	14½	100	830	45.00	58.00	
69	19	39	15	105	850	48.00	62.00	
69½	19½	40	15½	115	870	51.00	66.00	
74	16	30	12	75	440	32.00	42.00	
78	13½	26	12	55	400	30.00	39.00	
79	14	28	12	60	400	30.00	39.00	
80	14½	29½	12	65	440	31.00	40.00	
81	15	31	12	70	470	32.00	42.00	
82	15½	32½	12½	75	510	33.00	43.00	
83	16	34	13	80	540	34.00	44.00	
84	16½	35	13½	85	580	35.00	46.00	
86	12	30	12	60	420	30.00	39.00	
87	12½	32	12	65	450	30.00	39.00	
88	13	34	13	70	500	32.00	42.00	
89	14	35	13	75	550	34.00	44.00	
90	15	36	13	80	600	36.00	47.00	
92	16	38	14	85	650	38.00	50.00	

REMARKS.

For Canoes with larger carrying capacity, see page 16, 17.

We recommend the use of Air Tanks, see page 34.

Painted Canoes can be built with copper nails, for $2.00 and up, *extra*.

Torpedo Decks, instead of the ordinary style, $2.00 per Canoe *extra*.

Painting Canoes white, $1.00 *extra*. Stripes or names painted, $1.00 *extra*.

Cane Seats, instead of thwarts, $1.00 each *extra*.

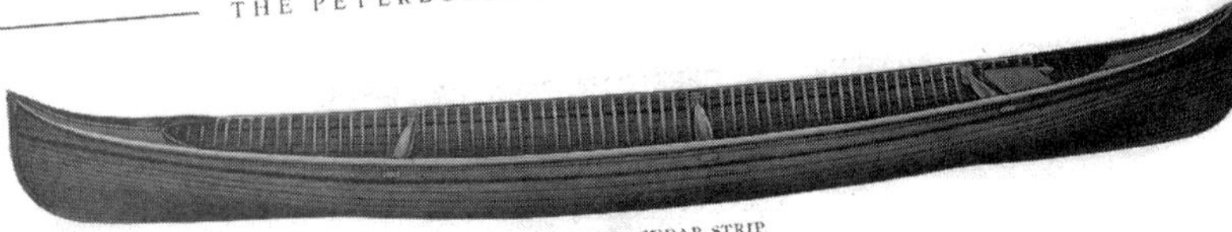

VARNISHED CEDAR STRIP

LONGITUDINAL STRIP CANOE.

THE LONGITUDINAL STRIP CANOE receives its name from the fact that the planking is made up of narrow strips about 2 inches wide which run longitudinally or lengthwise of the canoe from bow to stern. The narrow strips that form the planking are half checked together with what is known as the "ship lap joint" and is made of selected clear basswood, cedar, cypress, mahogany or spruce. The ribs in this construction are ¾ inch and ⅞ inch half round rock elm running from gunwale to gunwale. The spacing of these ribs is 3 inches from centre to centre, which makes a very strong canoe on account of the close spacing of the ribs and the shape of the planking.

SECTION LONGITUDINAL STRIP CANOE

The LONGITUDINAL STRIP canoe is one of our most popular methods of construction. The narrow planking is an important feature as there is no noticeable shrinkage and they do not check, split or open up when exposed to the sun and weather as do some of the wide planked canoes when unduly exposed. We would draw attention to fact that all our LONGITUDINAL STRIP canoes are put together with a ship lap joint, and this groove is first flushed with varnish before the strips are put on the boat as an extra precaution against leakage, and also as a great preservative for the wood.

Our large freight canoes in the XX size are also built of this construction.

GITUDINAL STRIP CANOES.

Number	Length	Beam	Depth	Painted Cedar	Varnished Cedar	Varnished Mahogany	REMARKS.
	Feet	Inches	Inches				
42	15	28	12	$44 00	$50 00	$60.00	
43	15½	29½	12	45.00	52.00	62.00	
44	16	31	12	47.00	54.00	65.00	
45	16½	33	12½	49 00	57.00	68.00	Extra Depth, $2.00 per inch.
46	17	35	13	52 00	60.00	72.00	
48	18	38	14½	57.00	66.00	78.00	Cane Seats $1.00 *extra.*
50	14½	29½	12	45 00	52 00	62.00	
51	15	31	12	47 00	54 00	65.00	Torpedo Decks, $2.00 per Canoe.
52	15½	32½	12½	49 00	56.00	67.00	
53	16	34	13	51.00	58 00	70.00	Use Air Tanks, see page 34.
54	16½	35	13½	53 00	60.00	72.00	
86	12	30	12	44 00	50.00	60.00	
87	12½	32	12	44.00	50.00	60.00	For FREIGHT CANOES in this construction, see pages 16 and 17.
88	13	34	13	45 00	52 00	62.00	
89	14	35	13	48.00	56.00	66.00	
90	15	36	13	51.00	59 00	70.00	
92	16	38	14	54 00	62.00	74 00	

THE PETERBOROUGH CANOE COMPANY Limited

VARNISHED CEDAR RIB

CEDAR RIB CANOES.

SECTION CEDAR RIB

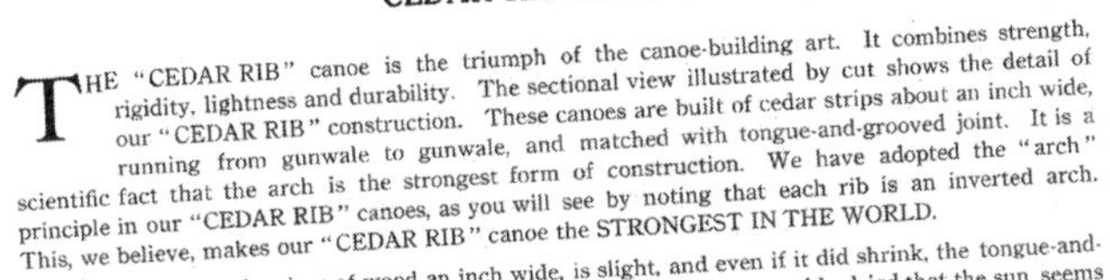

THE "CEDAR RIB" canoe is the triumph of the canoe-building art. It combines strength, rigidity, lightness and durability. The sectional view illustrated by cut shows the detail of our "CEDAR RIB" construction. These canoes are built of cedar strips about an inch wide, running from gunwale to gunwale, and matched with tongue-and-grooved joint. It is a scientific fact that the arch is the strongest form of construction. We have adopted the "arch" principle in our "CEDAR RIB" canoes, as you will see by noting that each rib is an inverted arch. This, we believe, makes our "CEDAR RIB" canoe the STRONGEST IN THE WORLD.

The shrinkage of a piece of wood an inch wide, is slight, and even if it did shrink, the tongue-and-groove joint would prevent any leakage. The cedar we use is so thoroughly dried that the sun seems to have little effect upon it. It takes about a month to build a "CEDAR RIB" from start to completion but we always try to keep our moulds full, so as to have a goodly number dry and ready to finish. After years of experience we are more than ever satisfied with the "CEDAR RIB" method of construction. We can produce "CEDAR RIB" canoes that have been in constant use for thirty-five seasons, and are in first-class condition. We claim for our "CEDAR RIB" canoe lightness, tightness, strength, and durability and beauty. They are the best and strongest canoe made, and require experience in building. They are canoes of the very highest quality, and have more strength for their weight than any canoe manufactured.

…GH CANOE COMPANY, Limited

…OF "CEDAR RIB" CANOES.

Number	Length	Beam	Depth	Weight	Capacity 6 inch Draft	Painted Quality	Varnished Quality	REMARKS
	Feet	Inches	Inches	Pounds	Pounds			
2	15	28	12	45	425	$55.00	$60 00	
3	15½	29½	12	55	460	57.00	62.00	
4	**16**	**31**	**12**	**60**	**480**	**59.00**	**64.00**	
5	16½	33	13	65	550	62.00	67.00	
6	17	35	13½	75	600	65.00	70.00	
8	18	39	15	95	820	75 00	80.00	
10	19	42	17	105	900	85 00	90.00	Extra depth, $2.00 per inch.
18	13	25½	11	35	350	55 00	60.00	
19	13½	27	12	40	380	55 00	60.00	
20	14	28½	12	47	400	55.00	60.00	Use Air Tanks in your Canoe. See page 34.
21	14½	30	12	55	420	57.00	62 00	
22	15	31	12	60	440	59.00	64.00	
23	15½	33	12½	65	480	61.00	66.00	All CEDAR RIB Canoes have cane seat in stern.
24	16	34½	13	70	550	63.00	68.00	
86	12	30	12	45	420	50 00	56.00	
87	12½	32	12	50	450	52.00	58.00	
88	13	34	13	55	500	55.00	60.00	
89	14	35	13	60	550	58.00	62.00	
90	15	36	13	65	600	60.00	65.00	
92	16	38	14	72	650	65.00	70 00	

THE PETERBOROUGH CANOE COMPANY, Limited

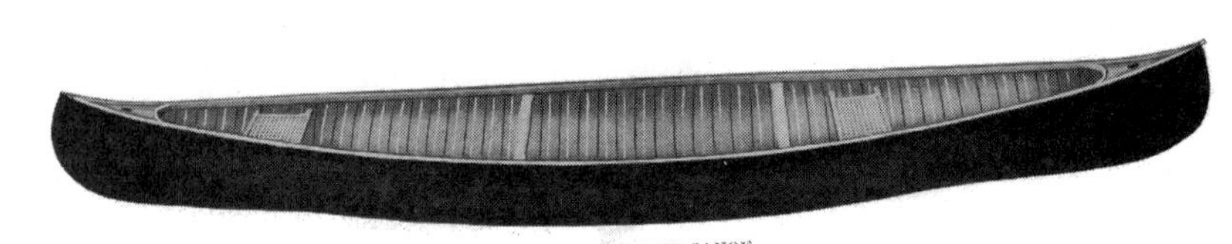

CANVAS COVERED CANOE

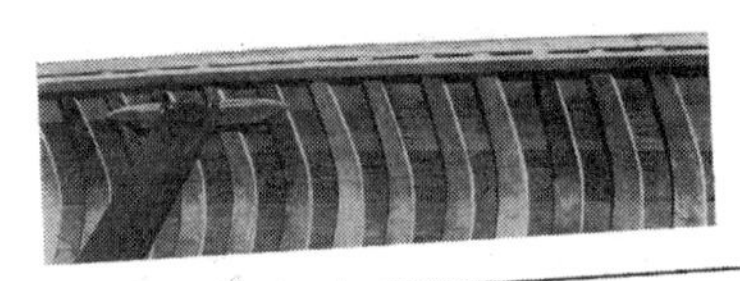

CANVAS COVERED CANOES.

OUR canvas covered canoes are essentially an all cedar canoe covered with the finest grade of special canoe duck in one piece. The ribs are 2¼ inch wide, ¼ inch thick, and are made of clear Ontario cedar bent from gunwale to gunwale and spaced close together. This frame is planked with a very light covering of cedar. This boat is then finished the same as the wooden canoe being varnished inside. Over the outside of the canoe is stretched the canvas all in one piece and it fits closely to the wooden shell. The canvas is then filled with a special preparation which is carefully rubbed down until a perfectly smooth surface is obtained. This is then painted and finished in colors as desired, and finally covered with spar varnish. The canvas covered canoe is tough and durable and is not affected by exposure.

THE PETERBOROUGH CANOE COMPANY Limited

PRICES OF CANVAS COVERED CANOES.

Number	Length	Beam	Depth	Weight	Price
86	12	30	12	50	$35.00
88	13	33	12	60	38.00
90	15	36	13	70	42.00
604	16	31	12	65	40.00
606	17	35	13	75	44.00
608	18	37	14	85	48 00

These canoes are made with two cane seats.

SPONSON CANOES.

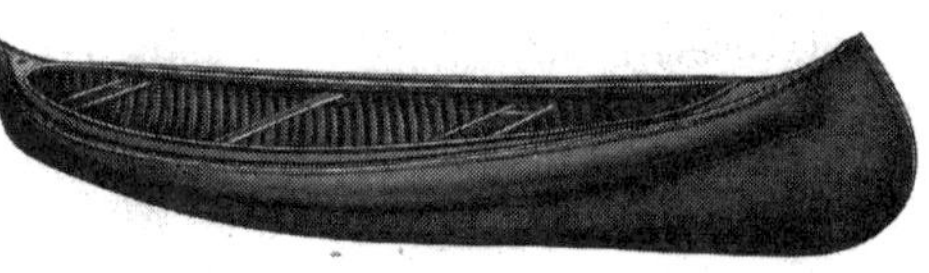

THE SPONSONS are the Air Chambers built along the sides of the canoe. This makes a canoe that is almost impossible to upset. Around summer resorts, for the use of children, and where every precaution is desired we recommend this style of canoe. Sponsons can be built on any Canvas canoe and they cost $20.00 extra. We carry the Sponson canoe in stock in No. 604 size.

CANVAS COVERED FREIGHT CANOES.

Number	Length	Beam	Depth	Weight	Price
66x	17	36	15	90	$53.00
68x	18	38	16	100	58 00
68xx	18	42	17	135	63.00
69xx	19	45	20	160	68.00
572	20	54	20	190	88.00
576	22	62	24	280	150.00

THE FREIGHT CANOES are all built with hardwood outside gunwales and long decks. The last four sizes on the list have inside gunwales as an extra reinforcement.

Carrying capacity of freight canoes given on page 17. When comparing freight canoes more attention should be given to the beam and depth, and carrying capacity than to the length.

Any of the smaller sizes as listed above can be built with hardwood outside gunwales and long decks like our ordinary wooden canoes for $5.00 extra. Keels on Canvas canoes $1.00 extra.

THE PETERBOROUGH CANOE COMPANY Limited

FREIGHT CANOES.

FREIGHT CANOES test the skill of the canoe builder. They have to be strong, and they have also to be light. The combination of strength and lightness, both pronounced characteristics of PETERBOROUGH CANOES, is one of vital importance for use in explorations or travel where there are rough shores and frequent portages. A heavy canoe delays travel, and a weak spot in construction might mean not merely loss of canoe and baggage, but even the abandonment of the trip. We build a lot of large canoes specially for heavy work, for Government survey, exploring expeditions, fur trading, etc.

The larger sizes have inside gunwhales and billestringers of oak which serve to stiffen the canoe without adding too much to the weight. For very heavy work when ordered especially, we put iron bolts under the thwarts to prevent the canoe from being spread and tearing away the fastenings, when under very heavy strain.

Our stock canoe is built in single X sizes of boards, "rib and batten" style, but the XX sizes are built of narrow strips, the same as the "Longitudinal Strip" canoes previously described in the catalogue.

CARRYING CAPACITY OF 69XX CANOE 2000 LBS. 12 INCH DRAFT

THE PETERBOROUGH C

PRICE LIST OF

No.	Code Words for Sizes	Length	Beam	Depth	Weight About	Approx 10 in. Draft.	
		Feet	Inches	Inches	Pounds	Pounds	F
66X	Bush	17	36	15	95	950	
67X	Voyage	17½	38	16	100	1000	
68X	Portage	18	38	16½	100	1100	1
68½X	Rapids	18½	40	17	110	1200	1
69X	Forest	19	42	17½	120	1250	1
69½X	Stream	19½	43	18	130	1300	1
68XX	Birch	18	42	17	130	1250	17
68½XX	Willow	18½	43	18	140	1300	18
69XX	Spruce	19	44	19	150	1400	19
69½XX	Pine	19½	45	20	160	1500	20
566	Martin	17	42	17	....	1250	...
567	Sable	17½	44	17½	....	1300	...
568	Mink	18	46	18	....	1400	1900
569	Otter	18½	48	18½	....	1500	2000
570	Moose	19	50	19	....	1750	2400
572	Beaver	20	54	20	....	....	3000
576	Lacseul	22	62	24	300	....	4200

..... 120 00 | 150 00 | Basswood, Cedar or Canvas Covered.

*576—Only built in Cypress Strip and Canvas Covered.

THE PETERBOROUGH CANOE COMPANY, Limited

DECKED CANOES.

FOR those who prefer a canoe decked in more than the ordinary open canoes shown in the previous pages, we would suggest any of the styles here illustrated. These are very desirable if the canoe is to be used for sailing, especially in rough water, as the extra decking and coaming makes them dry.

Our illustrations show the SOLID COMFORT Deck, which is about 30 inches long at each end, and 2½ inches wide along the sides, with the coaming 1¼ inches high around the cockpit.

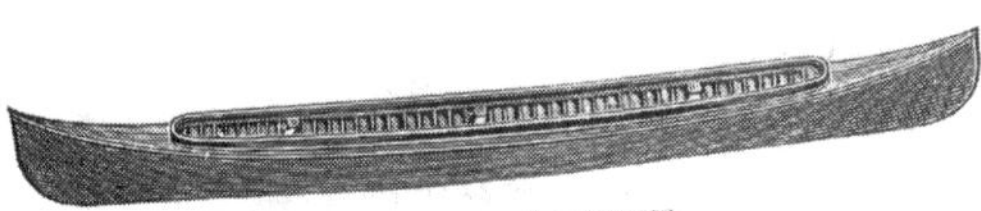

SOLID COMFORT DECKING

The JUNIPER Deck is 3 feet long at each end, 3 inches wide along the sides, with the coaming 1¼ inches high around the cockpit.

JUNIPER DECKING

The ONTARIO Deck covers the whole canoe, with the exception of the cockpit, which is usually 4 or 5 feet long.

We build these boats to order in any of the sizes listed for Open canoes.

For Prices add the following to the prices quoted for Open canoes in previous pages;

"Solid Comfort" Decking $8.00 *extra*.
"Juniper" Decking - - 12.00 *extra*.
"Ontario" Decking - - 20.00 *extra*.

ONTARIO DECKING

THE PETERBOROUGH CANOE COMPANY, Limited

PRICE LIST OF CEDAR SKIFFS, LAPSTREAK BUILD.

Number	Length	Beam	Depth	Painted Cedar Quality with Ribs 4 inch Centres	Standard Quality Varnished Cedar with Ribs 4 inch Centres	Special Quality Varnished Cedar with Ribs 2½ inch Centres Cane Seats, etc.	Special Quality Varnished Mahogany with Ribs 2½ inch Centres Cane Seats, etc.	REMARKS
	Feet	Inches	Inches					
501	14	38	13	$42.00	$46 00	$54.00	$66 00	We build special sizes of Lapstreak Skiffs to order when required, and also build them for use See page 24
502	15	40	13	44 00	49 00	57.00	70.00	
503	16	42	14	47.00	54 00	63 00	76.00	
504	17	44	14	50.00	59.00	68.00	83 00	
505	18	46	15	55 00	6			
506	19	48	16	60 00	7			

Prices include one p
a rudder or paddle.

EXTRA OARS and
pair on the two cheaper
pair on the two better q

CANE CHAIRS fo
extra.

Side Decks and co
any of the skiffs at $10.

For nesting orders
short and long so as to
feet to 17 feet in one ne

THE PETERBOROUGH CANOE COMPANY, Limited

RACING CANOES.

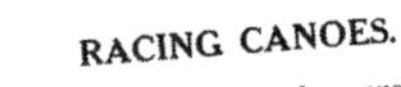

SINGLE OR TANDEM RACER

THERE is not a boatman whose eye does not kindle, his heart leap and his hands involuntary tighten, when he thinks of the thrilling moments of a canoe race. It is a great sport, and is at once a test of skill, strength and physical balance. Canoe racing is becoming more indulged in every year, and the keen competition for prizes and honors has kept designers busy evolving the fastest possible models. We have struck the best ideas yet embodied in any racing canoe in our racing models for the year 1914. We can arrange thwarts in any way to suit the paddles. Our No. 70, the Single and Tanden Racer, is our fastest canoe, and the fastest built anywhere. It is not necessary to say any more, as the racing results for years have proven the superiority of the Peterborough Racing Canoe.

Our Fours Racer is listed as No. 72, and what we have said of No. 70 applies in every way to this model. A trial of the canoe by men who knew will prove anything we may claim for it.

WAR CANOES.—The great events at all regattas are generally the war canoe races. For some years we did not build a racing war canoe as the models were changing every year and we did not wish to sell a Canoe to a club, knowing that the next year we would probably come out with a new and faster model. We are now putting out a 30 ft. war canoe that cannot be improved on. It is fast, and will stand up to the work that is required.

We Quote Prices as Follows without Paddles.

Number	Length	Beam	Depth	Weight	Painted Basswood	Varnished Basswood	Painted Cedar	Varnished Cedar	Varnished Mahogany
	Feet	Inch	Inch	Pounds					
70	16	30	12	45	$ 34 00	$ 40.00	$ 44.00	$ 52 00	$ 62 00
72	20	30	12	65	45 00	50.00	55 00	65.00	76.00
R	30	40½	19	200	125.00	160.00	175 00	200.00	225.00

For those desiring a Semi-racing Canoe we recommend our model No. 74 listed on page 9. It is designed to combine the 16 ft. racing and the ordinary 16 ft. paddling Canoe.

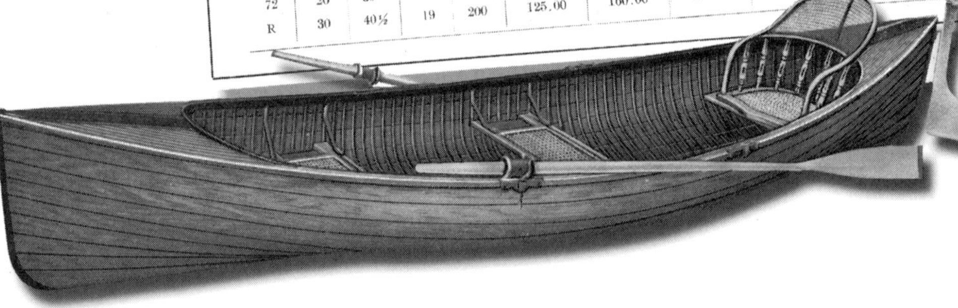

Not All Chestnuts Are Alike

Chestnut Canoe Co., Ltd. Edmonton, Alta., February, 13, 1933
Fredericton, N.B.

Dear Sirs:

I received your canoe catalogue some time ago, but wish to make further inquiries regarding your Indian Maiden and Pleasure models. Mr. Clinton Brown of our club, "The Voyageurs," purchased an Indian Maiden from you last spring which has won the admiration of the entire club. Mr. Brown won honors in every race in which he entered, coming first in the gruelling 250 mile marathon race from Rocky Mountain House last July and winning the Provincial Championship in the singles, doubles and mixed doubles in his first year as a canoeist.

Yours very truly, (Miss) L. E. SANSOM

Chestnut Canoe Co. Kamloops, B.C., July 21, 1929

Dear Sirs:

For more years than I like to think about I have used Chestnut canoes, during this time I have had to use others as necessity called for, but have found the Chestnut safest, lightest and most reliable canoe of the lot.

Yours truly, J. E. L. RICHMOND
Boy Scouts of America

Models and Classes of Chestnuts

While other canoe makers serviced a local community, Chestnut's mandate was to fill every conceivable canoeing need in a worldwide marketplace, in particular Canada's wide range of canoeing conditions. The result was the development of over sixty different canoes. By the 1940s these styles had codified into six distinct families that have become generic terms to canoeists everywhere. Pleasure canoes were designed for cottagers and recreational canoe tripping. The Cruisers and Guides' Specials were fast professional canoes, different from Ogilvy models which were the professional river canoes, flat-bottomed so they could be poled in shallow water of just a few inches, and extremely stable for standing while fly-fishing. Freight canoes with incredible carrying capacity became the staple transportation for the North. The Prospector canoes were meant to combine the agility and speed of the Cruiser with a wider beam and depth that rivaled the Freight for carrying capacity.

People generally refer to canoes by their generic names, such as a sixteen-foot Prospector or nineteen-foot Freight, not the "codes" Fort or Company. But these names were essential to ensure accuracy when ordering canoes by telegraph, when one wrong keystroke could make the difference between a twelve-foot Prospector and an eighteen-footer. The names weren't noted for their originality or sales appeal. In some cases, these names were never changed, even if the canoes were altered drastically through the years. In other cases, names were adopted in later years that lost much of the historic charm of the original ones.

Pleasure Canoes

Pleasure canoes were a major inspiration for the original Chestnut design. We have little information with which to study these early Chestnuts. One copy of the first Chestnut canoe catalogue (1905) and one canoe from this important era of Chestnut history still survive. Amazingly, that canoe is in pristine condition even with the original canvas. It was built at the turn of the century and shows prominently the excellent workmanship that went into Chestnut canoes from the start. It is likely that whereas the "professional" flat-bottomed fishing canoes were designed after the models seen from Maine, the Pleasure canoes were homespun and highly influenced by the local Malecite birchbarks. Also from the birchbark building tradition, in these early canoes the gunwales are capped, that is, the outer gunwale is quite thin and both inner and outer gunwales are covered by one thin batten. Capped gunwales, being a birchbark hand-me-down, were unneccessary for wood canvas canoes. Open gunwales, yet to be invented, had definite advantages: they made canoes easier to drain of water, eased dry rot problems, and the thicker outside rail eliminated the previous need for tapering the ends of the ribs to a feather edge.

Only as bark canoes drifted out of the picture were the capped gunwales replaced with the "new" open gunwale construction. In 1906 the Old Town Canoe Company in Maine introduced a new model with open gunwales. Other Maine builders soon followed. B. M. Morris made the system available on all his models by 1910. The 1914 Chestnut catalogue advertises Chestnut's "new" open gunwales. It is impossible to say exactly in which year this modification was first adopted in Fredericton, but it was likely before this date.

This birchbark tradition flirts with wood rot and is not at all desirable for the wood-and-canvas design; another indicator that the wood-and-canvas canoe evolved on the east coast independently of the earlier Peterborough invention.

Pleasure model.
(Courtesy: Jill Dean.)

Psyche

The oldest extant Chestnut canoe is displayed behind a modern cedarstrip built by Walter Walker. This earliest of Chestnut canoes has led a charmed life, owned by American cottagers north of North Bay, Ontario. It made a brief appearance at one of the Wooden Canoe Heritage Association assemblies, otherwise few people would know of its existence. It is the only capped gunwale Chestnut I have ever seen, although I have heard of one other still around. It seems to have been a cherished heirloom from the start, unusual for Chestnuts which were usually considered utilitarian canoes and well used, with no expectation of lasting one hundred years.

Chestnut canoes have changed substantially over the years, yet this canoe is distinctly "Chestnut" in appearance. Even the well-known Chestnut emblem was used, although in this earliest preserved emblem there is one less point on the leaf. The owners of the Psyche canoe had a letter preserved by their family from Maggie Jean Chestnut. As I recall, the reason for the communication was to offer advice on refinishing—not recanvasing—the canoe, and the letter was a confirmation of 1899 as the building date.

The 1899 Chestnut Psyche (background), with a modern Peterborough style built on a Gordon form (foreground) built by Walter Walker.
(Courtesy: Jeff Dean.)

In 1905 we know that Chestnut was still producing canoes for a local market because the canoes were large. The size is a result of the localized market of the St. John River, where few portages would be encountered. The smallest Pleasure canoe then was sixteen feet. In later years, sixteen feet was the largest model marketed.

Besides capped gunwales, another startling feature revealed by the 1905 catalogue is that the Pleasure canoes were narrower than the Cruisers—quite the opposite is the case in all subsequent catalogues. This speaks to evolving fundamental changes to both the Pleasure and Cruiser lines. In the case of Pleasure canoes, there seems to have been a long transition of them becoming wider and wider over the years, perhaps to match the general public's lessening expertise in canoeing and thus the market's need for a more stable canoe.

By 1910 Chestnut was producing a sponson canoe—a canoe with flotation chambers attached to the sides to reduce the possibility of upset. Even at the very end of the Chestnut Canoe Company's long life the "widening phenomenon" still prevailed.

In the 1950s the popular sixteen-foot Pleasure model, the Pal, was widened, leaving many disgruntled canoe enthusiasts confused, refuelling the legendary debate between Chestnut and Peterborough canoes. Because the new sixteen-foot canoes were radically different from the ones paddlers were accustomed to, people began to wonder if the canoes they had favoured had been Pleasure canoes at all, or if they had been built from the sixteen-foot Prospector or Cruiser form. The truth was the canoe was the same, but in the 1950s the form changed.

The sixteen-foot Pleasure was Chestnut's most popular model. It required the building of three forms to keep up with production demands. The Hudson's Bay Company had their own model, the Baycrest, which was in fact a Pal built with wooden seats and no. 10 PVC coated canvas, sold under their own label (Voyageur). We have two of the three forms in our shop today.

Eureka! The Pal returns to its original width. (Courtesy: The Author.)

Uncovering a True Pleasure Form

The sixteen-foot Pleasure was the model I grew up with. Summer camps in Ontario have literally thousands of them. Naturally, when I began canoe building, I immediately embarked upon building that model. But what came off the form was nothing close to the canoe I knew so well. I built one canoe, a second, a third, and my frustration grew with taking each canoe off the form.

As I lay awake one night fuming about this, I remembered that the twelve-foot Prospector form had been widened in later years to make the Mermaid, an obscenely wide fun boat. I went to my shop in the middle of the night to test my suspicion. Armed with a crowbar, a hatchet, and a small sledge hammer I hacked away at the problematic form. I removed a few of the metal bands and chopped away at the sheathing of the form. There shouldn't have been anything underneath except the bulkheads, or "stations" of the form, but I discovered more solid wood. I stripped off more and more of the metal bands. Soon enough, the original form was revealed with distinct markings of where metal bands had once been. Beneath approximately four inches of scabbed wood, two to each side, was the original, beautifully shaped, slender canoe form. We replaced the metal bands on the still good original wood and today it is the form we use more than any other, (although we have a second Pal form that has been left widened for such a canoe). My late-night discovery was comparable to buying a painting of little value and finding out that beneath the surface lay a rare and valuable Rembrandt.

Pleasure canoes were always built in two grades. Grade one was meant to emulate the finest in craftsmanship—an *objet d'art*—an unbridled attempt to win over the customers of the all-wood cedarstrip "poor man's yacht." Grade two was a less expensive craft intended to be rugged, inevitably scratched the first time out. Thus, less care was given to the final finishing. Also, the second grade canoe was built with wood that could not be used in first grade canoes—wood that had some knots or less than perfect grain.

Around 1919 Chestnut introduced the grade three canoe, a sixteen-foot craft that sold for as little as thirty-eight dollars. This canoe took the principle of a lower grade canoe one step further. In this case, wood that was not wide enough for normal rib stock (2⅜ inch) was milled into narrow rib stock (1½ inch) with the ribs placed closer together to retain strength. These ribs not only used up the scrap stock, but were also much easier to produce because they were so narrow they were not tapered at the ends, as was the normal practice. Because the stock was straight, the corners could be quickly rounded by molding machines. People liked the narrow ribs so much that requests were soon made for the narrow ribs in first grade canoes. Eventually, these narrow-ribbed Pleasure canoes became as popular as the wide ribbed version, including both Omer Stringer's famous canoe, *Omer* (15 foot Chum/Doe) and Bill Mason's first Chestnut (16 foot Pal/Deer). As youths growing up with these two styles of ribs, we didn't think about it too much either way, and called both versions the Pal and the Chum.

By the 1950s this two-tiered system was abandoned, although certain curious traditions remained. For many years a fifteen-foot "lightweight commercial canoe," the Bantam, was marketed. This was, in fact, a grade two Bob's Special, although by that time the factory had no provisions for a two-tiered system. The only difference, besides the name, was the price. George Birch joked about how many of these canoes were sold to canoe outfitters, just because of the term, "commercial."

The Featherweight and the Bob's Special

Although any Chestnut canoe could be ordered extra-light upon request, two models were specifically designed lightweight for many portages. Both models were produced since at least 1914. At eleven and fifteen feet, the Featherweight and the Bob's Special (originally called the Fifty-Pound Special) were extremely beamy for their length, giving them a surprisingly large carrying capacity. Weight was minimized in every way possible: extra care in construction, very light ribbing (¼ inch), and almost paper-thin planking (⅛ inch). Although not officially a "class of canoe," these two models were definitely conceived together as a pair.

In later years it was difficult to keep the weight down when Chestnut adopted an assembly line approach. In 1915 the Featherweight weighed 34½ pounds and the Fifty-Pound Special weighed just what its name indicated. Later, these canoes were listed in catalogues at 40 and 58 pounds, respectively, (necessitating a name change from the Fifty-Pound Special to the Bob's Special). In fact, they often weighed much more. The increasing weight was prevalent in most models, partly because of shortages of proper canoe materials, for instance switching from spruce to ash for gunwales.

The difficulty of obtaining proper canoe materials has plagued canoe builders since the days when suitable birchbark became scarce. An early Chestnut catalogue apologizes for a temporary shortage of cane for canoe seats. Along with Eastern white spruce, white cedar for planking and ribs was hard to obtain in quantity. Unlike other large canoe companies, Chestnut never made the switch to the lower grade Western red cedar, although near the end of the company's days, letters were sent out around the world in search for an elusive type of mahogany that reportedly copied the exact characteristics of Eastern white cedar. Today's canoe builders have much the same problem with acquiring materials.

The Featherweight and Bob's Special remained in a class of their own, never considered a true Pleasure canoe nor marketed under that class until 1955. They were considered more a working man's canoe for trappers in the deep bush because of their extremely wide beam and maximum carrying capacity. Now they are also appreciated by many nature photographers for their steadiness. Their forte as canoes was dipping in and out of beaver ponds. They are not a fast canoe and never were.

Cruisers and Guides' Special Canoes

These canoes, built in the same lengths as Pleasure canoes, form the other part of the original Chestnut canoe production as listed in the 1905 catalogue. They remained the same, with no additions or omissions to their class, for eighty-two years. Without wishing to tarnish that impressive record, it appears that the earliest canoes in this class were, however, substantially different from those in later years.

We have come to know the Cruisers and Guides' Specials as a fast and extremely responsive craft due to a narrow, rounded hull. But in the 1905 catalogue they are wider than the Pleasure models! Also, the 1905 description of the Guides' Special is that of a flatter-bottomed river canoe: "*Realizing that on rough, rocky streams there is need of a canoe practically indestructible, we build a second grade canoe with half or 'short' ribs between the long ribs, placing them throughout the entire length of the canoe. This so stiffens and strengthens the bottom that the canoe will stand almost any amount of hard usage, and is essentially the craft for canoeing on rocky streams in low water.*"

This is a direct importation of a design from the typical Maine "Guide" canoes. The half-ribs were needed to strengthen the very flat bottom of those canoes. They were also referred to as "walking ribs," for they added strength to the hull bottom for walking about while poling or fishing. (Chestnut sold setting poles in those years for poling, an art now almost entirely lost.)

This simply does not make sense. With their sharply curved hulls, the Cruisers needed this extra strengthening far less than other models. The later Cruisers are so curved that not only is extra ribbing superfluous, but standing in one is a risky proposition indeed.

If the original Cruisers and Guides' Specials were flat-bottomed, they probably became rounder as extremely flat-bottomed "fishing canoes" were introduced in 1918. What is interesting is that for the entire life of the Chestnut Canoe Company, the Guides' Specials, built on the Cruiser forms, continued to be marketed as a separate entity. All Chestnut canoes could be ordered with close ribbing. (About 1910 normal ribs placed closely together replaced the earlier, Maine-styled half ribs. Canoe forms were completely banded over with metal to facilitate various rib spacings.) Exceptional circumstances aside, the later Guides' Specials, round-bottomed and completely double ribbed, were a very overbuilt canoe.

Freight Canoes

Freight canoes are perhaps Chestnut's greatest contribution to the opening of Canada's vast northern wilderness. They became the staple of transportation, although to most paddlers these are one of the last craft to come to mind when thinking of canoes. In fact, a twenty-four-foot juggernaut with fifty-horsepower affixed to its transom is more akin to an

Freighters continue to reign supreme for serious work in Canada's north. These are from the fleet that still operate as taxis between Moosonee and Moose Factory. (Courtesy: The Author.)

icebreaker than a canoe. (The comparison is no accident. When I paddled the Missinaibi River to Moose Factory I talked to locals who mentioned that they recanvased their canoes every winter—a result of using their motorized "icebreakers" well into the fall hunting season.)

The final Chestnut catalogue stated that the first Freight canoe was built in 1898—a dubious claim—but sales records show that they were produced at least as early as 1908. (They are not listed in the 1905 catalogue.) It is clear Chestnut by then had entered the canoe market continent-wide.

The first Freighters were normal pointed canoes, sluggish to paddle but with incredible carrying capacity. The seventeen-, eighteen-, and nineteen-foot models were built specifically for the Hudson's Bay Company, using dimensions supplied by that company, and were called the Hudson, Bay, and Company, respectively. As the 1919 catalogue suggests: "*The Chestnut Freight canoes for freighters, prospectors, surveyors, etc., have proven so far superior to any others made that practically nothing else is now used.*" Freight canoes accounted for a large percentage of Chestnut's income.

Freighters required the greatest changes over the years, as they were a purely practical commodity that needed to keep up with the changing times and technology. In a tradition that anticipated the advent of the outboard motor, freighters were always built with a mast step as standard equipment. Motors were quickly adopted and Chestnut came up with an ingenious "hood" that could be placed over one end of the pointed form, producing the "vee" stern. The vee stern was a particularly good design for marrying a brand new technology—the outboard engine—with a canoe shape that was still pointed under the water line, making the craft handle the same under paddle. Eventually, all the pointed models were completely abandoned. When it became evident that the larger freighters were never going to be paddled, the vee stern was abandoned and new forms with full width transoms took over, allowing for both a much larger carrying capacity and larger engines. Producing new, large canoe forms was prohibitively expensive, and Chestnut's reluctance to keep abreast of changing requirements contributed significantly to the company's eventual downfall.

From Moosonee to Tuktoyaktuk they are still used extensively; even today, the long and narrow Freight canoe still provides the fastest and most fuel efficient form of transportation for large weights in Northern waterways.

Prospector Canoes

The name Prospector evokes images symbolic of Canadian tradition. Although a relatively late design, it has a place in history. It was glorified in the published canoe exploits of R. M. Patterson in 1928–29 on one of the great northern rivers, the Nahanni, in the Northwest Territories. Patterson's book, *Dangerous River,* was first published in London, England, with many subsequent publications and translations. It is still in print today. Patterson described the canoes for the journey: "*The outfit consisted of three Chestnut canoes: a sixteen-foot Prospector, which was the same size and model that I had used the summer before; a nineteen-foot Freight, a thing about the size of a fishing boat with a depth of nineteen inches and a fifty-one inch beam; and an eighteen-foot Freight that we had bought from the Bay at Fort Nelson—a shockingly battered antique with its canvas hide flapping loosely over its cedar frame, the sort of thing that a sane man would hesitate to use on a quiet lake, let alone on the Nahanni.*" Interestingly, Patterson bought a vee stern Olgilvy when he returned to the Nahanni many years later.

Freight canoes may have been Chestnut's most important contribution to the Canadian North but it is the Prospector canoe, for which Chestnut is most remembered today. The very name conjures up images of the solitary prospector alone in the wilderness for years at a time, in need of a canoe that could carry his complete outfit, that could run the meanest rapids, and could still be carried on his shoulders.

Prospector canoes were a late innovation, designed to fill this exact need. The Cruisers were fast and light, but didn't carry enough; the Freighters were too slow. The need for something in between was recognized as early as 1919: "*For those desiring larger canoes than our regular size, but something smaller than our Freight models, we suggest our Cruiser model, built two or three inches deeper than standard. We have had such a demand for these canoes that we now stock them in the three lengths....*"

In 1912 Ernest C. Oberholtzer undertook an extensive journey into the barren lands, to places

Prospector model.
(Courtesy: Jill Dean.)

unseen by white men since Samuel Hearne's explorations in 1770–72. It was one of these extra deep Cruisers that he used, and Oberholtzer wrote to Chestnut from Ranier, Minnesota, in 1917 to extol their virtues: "*I have just seen and admired the specially light and deep canoe which you made for my friend, Mr. Roberts, on my recommendation. My high opinion of the Chestnut canoe was formed in 1912 when I used one of your extra deep Cruiser models for a twenty-four hundred mile trip into a hitherto unexplored part of the barren grounds northwest of Fort Churchill.*"

By the mid-1920s Chestnut perfected its Prospector with a tremendous number of forms, from a tiny twelve-foot model to an eighteen-foot model that, although easily portaged with a weight of ninety pounds, could carry a payload of over half a ton. Even the fourteen-foot, as well as all the larger models, were marketed with a vee stern for use with an outboard motor. The smaller Prospectors were slowly phased out. The twelve-foot form was widened and added to the Pleasure class as the Mermaid. The fourteen- and fifteen-foot forms survived until the company's closure, although they were not listed in the last catalogue. Many of the forms were duplicated so that the builders could reserve one permanently for the vee stern model. This way the hood would not have to be constantly put on and taken off—an awkward and imperfect procedure.

Today many canoe companies have tried to capitalize on the fame of the Chestnut Prospector. Rarely is it authentically duplicated, and this may be good because many of the copies resemble more a Pleasure model, which for the modern canoeist, is likely a safer bet. (See Bill Mason, page 155.)

Ogilvy Canoes

After decades of designing canoes for a worldwide market, Chestnut looked homeward in its last major design innovation. Prompted by an important New Brunswick guiding family, the distinctive Ogilvy canoe was born.

For this local market, which was particularly concerned with fly-fishing for salmon, the flat-bottomed Fishing and Poling model had been the mainstay since it was first introduced in 1918.

The purpose of this canoe was unmistakable, by virtue of its name and by the fact that it was supplied with a permanent anchor pulley. But David Ogilvy was finding that his customers, the "sports," were becoming more and more irresponsible, moving about in the craft while he and his fellow guides did their best to keep them upright. He wanted canoes that were still wider and flatter. He gave Chestnut his requirements, and in 1931 Chestnut produced the first eighteen-foot model. Four other sizes were added, and

Chestnut Innovations

In its younger years, Chestnut was a small firm that took pride in its ability to meet the changing and varied needs of its customers. The fine craftsmen were inventive and ingenious in altering a canoe during its construction. Below are some of the "options" available at different times:

1921 .... Close (double) ribbed $16

1921 .... Fitted to take a sail (sail included) $24.50

1921 .... Fitted for oars $14

1921 .... Fitted with extra long decks $8–10

1921 .... Made into a sponson canoe, that is, fitted with flotation air chambers on the sides $20

1921 .... Built deeper $2 per inch

1935 .... Built extra light $6

1935 .... Built with a keel $12.50

1935 .... Built with an anchor pulley $2.40

1935 .... Built with a square stern for a motor $10

named after Ogilvy's brothers and sons. On the original eighteen-foot Ogilvy form, one can see the evolution of the design. Painted on one side is the name "Flat Poling" while on the other side the name was amended to include the new name, "Ogilvy."

The Olgilvies are a specific Maritime canoe built to meet a particular need. One won't find many elsewhere. As portaging was never anticipated, they are heavily built and double ribbed. Furthermore, in order to give strength to the extremely flat bottom, the ribs are often so thick that they had to be individually thinned at each side in order to take the steam bending for the sharp and sudden curve of the bilge.

The Labrador Canoe, Nestables and Other Oddities

Various aspects of canoe design through the nineteenth and twentieth centuries had nothing to do with canoeing but with the business of more efficiently shipping the craft to the widespread markets. Canoes must be one of the bulkiest products ever to be invented. Yet, they have had to be transported: as freight, in bush planes, over ice by dog sled in winter, on top of cars.... No matter how light a product is, freight charges are based on cubic footage; each cubic foot of space is billed at a specific weight. The problem of shipping the product was first addressed by the Peterborough area builders. With canoes so light, but so bulky, a means of shipping was devised by "nesting" canoes one inside another.

Nestable Canoes

For shipment to remote points where the freight is a great consideration, we have designed a line of canoes that have no tumble home and will therefore, nest one within the other.

They are built with our standard grade of materials, the finish being a painted one, both inside and out. They have double open gunwales and can be nested without removing the decks. To take out or replace the seats and bars is only the matter of a few minutes' work and after the arrival of a shipment the canoes are soon ready for the water.

The lowest classification under which canoes not nested can be shipped by rail freight, is three and one half times first-class rate but, nested canoes, when crated, may be shipped at one and a half times the first-class rate or when boxed, at the first-class rate, the minimum weight, when so shipped, being figured at 800 lbs. On long hauls it is easy to see the great saving in favor of the Nestable Model, provided several canoes are shipped in one nest.

For stock, we only build these canoes in the Second Grade, but will build them in the First Grade on special orders

With the complete line of Nestable canoes, Chestnut carried the concept to its fullest. Abandoned was the traditional "tumblehome" (or "home tumble"), where the sides curve back into the centre for a stronger side, and gunwales are closer to the body for ease of paddling—ubiquitous to Chestnut designs. Nestables had instead flared sides. By removing the seats and thwarts, up to six Nestable canoes could be stacked together, the outermost forming the packing crate. They had the quaintest names: the Chicken, Yolk, White, Egg, Nest, and Barn. Unfortunately, the resulting canoes, designed for transport and not for paddling, were quite ungainly in the water. (Indeed, they have a remarkable resemblance to some of the extraordinarily cheap polyethylene canoes found in stores today.)

Another transportation problem had less to do with freight than with usage. Canoes were still the best way to undertake geographical surveys and such in the far north, but by the first quarter of the twentieth century getting there was infinitely easier in a float plane. Hence, Chestnut embarked upon the question of how canoes could best be stowed in a small aircraft.

First there was the sectional canoe—any normal canoe cut into lengths and with bulkheads and rubber gaskets—so that it could be reassembled. Then there was the Labrador. Designed with the help of the Canadian Science Research Council of Canada, the Labrador was designed so that the raised ends were detachable, allowing it to fit tightly under the belly of the "Fairchild Hydroplane," the most popular float plane of the time. Finally there is our current strategy to put "carrying bars" on all the canoes we build, not for their original intent, but because nothing better holds a canoe to the top of a modern automobile.

The availability of these options put a strain on Chestnut. In later years, workers changed from being skilled canoe builders to assembly line workers on a piecework contract, who were often unskilled in anything but their specific responsibility. The art of canoe building from start to finish was lost, and that knowledge was essential to make these sorts of manipulations. Thus in the later years, a number of the hybrid options resulted in an unsatisfactory product. Slowly, the number of these types of options reduced to a trickle, and only those that were popular enough to warrant a permanent solution survived. (For instance the "extra deep Cruiser" became the Prospector line.)

Labrador model strapped to hydoplane.
(Courtesy: Jill Dean.)

A number of canoe designs came and went. Many forms stayed in storage decades after they had been discontinued. The forms for the larger Pleasure canoes, the Trapper canoe, the fourteen- and fifteen-foot Prospectors, the Indian Maiden, among others were dusted off only when they were catalogued for sale at the demise of the Chestnut Canoe Company. The Indian Maiden canoe, for example, is a design with highly curved stems, gunwales, and decks that was intended to emulate a preconceived notion of an Indian canoe. This form was dusted off in the last days of Chestnut and had the distinction of being the model last built in New Brunswick. In 1967 Chestnut printed a Canadian Centenary Catalogue. Featured on the front cover is the Centennial, a twenty-five foot war canoe, which was designed specifically to be used in Canada's Centennial celebrations.

Indian Maiden.
(Courtesy: Jill Dean.)

Serial Numbers and Decals

As a Chestnut canoe builder I am asked many questions by canoe owners: Is my canoe a Chestnut. What model is it? When was it built? Often the owner is adamant the answer lies stamped in one of the stems, where a series of numbers has been discovered. Unfortunately, they don't usually mean much.

The Old Town Canoe Company still has complete records of virtually every canoe they have built in the last century. Why are the Chestnut records so poor? Perhaps it was a by-product of the company's status as a major canoe builder with so many different labels affixed to Chestnut canoe decks. A canoe would be painted and ready to go, but it was still not determined whether it would be a Chestnut, a Peterborough, a Canadian Watercraft Limited, or a Hudson's Bay Voyageur. Keeping track of the serial numbers would have been more than difficult.

However, in the post Peterborough years, Chestnut did codify things somewhat. Two digits were set off in a series by a hyphen.The reverse of those two numbers gave the year of construction; thus 36-4638 meant that canoe was built in 1963.

For the record, we have established a record-keeping method. Stamped in our cherry wood stems are the following: two numbers that state the year of manufacture and further numbers that reveal exactly which canoe it is in

chronological order since we began building canoes. Hence 96052 was built in 1996 and is our fifty-second canoe.

As for the decals the distinctive leaf deck decal is arguably the single Chestnut icon that is most recognizable today. Many old canoes are identified as Chestnuts simply by the unique outline of an old decal that remains visible on an old deck. We have had the decals reprinted—no small feat as the art of industrial silk screening isn't what it used to be—with both "Fredericton" for rebuilds and "Cold Springs" for new canoes. The side decal that came out in the sixties and seventies does not have much of an historic ring to it, suggesting as it does that the canoe was built during Chestnut's infamous days of poor canoe building. Readable from a distance, it made good advertising, and now most other canoe companies use a similar decal. To date, we have resisted its allure, but many customers ask for it. Perhaps we will reprint it in the future.

Chestnut Canoe Co.,
Fredericton, N.B.

Island Lake Indian Mission, Rev. R. T. Chapin.
Island Lake Manitoba, October 8th, 1928

Sirs:

Will you please send me your latest catalogue of Chestnut Canoes, and a price list. I have been using your Freighting Canoes for a number of years and find that they work better than any other canoe. Also two years ago I got a Prospector model fitted with sponsons. With an outboard motor on this I have had wonderful service. Only once in these two years have the seas been bad enough to prevent me from going where I started for.

Yours truly,
R. T. CHAPIN

The Canoe For You

As a canoe builder I am faced with would-be customers wanting help in choosing the canoe that is just right for them. Many have already made up their minds as to which canoe is for them based upon preconceived bias, often before seeing our catalogue. I ask them to describe their canoeing conditions so that I can best advise them on their choice.

In my experience the best all-round canoe, of the models available in Chestnut's later years (I use these model names because these are what people will be most familiar with) are the fifteen- and sixteen-foot Pleasure models—the Chum and Pal—whether for cottages or summer camps or two-week canoe trips with moderately moving water. One of these two models suits most people's needs.

Canoes built by the author and the current Chestnut Canoe Company. In the foreground is a Chum (note the narrow ribs). Behind it is a sixteen-foot Prospector, the Fort. After release of this book Chestnut will return to older canoe names, for example, the Chum reverts to the Twozer. (Courtesy: The Author.)

For experienced paddlers who enjoy a faster, cleaner tracking canoe, the slender Cruiser is perhaps preferable. In the later years it was the only one of two available in longer lengths. But its narrow beam makes it considerably harder to turn and more prone to tipping. This is not a canoe for children, unless they are serious about paddling. Of the many summer camps I am acquainted with, most use the Pleasure models. Only one, a camp that specializes in hard, serious, lengthy canoe trips, use Cruisers.

For photographers and those who enjoy travelling at a leisurely pace, the lightweight models are excellent. For fun I have taken a short canoe trip with two people and a dog in a Featherweight. With virtually nothing on our backs, we enjoyed ducking into every little creek and puddle, taking long portages just for the hike, but this is an exception. The Featherweight canoe is really designed for one person. If one wants a truly stable canoe the widened Pal is also a possibility with a thirty-seven inch beam rather than the original thirty-three.

Bill Mason contributed greatly to the popularity of the sixteen-foot Prospector. While doing much for the sport of canoeing and for the Chestnut name, I believe he has done the canoeing public an injustice. In many modern conditions people can be in danger paddling a Prospector as lightly loaded as we often are nowadays—they were designed to carry a prospector's load after all, and can be easily windswept without enough ballast. They are extremely rockered, that is, the ends rise up on a higher plane than the centre. Thus, lightly loaded, it is more like paddling a twelve-foot canoe with a sixteen-foot sail. If unencumbered by portages, trippers wanting to carry the amenities of modern life will find the Prospector can still be an excellent choice. It will carry almost any weight, and later, when camped, its large amount of rocker makes it easy to manoeuvre on the still water for an idyllic moonlit paddle.

Mr. Jobidon
Quebec

June 21, 1929

Dear Mr. Jobidon:

This letter is to tell you how satisfied I am with my canoe: The Labrador model Chestnut. I find it roomy and very light for its size. I was a bit afraid that it would be unsteady, but to my great pleasure the contrary is the truth, even when I put in my lateen sail.

To finish I will say that this canoe is the real thing I needed for my lake; it is the best canoe I have ever used.

Yours truly,
CHS. A. KIRUAC, M.D.

Where the Chestnut Forms are Today

When the Chestnut Canoe Company closed its Oromocto factory doors in 1979, canoeists around the world thought they were seeing the end of an era. However, the Chestnut forms were dispersed across North America. As long as the forms over which the canoes had been built survived, there was still hope for the continuation of the Chestnut tradition.

Attempts were made by two aboriginal bands to rebuild a canoe building company of stature. The Pays Plat band, near Thunder Bay, Ontario, was a promising candidate. It was a natural move; they had earlier acquired the Chestnut Snowshoe line from Sportspal, to whom Chestnut had originally sold a few years earlier. (Sportspal, like Chestnut before it, found it difficult to find skilled employees to lace the rawhide snowshoes.) The Pays Plat band negotiated with Lock-Wood, through businessman Carl Hagstrom, for not only a number of forms but also the Chestnut name; however, the canoe shop was never set up. Before production began, it was converted to one of the first aboriginal casinos in Canada.

Through Edmonton businessman Ellis Gnapp, George Birch, still trying to have a hand in things, organized the largest package of forms and materials to be sold to the Wabasca Indian band, far north of Edmonton, Alberta. The Wabasca band hired a former Chestnut employee, Jamie Thompson, who had worked for Chestnut only a few weeks one summer, and learned more about canoe building at the Langford Canoe Company in Dorset, Ontario. With Thompson as the foreman, he and members of the band set up a plant with over twenty Chestnut forms, produced a catalogue, and went into production. The Wabasca Canoe Company could not find a large enough market to support a full-scale canoe factory. Operations ceased almost as quickly as they began.

During the time it took to organize these two major sales, many of the popular Chestnut forms were sold off in small packages. Two Chestnut employees, Donald Fraser and Carl Jones, each bought a handful of forms and set up their own shops. Hugh Stewart of the Headwaters Wilderness Camp in Temagami, Ontario, that is now located near Meech Lake in

Quebec, purchased three forms. A few others were purchased individually. The record of sales in these dying days were poor, and there are a couple of important forms missing.

The trademark change of hands is unresolved to date. Just about everyone in the canoe business has tried to capitalize on the Chestnut name. There is confusion about which model is which, partly because forms were sometimes duplicated and are now in the hands of different builders. The issue of distinguishing models is made murkier by some unscrupulous builders who advertised canoes for which they did not have the forms, or built canoes on other forms, modifying them after they came off the forms to resemble the ones advertised. The form lists below may help clarify who has what. The ongoing popularity of Bill Mason's work gives the Chestnut Prospector a near mythical image, and many canoe builders, in wood and in plastics, have capitalized on Chestnut's fame by marketing their own copies. Though some copies are better than others, the result is utter confusion for the canoe enthusiast today as to just what an authentic Chestnut canoe is.

Genuine Chestnut canoes are again being built, and many are of superb quality, produced by various dedicated craftsmen, who either purchased Chestnut forms upon the company's dissolution or, as in our case, received them from the two Indian bands. For them, building true Chestnut canoes is a labour of love. As a result of their efforts, almost the entire Chestnut line is again available for sale. However, interested buyers cannot simply walk into a store and buy one. For some models, waiting lists can be as long as two years, and locating the builders may not be easy as most do little advertising other than by word-of-mouth.

Chestnut Canoe Co. Quebec, P.Q., March 20, 1929
Fredericton, N.B.
Dear Sirs:

The snow shoes arrived this morning. I find them of the same excellent stuff you have always supplied me with since I have been dealing with you, whether it be canoes or snow shoes. Hence my entire confidence in your firm and absolute satisfaction with its products.

Faithfully yours,
C. O. PELLETIER, Col.

Chestnut Canoe Forms

The following charts concern the famous Chestnut canoe forms. The first chart below showing forms and their shapes was compiled by comparing six different catalogues that span Chestnut's history. A word of caution: This chart compares given dimensions, not measured ones. For instance, the sixteen-foot Pleasure model's name changed, but did its form? The first catalogue listed the Ajax/Moonlight (grades one and two) as having a beam of 34⅛ inch and a depth of 11¾ inches. In 1922 and 1934 they had a beam of 34 inches and a depth of 11¾ inches. The names Pal and Deer emerge in 1955 with a beam of 34 inches and a depth of 12 inches. Undoubtedly, these were all the same canoe; canoe measurements vary depending upon the precision in measuring the canoe. In 1976 the Pal suddenly had a beam of 36 inches and a depth of 12¾ inches. This is a radical difference, and the form, as we now know, had definitely changed. Later Chestnut catalogues became less and less meticulous in their descriptions of the models.

Chestnut Canoe Dimensions Extracted from Catalogues 1905–55

TELEGRAPH CODE	CLASS	L	W	D	NOTE	1905	1922	1934	1950	1955	1976
Ajax	Pleasure	16	31	11		X					
Aster	Pleasure	17	31	11½		X					
Alpha	Pleasure	18	32	12½		X					
Premier/Kruger	Cruising	16	32	11½	1.	X					
Primus/Cronje	Cruising	17	33	11½	2.	X					
Leader/Stoessel	Cruising	18	34	12		X					
Boone	Special Guides	16	32	11½	3.	X					
Crocket	Special Guides	17	33	11½		X					
Moses	Special Guides	18	34	12		X					
Featherweight		11	34	11¾			X	X	X		
	Pleasure	11	34	12						X	X

TELEGRAPH CODE	CLASS	L	W	D	NOTE	1905	1922	1934	1950	1955	1976
Teddy/Trapper	12′ Canoe	12	34¾	14			X				
	12′ Canoe	12	34	14				X	X		
Bob's/Bantam	Fifty pound Special	15	37⅝	12			X				
	Fifty pound Special	15	37½	12				X	X		
Bob's Special	Pleasure	15	37	12	15.					X	
	Pleasure	15	37	12½							X
Little/Peach	Pleasure	14	33	10¾			X				
	Pleasure	14	32	11¼				X	X		
Playmate	Pleasure	14	32	12						X	
Playmate/Fox	Pleasure	14	32	11¾	21.						X
Twozer/Gooseberry	Pleasure	15	32⅜	11⅝			X				
	Pleasure	15	33	11½				X	X		
Chum	Pleasure	15	33	12	16.					X	
Chum/Doe	Pleasure	15	34	12½	21.						X
Ajax/Moonlight	Pleasure	16	34⅛	11¾			X				
	Pleasure	16	34	11¾				X	X		
Pal	Pleasure	16	34	12	17.					X	
Pal/Deer	Pleasure	16	36	12¾	21.						X
Moonlight	Pleasure	16	34	12	18.					X	
Glider Sponson	Pleasure	16	34	12	19.					X	
Aster/Winter	Pleasure	17	35⅛	11½			X				
	Pleasure	17	35	12				X	X		
Alpha/Evening	Pleasure	18	37	12¼			X				
	Pleasure	18	36	12¼				X	X		
Premier/Kruger	Cruising	16	33⅞	11¼	6.		X				
	Cruiser	16	34	12	6.			X	X		
Kruger	Cruiser	16	34	12						X	
	Cruiser	16	33	13¼							X
Primus/Cronje	Cruising	17	35¼	11¼	6.		X				
	Cruiser	17	35	12¼	6.			X	X		

TELEGRAPH CODE	CLASS	L	W	D	NOTE	1905	1922	1934	1950	1955	1976
Cronje	Cruiser	17	35	12 1/4						X	
	Cruiser	17	34	13							X
Leader/Stoessel	Cruising	18	35 5/8	12 1/2	6.		X				
	Cruiser	18	36	12 1/2	6.		X	X			
Leader	Cruiser	18	36	12 1/2						X	
	Cruiser	18	35	13 1/4							X
Boone	Guides' Special	16	33 7/8	11 1/4	4.		X				
	Guides' Special	16	34	12				X	X	X	
	Guides' Special	16	33	13 1/4							X
Crocket	Guides' Special	17	35 1/4	11 1/4			X				
	Guides' Special	17	35	12 1/4				X	X	X	
Moses	Guides' Special	18	35 7/8	12 1/2			X				
	Guides' Special	18	36	12 1/2				X	X		
	Guides' Special	18	37	12 1/2						X	
	Guides' Special	18	35	13 1/4							X
Hudson	Freight	17	45 3/8	17 1/4			X				
	Freight	17	45	17	10., 20.			X		X	
	Freight	17	45	17	11.				X		
	Freight	17	45	18 1/2	22.						X
Bay	Freight	18	46 3/8	18			X				
	Freight	18	46	18				X	X	X	
	Freight	18	46	18 1/2	22.						X
Company	Freight	19	51 1/4	19 1/4			X				
	Freight	19	51	19				X	X		
	Freight	19	51	21						X	
	Freight	19	51	19 1/2	22.						X
Traffic	Freight	20	45	19 3/4			X				
	Freight	20	52	20				X	X	X	
	Freight	20'2"	52	20	22.						X
Daddy	Freight	22	62	24	22.			X	X	X	X

TELEGRAPH CODE	CLASS	L	W	D	NOTE	1905	1922	1934	1950	1955	1976
Giant	Freight	24	67	28							X
Northman	Freight	16′2″	39	13	23.						X
Rupert	Freight	25	50	23				X	X		
Chicken	Nestable	14	33 1/4	13 3/4			X				
	Nestable	14	32	12				X			
Yolk	Nestable	15	36 3/4	15			X				
	Nestable	15′3″	36 1/2	13 1/2				X			
White	Nestable	16	37 1/2	14			X				
	Nestable	16′6″	41	15				X	X	X	
Egg	Nestable	17	41 3/4	16			X				
	Nestable	17′9″	46	17				X	X	X	
Nest	Nestable	18	45 5/8	17 1/2			X				
	Nestable	19	51	19	9.			X	X	X	
Barn	Nestable	19	51 1/4	19 1/4			X				
Indian		16	33	12	12.			X			
Maiden		16	33	12	13.			X			
Forest	Prospector	12	32	12				X	X	X	
Fire	Prospector	14	34	13				X	X		
	Prospector	14	33	13 3/4							X
Elk	Prospector	14	34	13	vee					X	
Ranger	Prospector	15	35	13 1/2				X	X	X	X
Bear	Prospector	15	35	13 1/2	vee					X	
Fort	Prospector	16	36	14	10.			X	X	X	
	Prospector	16	36	14 1/2							X
Fawn	Prospector	16′3″	36	14 1/2	vee						X
Fawn	Prospector	16	36	14	vee					X	
Garry	Prospector	17	37	14 1/2				X	X	X	
Marsh	Prospector	17	37	14 1/2	vee					X	
Voyageur	Prospector	18	38	15				X	X	X	X
Birch	Prospector	18	38	15	vee					X	X

TELEGRAPH CODE	CLASS	L	W	D	NOTE	1905	1922	1934	1950	1955	1976
Henry	Ogilvy Special	16	36	13	7.			X	X	X	
	Ogilvy	16	36	13½							X
Parr	Ogilvy Special	16	36	13	vee					X	
Dave	Ogilvy Special	18	36	13				X	X	X	
	Ogilvy	18	36	13½							X
Grilse	Ogilvy Special	18	36	13	vee					X	
Jock	Ogilvy Special	20	37	13				X	X	X	
	Ogilvy	20	37	14							X
Pool	Ogilvy Special	20	37	13	vee					X	
	Ogilvy	20'5"	37	14	vee						X
Alex	Ogilvy Special	22	39	14				X	X	X	
	Ogilvy	22	38	15							X
Trout	Ogilvy Special	22	39	14	vee					X	
	Ogilvy	22	39	15	vee						X
Joe	Ogilvy Special	24	40	14					X	X	
Salar	Ogilvy Special	24	40	14	vee					X	
Chief	Ogilvy Special	26	40	14				X	X	X	
Salmo	Ogilvy Special	26	40	14	vee					X	X
Trout	Poling & Fishing	18	33	13				X			
Grilse	Poling & Fishing	20	36	14				X			
Salmo	New Model/Poling	22	37½	14½	5.		X				
	Poling & Fishing	22	38	14½				X			
Salar	Poling & Fishing	24	41	15				X			
Manitou	Labrador	15	34	15				X			
Mingan	Labrador	16	38	16				X			
Moisie	Labrador	18	40	17	8.			X			
Robinson/Crusoe	One-Man Canoe	15	28	12				X			
Solitaire	One-Man Canoe	13	26	11¾				X			
Dugout	Dugout Class	20	33	13				X			
Pirogue	Dugout Class	26	37½	15				X	X		

TELEGRAPH CODE	CLASS	L	W	D	NOTE	1905	1922	1934	1950	1955	1976
New Champion		16	34	12					X		
Playtime	Ogilvy Gadabout	16	40	14	14.				X		
Sport	Ogilvy Gadabout	18	40	14					X		
Prince	Ogilvy Gadabout	20	40	14					X		
Bantam	Lightweight Comm.	15	37	$12^{1}/_{2}$							X
Mermaid	Lightweight Comm.	12	40	$12^{3}/_{4}$							X
Nestable	Group Paddling	19	51	19							X
Selkirk	Group Paddling	22	38	18							X
Centennial	Group Paddling	25	51	19							X

Notes:

1. Forms for canoes Ajax through Moses (above dashed line) were destroyed in first fire.
2. Forms for canoes Ajax through Moses (above dashed line) were measured in a different system than those below dashed line.
3. The Boone had half ribs.
4. Guides' Special Boone, Crocket, and Moses were available in second grade only.
5. First introduced as a poling canoe in 1918.
6. Pages nine and ten are missing from the 1934 catalogue. Assume the Cruising model would have been listed.
7. First produced in late autumn of 1931; modified in 1932. Offered with pointed ends only.
8. Featured removable ends or "hoods" to form a straight top to be lashed to airplane underside.
9. Nest takes the place of Barn; original Nest is deleted from catalogue.
10. Vee stern offered in 1934 catalogue on all Freight and sixteen-, seventeen-, and eighteen-foot Prospector models.
11. Hudson offered in 1950 only with vee stern and keel.
12. Indian finished with mahogany gunwales, thwarts, seats, decks, and so on.
13. Maiden finished with spruce gunwales, thwarts, seats, decks, and so on.
14. All Ogilvy Gadabouts offered with square stern, keel, and keelson only.
15. Bob's Special has $^{1}/_{4}$ inch x $2^{3}/_{8}$ inch ribs spaced $1^{1}/_{2}$ inch apart.
16. Chum has $^{3}/_{8}$ inch x $1^{1}/_{2}$ inch ribs spaced 2 inches apart.
17. Pal has $^{3}/_{8}$ inch x $1^{1}/_{2}$ inch ribs spaced 2 inches apart.
18. Moonlight has $^{3}/_{8}$ inch x $2^{3}/_{8}$ inch ribs spaced 2 inches apart; also no.8 canvas.
19. Glider Sponson same as Moonlight but with sponsons.
20. Freight canoes offered with vee stern only in 1955.
21. Fox, Doe, and Deer are Playmate, Chum, and Pal with $1^{1}/_{2}$ inch ribbing.
22. Offered in the 1976 catalogue with both vee and flat wide sterns.
23. This canoe with flat wide stern was a Peterborough form called the "Northboy."

The next chart is the one used by Lock-Wood in dispersing the Chestnut forms, after they gave up on finding one buyer. There are forty-one listed forms in use and twelve discontinued for a total of fifty-three forms. It is an interesting document because it shows how many forms had been in storage (compare to canoes actually built as shown in the 1976 catalogue column in the first chart). It gives what was considered the merit of each form with the handwritten addition of P (Popular), S (Build only to special order), and D (Discontinue). One can see which forms are missing entirely.

There are a number of handwritten annotations as well. This first list is not dated. There is a further, shorter list that is dated May 29, 1980, with the handwritten addition: "These molds still available July 10, 1980," and a final list of "Molds Available as of September 10, 1980." (These are forms, not molds, as are used in plastic boats. It appears whoever at Lock-Wood was writing this up did not know the difference.)

The following is a compilation of what is found on those pages, at least all that is legible. From all the references, plus additional research, the final column lists where the forms were dispersed. Some forms are marked with a price, although it does not specify whether it is an asking or final price. A number of forms have two or more copies.

Who Bought What

*P (Popular), S (Build to special order), and D (Discontinue). Sometimes model names are listed, sometimes not. Sometimes there are other descriptive comments. There are obvious typographical errors. The following table is duplicated here as it was found. [Note: Forms purchased by the Wabasca and Pays Plat Indian bands were subsequently purchased by the author.]

LENGTH	NAME & MODEL	P/S/D*	MAY 29	SEPT. 10	SOLD TO
	Pleasure Canoes				
12′	Mermaid (*the old prospector*)	D	*	*	Wabasca Indian Band
14′	Playmate	?	*	*	Wabasca Indian Band
15′	Chum	P		*	Carl Jones
16′	Pal	P	*	*	Wabasca Indian Band

LENGTH	NAME & MODEL	P/S/D*	MAY 29	SEPT. 10	SOLD TO
16′	Pal	P	*		Pays Plat Indian Band
16′	Pal	P			Carl Jones
14′	Fox	D	*	?	
15′	Doe	D		*	Wabasca Indian Band
16′	Deer	D	*(2)	*	Wabasca Indian Band
11′	Featherweight	S	*	*	Wabasca Indian Band
15′	Bob Special				Pays Plat Indian Band
15′	Bob Special				Donald Fraser
16′	North Man (not in first list)		*	*	Wabasca Indian Band
12′	Teddy & Trapper (")		*	*	Wabasca Indian Band (note below)
16′	Indian Maiden	?			Carl Jones
17′	added in hand writing when ...	–			Carl Jones
18′	discovered, forgotten in storage	–			Carl Jones
	Prospector Canoes				
14	Fire	D	*	*	Wabasca Indian Band
15′	Ranger	D	*	'sold'	?
16′	*Fort	P	*		Hugh Stewart
16′	*Fawn	S			Pays Plat Indian Band
17′	*Garry	P			Donald Fraser
18′	*Voyageur	S			Hugh Stewart
	Ogilvy Canoes				
16′	Henry	S			Donald Fraser
18′	Dave	S			Donald Fraser

LENGTH	NAME & MODEL	P/S/D*	MAY 29	SEPT. 10	SOLD TO
20′	*Jack	S			Donald Fraser
22′	*Alex	S			Donald Fraser
26′	*Salmon	S			Carl Jones
20′	Gadabout (F. W. Ogilvy)	S			Carl Jones
	Cruiser Canoes				
16′					Hugh Stewart
17′					Donald Fraser
18′					Big Cove Indian Band, later bought by Carl Jones
	Freight Canoes				
17′	Vee	P	*		Pays Plat Indian Band
17′	Wide	P	*		Pays Plat Indian Band
18′	Vee	P	*(2)	*	Wabasca Indian Band
18′	Wide	P	*(2)	*	Wabasca Indian Band
19′	Wide	S	*	*	Pays Plat Indian Band
20′	Vee	S	*	*	Wabasca Indian Band
20′	Wide	P	*		Pays Plat Indian Band
22′	Vee	S	*		?
22′	Wide	P	*		Pays Plat Indian Band
24′	Wide	P	*		Pays Plat Indian Band
25′	Pointed (The "Centennial War Canoe")	S	*	called 'Vee'	Wabasca Indian Band
16′	Nestable			*	Wabasca Indian Band

LENGTH	NAME & MODEL	P/S/D*	MAY 29	SEPT. 10	SOLD TO
17′	Nestable			*	Wabasca Indian Band
19′	Nestable	S			
12′	Cartop Boat (3 with different widths)	D		*	Wabasca Indian Band
13′	Cartop Boat			*	Wabasca Indian Band
15′	Marvel		*	*	Wabasca Indian Band

Notes found at the end of above list:

* Denotes hood available for 'vee' stern.

All of the above molds are in good operating condition. There are twelve additional molds which would require restoration prior to use. None of these are for catalogue items.

There is a final page where seven fibreglass boat molds are listed: Regent, Monterey, Pathfinder, Chaleur, Wayfarer, Imperial; and four fibreglass canoe molds: fourteen-foot Hudson's Bay, sixteen-foot Clippercraft (2), sixteen-foot Champlain (2), seventeen-foot Falcon. It appears they were considered unsaleable.

The second and third lists seem to include the forms for those canoes that were not in serviceable repair. A number of older and/or experimental forms appear only in these last pages, suggesting that at first the Lock-Wood employees didn't know these forms existed:

Miscellaneous Quantity Available

17' Nestable 1

19' Nestable 1

12' Cartop Boat 3

13' Cartop Boat 1

15' Marvel 1

How We Build Chestnut Canoes Today

Upon the purchase of the two groups of forms from the Pays Plat and Wabasca Indian Bands, I embarked upon my work as a true canoe builder. There are excellent books on wood-and-canvas canoe construction, particularly Jerry Stelmok's and Rollin Thurlow's *The Wood & Canvas Canoe,* or Jerry's earlier book *Building the Maine Guide Canoe.* Rather than duplicating their work, this chapter is a discussion of building methods that were peculiar to Chestnut in the past, and methods and materials that are unique to us today in building Chestnuts.

In our shop we see our role as preventing the further evolution of a product in order to preserve the past. It is arguably not a sound premise on which to build a profitable business. Nevertheless, we tend to do things the traditional way but will adapt new ideas and technologies where they show a marked improvement.

For example, the development of polyester resins and fibreglass cloth is a good example in which tradition is not improved by advances. We would never replace canvas with a covering of fibreglass and polyester resin (which other builders often do), for this shatters the basic premise of what makes the wood-and-canvas canoe work so well—the two hull system. During the sixties a number of summer camps, not knowing how to recanvas canoes, took whole fleets of canoes and replaced the canvas with fibreglass/polyester. The result was a monohull. Fibreglass does not allow the wood to breathe, forcing even white cedar to rot, and the covering can no longer be removed for a major repair such as broken ribs. Those canoes are now worthless shells of fibreglass, barely holding together bits and pieces of rotting wood.

Other skins bear some merit. We have used Seconite, the very thin dacron material used to cover ragwing airplanes, and were able to make our Featherweight under twenty pounds. It worked very well for such a little canoe, but I certainly would not recommend it for any large, fast canoe because collisions with sunken logs and the like could easily tear it. Also, it is so thin you clearly see the outline of the planking. A product called Verilite, manufactured in Montreal (it may still be produced), could be purchased as an optional covering in the later Chestnut catalogues. The material is PVC, a rubber type substance, impregnated into canvas. The principle was great, just canvas and paddle; the PVC impregnated canvas was even pre-painted. The material stood up quite well at first, but as demand for the product waned so did the care in its manufacture. Later samples showed that the canvas was no longer impregnated, just covered with PVC. Thus the rubber coating could wear away quite easily from any abrasion, and then the canoe would leak.

One glue that is an improvement to traditional methods is epoxy. Having rarely seen an old canoe seat that was still solid at its dowelled or mortise and tenon joints, I think I would be doing my customers an injustice not to use it. Making fillers of epoxy with sawdust from the wood being treated, allows me to use wood that I otherwise could not. For instance, it would be environmentally sacrilegious to reject a sixteen-foot gunwale because of a small worm hole, when the flaw could easily be fixed with such a filler; it would take truly careful examination to find the flaw in the finished canoe.

One difficulty that has continued through years of canoe building is that of obtaining the necessary quality and quantity of canoe woods. This problem has been significant since the wood-and-canvas canoes were first built, indeed, it precipitated their invention. One of the driving forces behind the invention of the wood-and-canvas canoe was the lack of birchbark. Lack of quality cedar soon followed.

The Chestnut canoes we build today are nineteenth-century designs built near the twenty-first century. All the materials are simply not readily available. For example, cedar is the basis of the canoe. It is difficult to imagine what cedar bushes two hundred years ago must have looked like. Today we generally see the Eastern white cedar (*Thuja occidentalis*) only in swampy land, growing so close together that not enough sunlight gets in to allow the trees to grow much beyond a size suitable for fence posts. It takes a large tree to make clear wood for only as branches die off and new rings of wood form over them does the tree develop outer rings that will produce knot free wood. Even today, in our most modest revival of cedar canoes, canoe builders are finding it increasingly difficult to find enough cedar even though the wood has no other commercial value today other than as fence posts. And the quality of the wood had decreased drastically.

I like to work with full-length planks for the garboard (middle) strakes especially, and if possible the rest of the strakes, until the gore pattern, should not be made of more than two planks in a sixteen-foot canoe. Also, traditionally Chestnuts were made with four-inch wide planking which we try to retain, but finding a four-inch wide plank free from knots is infinitely more difficult than a three-inch knot-free plank.

Admittedly, this is rather an eccentric fanaticism on my part, and it is increasingly difficult to maintain. I have seen other builders who make no effort, and scab together their planking with pieces no longer than three feet. Western red cedar (*Thuja plicata*), a giant rain forest tree, is certainly available in long, clear lengths, but it simply is not a suitable substitute, being not nearly as rot resistant. The Peterborough Canoe Company did use some red cedar planking in some of its later canoes with unsatisfactory results. (And because of difficulty in steam bending, red cedar cannot be used in ribs.) I once rebuilt a small Peterborough motor canoe (Northboy, later made in Fredericton and called Northman by Chestnut) made from red cedar planks. Almost all of the planking had rotted to nothing, while the ribs of local white cedar were well intact.

White cedar was not always so scarce. Much of the resource—valued again for its decay resistance—was used in building the Canadian railway system in the form of ties and telegraph poles. Although by 1899, a contemporary "wanted" poster calling for white cedar suggests that railway builders were having trouble finding enough wood. I also came across a letter in the Chestnut archives that was sent out to a number of addresses in the Philippines in response to a rumour that had surfaced about a rain forest mahogany that exactly imitated cedar's characteristics. Nothing came of it.

Cedar isn't the only endangered canoe wood. Early on in Peterborough, rock elm, used for the thin, half round ribs in cedarstrips, became scarce. Swamp elm was tried with poor results. Later, white oak became the norm.

In early years Chestnut used spruce for the gunwales. (I prefer it because it has flexibility and resilience and is lightweight. But finding full lengths of sixteen, seventeen, and eighteen feet or longer of clear spruce has become impossible.) There were three solutions: splice shorter pieces together; use another wood—ash was a good candidate, or white oak; or import rain forest sitka spruce from the British Columbian rain forests. In its last years Chestnut used the first two; in the worst years it even combined them, gluing together two or more pieces of ash.

Among nearly all of the canoe companies ash eventually became a preferred canoe wood for stems, and often for gunwales, seats, decks, and thwarts. It grows straight and tall with a high canopy, and remains one of the easiest woods to find in suitable quality. As it is one of the best bending woods, ash was also used extensively for Chestnut's line of snowshoes. However, ash has a serious flaw that early companies did not really worry about—it has very poor rot resistance. One of the most common and troublesome repairs on old canoes is rotted stems caused by leaving canoes flipped over in the grass. In years gone by the canoe companies thought of their products as commodities, not family heirlooms. Indeed, naturally occurring obsolescence was perhaps a good thing for business.

Aside from the availability of quality materials, another important factor in the business of building canoes has changed: labour costs. It takes such a long time to build a canoe that the raw materials, while difficult to get, no longer present nearly as high a percentage of the value of the finished craft. On a more personal note, it has been my philosophy for the past decade that since we were going to have to charge a great deal for our canoes due to the amount of time invested in building them, that the materials we use should be the best. For this reason, we rank ash as a poor alternative.

The pre-canvas stage of canoe construction at Chestnut's York Street factory is shown here: Cedar planking over cedar ribs.
(Courtesy: The George Taylor Collection, The Provincial Archives of New Brunswick.)

To accommodate our self-imposed high standards for materials—our woods of choice are cedar, spruce, and black cherry—we invested in our own small saw mill. Working with local independent loggers, we found a small grove of magnificent local spruce that has lasted us a decade for inwales. When it runs out there are independent loggers that do selective logging in British Columbia and can get satisfactory western or sitka spruce. Though I regret cutting any tree in the rain forest, I feel better that some selective trees get cut and used for a noble purpose rather than clear-cut and wasted for pulp.

As for the stems, cherry is ranked high on the charts for good rot resistance. However, it does not bend well. No matter how much one steams a piece of cherry that has been air- or kiln-dried, it will never get back the elasticity that would allow it to bend into the sharp curve of a stem. Our solution? Cut the trees in the spring, when the sap is flowing, and then store the wood cut as logs in our pond. When the log is finally cut open it is steamed and bent immediately. This method works remarkably well.

The stem is an example of a Chestnut idiosyncrasy that I don't think was the best in wood-and-canvas design. Chestnut builders devised a method of wedding the deck, the inwales, and the stem using a mortise and tenon joint, whereas the top of the stem was cut into an extremely thin tongue and each inwale had taken out of it one half of the mortise. There are two problems with this. First, in every old Chestnut I have ever worked on that thin tongue of ash was rotted away. Second, by cutting mortises into the inwale the builder is severely limited in being able to check the alignment of the top of the stem. To check the alignment, we use "the Maine way" of running a string down the middle of the canoe once one side has been fastened, checking the alignment carefully until we are sure the alignment is true, then fastening the other side. The traditional Chestnut method doesn't allow for this much fiddling. With older canoes and the best craftsmen in the long Chestnut history, this was undoubtedly never much of a problem. The craftsmen were so skilled the canoe naturally turned out straight from their ample experience. Later, with piecework contracts and less skilled workmanship, this was certainly a difficult method. Considering we don't build as many canoes today, we have humbly adopted the more reliable method.

Our seats, thwarts, and decks are made with furniture grade cherry. Our patterns for all these parts were taken from older canoes in our collection. Thwarts are graceful and slender, shaped with beautiful curves. The decks are heart shaped, intricately carved, domed on top and hollowed out underneath, again a copy of a favourite old Chestnut. These copies of the earlier style take over one hour each to carve. Later canoes have just a simple, flat, chunky deck. It would take about five minutes (far less in an assembly line) to run a board through the planer, cut one of those simple decks, and sand it finished. To be sure, however, our intricate decks and thwarts could be modernized, but I rather enjoy hand carving these pieces with a spokeshave, and we build so few canoes it is simply not practical to modernize. If we were to build significantly more canoes we would have to change to a copying router. The work would no longer be enjoyable, but it would be quicker and indistinguishable from hand carving in the finished product.

Our inwales are always made of spruce because the canoe needs the flexibility. However, we offer buyers the choice of spruce or cherry for the outwale, and most buyers tend to go for the cherry. It is beautiful, matching the rest of the trim, and stands up better to the abuse of paddles slapping against them (although of course, a good paddler doesn't do that). The price one pays is approximately one or two pounds of additional weight.

I would not be against using white oak for stems. It is a heavy wood, but the finely carved stem is small enough that it would not add much weight. It is, after all, the boatbuilder's wood, renowned for its strength, flexibility, and rot resistance. My argument against it concerns aesthetics. Visually, a canoe benefits from simplicity—just cedar, spruce, and cherry, as opposed to a dazzling display of different woods.

We have also continued the undeniably outdated practice of hand caning seats, a task that most builders have forsaken. If a caned seat is desired it is far easier to use machine woven, "pressed" cane. We even use a weaving pattern that is more complicated and tighter than the method Chestnut used because it lasts much longer.

I also do not build modern styled carrying yokes (although I have installed one for a customer) as I have many arguments, both practical and aesthetic, against them. The traditional method of installing permanent string or leather lashing to the thwarts to hold paddles during portaging is simply a superior method. Now, this conviction dates back to my youth when as a camper I had the job of carrying the surplus paddles, of which there were many, on portages. The bundle was awkward far beyond the weight of a pack.

Furthermore, I find the simplicity of paddles and thwart lashed together make it easier to use a towel or a lifejacket for a far more comfortable position than a hi-tech carrying yoke, which gives you little room for padding or adjustment. (Although it is true that the traditional shape of the centre yoke is widest in the middle, where the carrier's neck would go.) But most of all, I find the inclusion of a carrying yoke visually disturbing, a modern affront to the beautiful lines of a traditional canoe. I would miss terribly the graceful lines of a well-carved centre thwart.

Paramount to our canoe building philosophy is keeping the weight low, and the greatest weight factors in a canoe are the canvas, filler, and paint. The Cree, when they used canvas as a replacement for birchbark, simply painted the canvas with whatever they could get from the local Hudson's Bay Company outlet, and the canoes were waterproof. Over time, builders tended to use heavier and heavier canvases, more and more filler and paint to produce a finish "like glass." It appears this trend gained popularity in the postwar era as they tried to make the canoe's outside finish resemble fibreglass. The Canadian Canoe Museum has a Chestnut from these last days; it is one of two or three canoes which different people refer to as the last Chestnut built. It is an Indian Maiden with the high sweeping ornamental ends and it comes from the time when Chestnut boasted of its "oven baked" finish. This was simply an attempt to speed up the drying of the gobs and gobs of filler, which could take a year to dry naturally. The canoe in the museum has never been in the water. Yet, the oven baked finish is riddled with cracks, similar to the crazing sometimes used as a special effect in pottery glazes, in this case caused by the forced drying.

We now tend to use a lighter canvas which requires less filler to make smooth. We also recommend that we apply fewer coats if a customer prefers flexibility to a glasslike finish. Some graduate students at the Massachusetts Institute of Technology made a study of types of finish on racing canoes and discovered that a slightly rough finish actually improves the craft's speed.

At the time Chestnut was using heavier canvas and gobs of filler, it made references to a secret filler formula. Omer Stringer gave me a formula that he said was identical but made was from off-the-shelf products:

1 qt boiled linseed oil
5 lbs window glazing putty
1 lb white lead
(or substitute another pound of putty)
4 oz Japan dryer
1 qt turpentine
Top up with more linseed oil to make one gallon

We used that recipe for some time, but it did not satisfy me. A filler's purpose is to waterproof the boat while keeping it flexible, and this filler was too rigid for me. I also worried about the fire hazard posed by having rags of filler ingredients lying around after the job of rubbing the filler into the canvas, knowing how many of the canoe companies had burned to the ground, often more than once. And the white lead in the filler is rather poisonous and difficult to obtain.

To circumvent these problems, I have devised the following improved formula which is very easy to obtain. For the filler I simply use a latex undercoat, available from a paint manufacturer. Latex is the active ingredient of rubber (although in this case it is probably synthesized). If flexibility is the objective, there isn't anything better. However, latex does not sand particularly well with electric sanders because it gums up. It also is not rot resistant, a quality that the white lead provides. To create rot resistance, we first coat the canvas with a canvas preservative—this is the most unpleasant and toxic operation in our shop—then between two and six coats of rubbed in "filler" goes on. On top of this, our next layer is another commercial paint undercoat, this time an oil-based one that is designed to be an undercoat to either latex or alkyd (oil-based) paint, which works well to wed the first layer of latex and the final layers of alkyd paint. This process creates a surface that sands well.

Finish materials have improved dramatically. The modern varnishes we use have ultraviolet prohibitors. Although they are very expensive, they add years of life to the varnish. For me, the jury is still out concerning

Canvas duck stretched over cedar planking. After waterproofing and curing under heat, the canoe is painted and prepared for market. (Courtesy: The George Taylor Collection, The Provincial Archives of New Brunswick.)

paint for the final finish of the canvas. For years I used an old-fashioned alkyd house paint on the simple pretext that the longer a paint takes to dry, the more flexible it will be. But this paint line was discontinued. I have been advised by numerous chemists for the paint manufacturers to use products often called "liquid plastic" (for the amount of polyurethanes or plastic in the mixture), which they say should give me the flexibility I want. Reluctantly, I am following their recommendation, but it is too early to give a final report. I would love that fibreglass-like finish, but I am not willing to sacrifice low weight and flexibility.

A word about keels: In all the canoes I have built I have yet to put one on because to do so requires drilling fifteen holes into an otherwise seamless, watertight skin. One of the myths about the keel is that it protects the boat. In fact, the bottom of a cedar canoe is inherently flexible and just covered in canvas it can run over logs, rocks, and beaches without concern for tears in the canoe. Put a keel on and every time the craft hits something, the obstacle is not pushing against a flexible hull but against a rigid keel. Inertia halts the keel, while the boat pulls forward. Soon the screw holes enlarge and leaks begin. (Careful caulking of the keel will certainly help, by why flirt with trouble.) During the sixties, when we all complained about leaky canoes, they were almost all leaking through those holes for the keel. The notion of a keel helping to keep the boat straight is another myth prompted by a poor J stroke. Most keels are too shallow to have much effect, except perhaps when performing the "ferry"' during white water manoeuvres. There are times when keels are favourable, for example in motor canoes. The Freighters are lined with up to seven keels from side to side, to stiffen the hull and protect the craft from the pounding produced by high-powered outboard motors.

Last, but certainly not least, there are various small materials used in the production of quality canoes that were used almost two centuries ago, and now they are either difficult to get or changes in the building industry have made them obsolete. For instance, building a canoe requires hammering about two thousand brass tacks. In any other construction that task would be aided by a pneumatic nailer (air gun); however, the low demand for brass canoe tacks designed for air guns, and the fact that brass does not mold consistently enough to prevent them from getting stuck in the gun, makes the otherwise efficient air gun unavailable.

For the past ten or so years, my wife and I have been slowly churning out Chestnut canoes, calling it more of a hobby. Hugh Stewart and Donald Fraser have been doing much the same. Each of us has our own building styles.

Carl Jones, shop manager in Chestnut's declining years, has made the only successful attempt at full-scale production. He wanted to call his company Chestwood, but Lock-Wood's lawyers stopped him, and his company is called Cedarwood. Although he has many good forms, he does not have the original forms for all of the canoes he advertises, and thus he has helped continue the elusiveness of the Chestnut story.

Perhaps our fanaticism for preserving the historic qualities of Chestnuts is best left at the hobby level of production. I have entertained thoughts of expansion. However, issues of trademark, quality, and economics seem to get in the way. We keep an open mind, as every year preservation of the Chestnut tradition becomes more important. Watch for updates at our web site: www.eagle.ca/~chestnut.

One of the last of the thousands of Chestnuts that were built in New Brunswick for over seventy-five years.
(Courtesy: The George Taylor Collection, The Provincial Archives of New Brunswick.)

The Saga of the Chestnut Canoe Trademark

"*A key way of protecting your corporate identity is through a registered trademark. Registration of your trademark is the legal title to intellectual property in much the same way as a deed is title to a piece of real estate.... A trademark is a word symbol, a design or a combination of the these to distinguish the wares or services of one person or organization from those of others in the marketplace.*" (from *A Guide to Trademarks,* The Canadian Intellectual Properties Office)

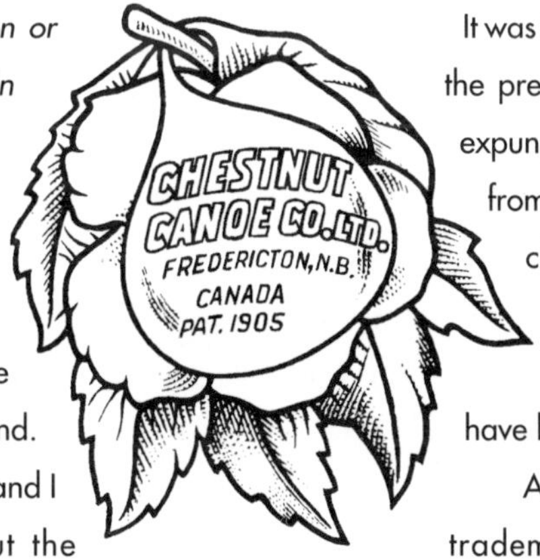

When Chestnut dispersed its assets, the trademark went with the canoe forms sold to the Pays Plat band. When I purchased these from the band I sought a lawyer's advice about the purchase, and since we were not planning to make a big deal of the business, his advice was to not get "too concerned" over trademarks, that all I would need was a vendor's permit from the Government of Ontario. Bad advice!

A couple of years later, in the summer of 1984, I received a phone call to inform me that an advertising company in Toronto was hours away from taking over the name. Off I went, in a mad fury to Ottawa.

CHESTNUT CANOE CO. LTD.
FREDERICTON, N.B.
CANADA
PAT. 1905

It was true; this Toronto company had had the previous ownership of the trademark expunged, that is, ownership was erased from the record. Had I simply filed a change of ownership when I made my purchase from the Pays Plat band, none of what follows would have happened.

A sympathetic staff member of the trademarks office helped me file for ownership of the trademark based on "previous use." I thought I had caught it in time. Later, I received notice that my ownership of the mark was being opposed by the same Toronto advertising company, in the name of Robbie Sproule, who had set up a store in Muskoka, Ontario, called Muskoka Fine Watercraft. And this time, there was a third party. The person who had originally called me, Roger MacGregor, who owned the Ivy Lea Shirt Company, had applied for the mark as well.

The ensuing oppositions involved years of depositions and counter depositions. It soon became obvious that if I wanted to pursue the matter it was going to take years and cost a small fortune, and it seemed likely that against these big guns that had unlimited opportunity to advertise the Chestnut name I could even lose. It seems getting a trademark (and keeping it) after it had been expunged had little to do with who legally purchased it, or who owned the forms or any such aspect of integrity, but simply who spread the name around most. So I quietly gave up. It didn't seem to affect our small business of building five or six canoes a year anyway.

Nearly a decade later and completely out of the blue in late 1996, I received a letter from the trademarks office. It seems the others had either given up or simply not filed the paperwork, but asked to send two hundred dollars and I could have the trademark. I was elated. By then, this book was close to finished, and I would be able to write a definitive final chapter.

However, it turns out, the good news was a clerical error from the trademarks office; they had sent me the wrong form letter. After months of straightening out the mess, I learned what they meant to send me was notification that I was no longer in the running. Ivy Lee and Muskoka Fine Watercraft, neither of which own a thing "Chestnut," are still battling it out. As this book goes to press, on checking with an Ottawa trademarks lawyer, the case is unresolved.

So who owns the Chestnut trademark? Right now no one. We continue to use the name Chestnut Canoe Company without impunity and remain true to the quality and style it symbolizes.

A Tale of Two Paddlers

Canada is the land of the canoe, so it should come as no surprise that this country produced two of the most important—and by most standards, the most famous—paddlers of the twentieth century. What is even more interesting is just how different these men were. Omer Stringer and Bill Mason shared a love of the canoe, especially Chestnuts, had diminutive physiques, and even died in the same year—Omer well-seasoned and Bill well before his time—though the similarities end there.

Omer Stringer, whose shadow I grew up in, was of the original, traditional guides' heritage. No one made a film about him, but he was well known for his unsurpassed paddling style, what people came to know as canoe ballet.

Bill Mason, on the other hand, was a man of the media. His "real" job before making a living as a canoe guru was as a commercial artist and ad-man. His chosen media became film and through it, and his books, he became known by canoeists worldwide. He is already the subject of an autobiography.

Omer Stringer

Omer Stringer,
master of
canoe ballet.
(Courtesy: Barry Wright.)

Omer Stringer, born in 1912, was the son of a forest ranger in Algonquin Park, Ontario. He and his ten siblings grew up near the juncture of Canoe and Joe Lakes, in the then logging town of Mowat, a place better known as home of Tom Thomson, one of Canada's famous painters, who died mysteriously in his canoe when Omer was just five. The one-room schoolhouse Omer attended in Mowat provided less than basic education; most of his young friends grew up illiterate. However, Omer's father was an avid reader and was instrumental in cultivating his son's creativity and curiosity.

At the age of twelve, Omer was a professional guide, first at Northway Lodge, a girls' camp on Cache Lake, and then at the town's prestigious Algonquin Lodge, part of the rail line's chain of wilderness retreats that offered luxury in the turn-of-the-century Canadian bush. I first met Omer when he worked as canoe instructor at my grandmother's camp—the first co-educational children's camp in Algonquin. He became a friend to my family, especially to my grandmother.

At twelve, he was already notoriously small for his age, but his stature inspired him to create his own paddling style. In his later years, he referred to himself as a "lazy perfectionist," explaining that he had to figure out how to do everything in the most efficient way since he lacked the muscles of his guiding competition. He recalled his early paddling experiences this way: "*I'd canoe fifty miles in a day. All the old people paddled from the stern with a weight in the front. Well in lots of places you couldn't find stones. On a windy day, you couldn't get across a beaver pond with the front up. So I'd sit in the middle of the canoe and sneak over to one side to paddle. No one else did it that way, so I wouldn't let anyone see me. Older guides, if they saw that, would hit you over the head with a paddle."*

As it happens, the style he created was taught to a generation of paddlers. Omer claimed he alone "invented" his trademark technique. However, there are pundits who say that his style must have been "discovered" by aboriginal paddlers in the millennium of canoeing experience before white men ever set foot in a canoe. Who is to tell. It is certain Indian paddling techniques generally were not highly sophisticated in the early twentieth century. But were they perhaps remembered by only a few elders whom Omer might have copied? Whatever influences he had, Omer made them his own and perfected them.

By the time he was a young man, Omer was working as a guide with the largest of the Algonquin children's camps, the Taylor Statten Camps on Canoe Lake. The boys' camp, Ahmek, was on the mainland, and a separate girls' camp, Wapomeo, was on nearby Wapomeo Island. Taylor Statten took a liking to Omer. It is said that he paid for Omer to later attend a private residential college, where he finished high school and got involved in his future passion: electronics.

A man of many talents, Omer built canoes as well as paddled them—with fleets of canoes to keep in repair at camps one couldn't help but figure out how they were put together. In fact, he was a seasoned canoe builder by the tender age of fourteen. At many of the camps, Omer would build a form and camps would save money building their own canoes. I remember Omer disdainfully telling me of the earlier all-wood canoes, which he regularly sank in the spring so that their seams would swell. They would stop leaking but double their weight in the process; he quickly became a proponent of the wood-and-canvas canoe and Chestnuts in particular.

He also taught the campers paddle making. He became particularly close to my brother Jeff and influenced what I still believe is the only decent paddle shape around. Today Nashwaak paddles can be found at most good canoe stores. Jeff and Omer wrote a substantive paddling book, although it was never published. Omer did, however, publish a concise method book that is a must for any paddler. He produced the first canoeing guidelines for the Canadian Red Cross, which were adopted across the country.

Omer was truly at home in the wilderness. I remember Omer said he never carried an extra paddle. If anything ever happened to his, he could find a suitable piece of wood and make a new one in an hour with an axe. He was often called upon by the park rangers as a tracker to help find people lost in the bush, among them were my father, my sister, and a camp horse lost by a riding instructor, Chucky (Lorne Green's son). He also helped develop the Outdoor Education Program for Ontario teachers. At every camp where he taught he left a tradition of excellence that endured for decades.

Omer was enlisted to help build a new camp called Camp Tamakwa, organized by a group of ex-Taylor Statten campers from Detroit that was led by Lou Handler. Thus began his long association with Tamakwa. A close friend of the Handlers', Edie from Detroit, often ran the camp office. Omer and his canoe must have made quite an impression on Edie for they began courting. Although he continued to be associated with Taylor Statten Camps and my grandmother's camp, his main alliance remained at Tamakwa. The camp may be familiar to modern movie-goers as the location for the Hollywood film "Indian Summer." (Omer's son David is still deeply involved as one of Tamakwa's directors.)

Omer served overseas during World War II with the Royal Canadian Air Force. He worked his way up to Chief Electronics Advisor for Airborne Radar in Southeast Asia. After the war he married Edie. The newlyweds settled in Michigan where Omer taught himself a variety of skills, such as repairing TVs and servicing furnaces. He returned to Canada for various kinds of jobs: work in northern Ontario lumber camps, to map bush in Quebec for the federal government, and to serve as a geologist for a mining company.

In 1964, at the age of fifty-two, he enrolled at the Ontario College of Education (University of Toronto) and received an Ontario Teacher's Certificate in electronics. He went on to teach electronics and a host of other subjects (including canoeing) at a suburban Toronto high school. He is remembered fondly by students, one of which is Canada's pre-eminent woodworker and furniture designer Michael Fortune. Many of Michael's designs involve steam bending, perhaps a carry-over from being a pupil of a renowned canoe builder and paddler.

Omer officially retired in 1978, after which a group of ex-Tamakwa campers, the same people who built the Roots Shoes empire, involved him in a new venture: Beaver Canoes. Now, Omer used two canoes, both Chestnuts: his Chum for solo work, namely, the "canoe ballet" for which he will always be remembered, and the foot longer but same Pleasure model, Pal, for tripping with the camps. (Omer's Chum, named *Omer,* was narrow ribbed and therefore technically a Doe.) At the time Beaver Canoes was starting up, it appeared Chestnut was gone forever, so Omer built copies of the Chestnut forms, and was set up in a fancy shop in Toronto. The Beaver Canoe business never caught on, but a clothing line bearing the logo "Beaver Canoes—Built by Omer Stringer" was a teenage fad for almost a decade, particularly in Toronto. It seems Beaver Canoes didn't even completely catch on with Omer. Although he was operating a company that built his canoes, whenever he gave a paddling demonstration Omer still used his faithful Chum: red-orange with a white stripe along the gunwale and the name "Omer" painted on it.

Omer was the master of what he called "canoe ballet." His *tour de force* was to paddle his canoe within the confines of an Olympic size swimming pool while a sound system poured out ballet music to which he "danced" his canoe from edge to edge, using strokes most paddlers only dreamed of. Once, when Omer was giving a paddling demonstration at a canoe exposition in Ottawa Omer met Bill Mason. Bill watched with apparent awe, hardly able to restrain his enthusiasm. As soon as Omer finished, Bill jumped in his canoe to try to copy Omer's moves, and quickly dumped. No problem for Bill; he didn't mind getting wet and he didn't have an ego that was easily bruised. He held the highest regard for Omer's skills.

The last time I saw Omer was in the States at the 1986 annual assembly of the Wooden Canoe Heritage Association. I remember this meeting especially well. He was there to give a canoeing demonstration. Of course, he had his famous Chestnut Chum with him. I had a brand new one—one of the first canoes I built upon obtaining Chestnut forms. One of Omer's well-known tales was that his canoe was no ordinary Chum. He had supervised the construction of it himself in Fredericton, and liked to say that it wasn't even built on the Chum form. Curious about the validity of his tale, I seized the opportunity to compare my Chum with his supposedly unique model.

Good-naturedly, Omer came clean; he really couldn't avoid it for the only difference was that he had cut two inches off the thwart, narrowing the beam. It suited his magnificent precision paddling, but from a builder's point of view I didn't like the modification. By pulling in the sides, against the shape of the form the canoe was built on, the gunwale lines were pulled straight with angular bends at each end, breaking the paramount boatbuilder's rule of "the fair curve." But who's to complain. After all, he delighted so many with his paddling skill.

Too soon, in 1988, Omer was hospitalized repeatedly. He was still helping source cedar for Beaver Canoes and had been named "Man of the Year" by the Friends of Algonquin Park. It was expected he would recover, and he was looking forward to the presentation. It was not to be. He died peacefully in his home on April 24, 1988.

Bill Mason

Bill Mason, Canada's pre-eminent paddler. (Courtesy: Canadian Press.)

Born in Winnipeg on April 29, 1929, at the onset of the Great Depression, Bill was the first born of Sadie and Bill Mason, Sr. A frail baby, he was plagued from the start with respiratory problems that led to asthma, and special care had to be taken with this tiny child. Bill survived his early uncertain days and flourished in a stable, conservative home. Throughout the Depression his father and both grandfathers had work, avoiding the devastation that many Winnipegers experienced.

The overriding influence early on for Bill and his younger sister, Elizabeth, was their paternal grandmother, Granny Mason, as described by James Raffan in his biography of Bill Mason titled *Fire in the Bones*: "*Granny Mason's world was a grim amalgam of guilt and servitude to her God, a world of fear and retribution. It was a world of black and white; no grey. You were either going to heaven or going to hell. With the exception of reading the Bible and worshipping the Lord, almost everything else—books, films, games, secular music, cards—was the work of the devil.*"

From his childhood, Bill's life had at least two major influences: religion and art. It is said that each Sunday he would attend church with his parents, where he would sit on the floor, and using the pew as an art table he would draw. Art and spirituality continued to be driving forces throughout his life.

If Bill's paternal grandparents helped to develop the spirituality that formed his life work, his maternal grandparents helped him experience the out-of-doors. Inevitably, Bill learned to bring the two elements—spirituality and nature—together. For years, the Fairs spent their summers at Grand Beach on Lake Winnipeg. Like Algonquin, where Omer Stringer was renowned, Grand Beach was developed by the Canadian National Railway as part of their series of wilderness resorts. (In the thirties the railway was advertised as the gateway to the wilds, with a series of resorts across the country, perfect places to launch canoe trips. Promotional materials often showed an empty red wood-and-cedar canvas canoe sitting in sublime solitude, an image which became one of Mason's most famous paintings.) While at Grand Beach, Bill insisted his father rent a canoe for a week. It was the beginning of an enduring passion for Bill. When he was thirteen he built his own boat—a kayak. He took this kayak on his first overnight trip alone in the woods.

In 1944 his grandparents' cottage at Grand Beach was sold, forcing fifteen-year-old Bill to find other access to the wilderness. The timing was good: Bill's Winnipeg church community was just starting Pioneer Camp on Shoal Lake, 150 kilometres east of Winnipeg. After Bill's persistent pleas, he went to camp. This trip marked the merger between spirituality and wilderness that would shape Bill's work for the rest of his life.

Canoeing during the first years of the Manitoba Pioneer Camp was done in Olympic racing boats in the kneeling racing style, definitely not wildness canoes. Bill's influence at Pioneer Camp was strongly felt. He completely changed the camp's ideas about the canoe and he made his first film for the camp. (He liked the camp so much, he had his honeymoon there.)

At the age of seventeen, Bill's diminutive size was still a major concern to his parents. He had the physique of a twelve-year-old at four feet seven inches tall and sixty-five pounds. It didn't seem to phase Bill. He was a popular kid with an uncanny talent for drawing. At the completion of grade eleven, Bill was invited to take the unorthodox step of spending his next year entirely under the guidance of his high school art teacher. There was no specific academic requirement for entry into the commercial art program at the Winnipeg School of Art, and it had been clear for a long time that this was where he was headed. Fortuitously, during Bill's second year the school was taken over by the University of Manitoba, putting him in line for a university diploma and enabling him to increase his range of study.

Bill received his Diploma in Commercial Art in 1950 and immediately went to work for a local firm. He spent his first pay cheque on a camera, and honed his skills as a still photographer. He brought home images for further treatment in the medium of paint, and was unwittingly preparing for the world of film. He was indulgent when summers came. Come canoe season, Bill had other priorities, in particular his continued devotion to Pioneer Camp.

Interestingly, Bill's first canoe marked the onslaught of postwar technologies. Made of the same molded plywood that was adapted for use in airplane bombers by the Montreal aircraft company, Vickers, this canoe brought home to Bill the merits of the wood-and-canvas design because of an accident which he claimed was the closest he ever came to getting killed. He wrote a highly understated account of the event in his diary: "*Just bought a car (a Nash Rambler.) Slept at Betula. Let out with canoe (the old Plycraft) loaded very light. Shot first and second rapids, portaged falls. Portaged gear over third rapid, then proceeded to shoot them as customary. Got on wrong side of rock in middle of rapids and canoe was swamped then smashed to pieces. Left it on shore and walked home a little wiser.*" He bought a Chestnut canoe next.

Bill ventured into filming at the side of Toronto filmmaker Christopher Chapman. By then Bill had already garnered respect among a small circle of wilderness buffs, and when Chapman was asked by the Quetico Foundation to make a film to promote the wilderness values of the newly formed Quetico Provincial Park, he sought Bill Mason to work with on the project.

Working with Chapman amounted to a three-week crash course, and it was the only formal training Bill received in filmmaking. The skeleton crew—one filmmaker, Chapman, and one actor, Bill—also cemented Bill's eventual style of putting himself in his films. This project launched Bill into the world of film full time. He travelled to Ontario to film with Chapman on the French River, and met Budge Crawley. Soon after, on Chapman's recommendation, Bill took a full-time position in the animation department at Crawley Films.

Bill made his first home in Ontario in his sleeping bag on the shores of Meech Lake, just across the border into Quebec. (Meech Lake continues to be the home of the Mason family today.) In November Bill moved into a rented cabin. He was awash in projects. There was the animations job for Crawley, along with his first film project for the Manitoba Pioneer Camp. Aside from film work there was his upcoming marriage to Joyce, a student nurse he had met through the church youth group.

From there on projects kept coming. In the middle of an extremely successful commercial animation for Crawley of the "Wizard of Oz," Bill met Blake James, another filmmaker with whom he would work extensively, including his first project for the National Film Board (NFB). Meanwhile, Bill quit the "Oz" project to help Chapman, who was making a documentary about an archaeological dig of an Iroquois village. While there, Crawley invited Bill on a filmmaker's dream of a lifetime: a pan-Arctic filming expedition. When he returned, his wife would be eight months pregnant. He filmed more on that trip than he could have ever imagined, including one of the last great igloo villages of the north. Filmmaking opportunities continued to accumulate. Crawley wanted him back on the "Oz" project. His old employers in Winnipeg wanted him to be their commercial art director. Bill took everything he could. Baby Paul arrived in July.

In the summer of 1962 he headed for the wilderness with his canoe. This was his first of many solo trips to Lake Superior. He sold the story of that first trip to *Star Weekly* magazine.

Filmmaking became an ever increasing part of his life. "Wilderness Treasure," the final title for the Manitoba Pioneer camp film, was completed in 1963 and won first prize in its class at the Canadian Film Awards. Bill's career as a filmmaker was firmly launched. One source of frustration in Bill's life at this stage in his career was his inability to win over the National Film Board of Canada producers in Montreal. The success of "Wilderness Treasure" helped sway the NFB, and four years later Bill was offered a contract in the animation department. It was not what he wanted, but it was a foot in the door. After a disastrous film on the Voyageurs with which Bill was involved (although his recommendations went unheeded), Bill made his first NFB film "Paddle to the Sea" between 1962 and 1964. It was a huge success and garnered numerous prizes, including an Academy Award nomination.

Bill's reputation broadened, along with the respect from the Canadian canoeing community and his opportunities for more adventurous projects. For example, his film project on wolves ("Wolf Pack," 1971) meant bringing home a litter of wolf cubs to his Meech Lake home. The howling attracted the attention of a summer resident—Prime Minister Pierre Elliot Trudeau—who knocked on the door.

Daughter Becky was born in 1963 and the Masons purchased a permanent home at Meech Lake. Around this time, at the age of thirty-six, Bill almost died of coronary failure while in Winnipeg. Bill's main concern was when he could return to the bush and whether he would still be able to portage a canoe.

The heart attack didn't slow him down. For the next twenty-five years, Bill continued to paddle with an impressive list of experts, dignitaries, and his own children. But for Bill, the epitome of the spiritual canoeing experience was solitude in the bush, paddling a red Chestnut canoe.

He made fourteen films with the NFB, the culmination of which was "Waterwalker," made in conjunction with Imago in 1984. The success of his movies helped make it possible to publish his books on canoeing skills that are the cornerstone of how-to literature on white water paddling techniques.

By the early 1980s the more his films and books succeeded, the more Bill felt the urge to return full time to painting and to the solitude of the bush. He found his compromise in his final film, "Waterwalker," a full-length feature film that would embody everything that mattered to him: solitude, the bush, canoeing, and painting. This was to be his ultimate expression of his spirituality. The production was rife with conflict and met with mixed if not antagonistic critical review. Some called it narcissistic.

In any case, after the film's completion, Bill turned to painting full time. Until then, his artwork had not received much attention, outside of a show in 1980. Perhaps Bill sensed it was time to give painting his full attention for shortly after he shifted his focus, in June 1988 he was diagnosed with inoperable cancer. In July, Bill and twelve of his closest friends and family members made one last trek to the great canyon of the Nahanni River in the Northwest Territories. On October 29, 1988, at the age of fifty-nine Bill died.

In conducting research for this book, I visited Bill Mason's daughter Becky at the Mason home, where her mother, Joyce, still lives on the shore of Meech Lake. My purpose was to determine just what was Bill's famed Chestnut sixteen-foot Prospector canoe, which he enthusiastically coined "the world's best all-round canoe." To be honest I went with a differing opinion on that score. I have the original Chestnut sixteen-foot Prospector form and I understand its limitations, I had serious concerns about such an awe-inspiring title being attached to the Prospector, for modern canoeists rarely carry the necessary ballast to keep this highly rockered, deep canoe from becoming windswept. I was curious to see Bill's Chestnuts to determine what model they were because many of the canoes portrayed as Prospectors in his films and books were not clearly Prospectors. In his final writings, Bill acknowledged that many of the canoe photos he used were not of the Prospector, but of the sixteen-foot Pleasure model, the first "real" canoe he owned. Mason enthusiasts who want to see for themselves, should examine either the books or the films. The Pal has cane seats and narrow ribs. The Prospector has slat wood seats and wide ribs.

With Becky, I examined the two red Chestnuts. The two canoes bore the signs of much use. The Pleasure model, Bill's first canoe, was officially not a Pal but a Deer because of its narrow, rounded ribs. This is a Chestnut trademark I have not seen in any other maker—except in Omer Stringer's designs for Beaver Canoes—and is the definitive element that identifies the canoe and dates it as well. Upon measuring the beam, I was more amazed to learn that this was a later, widened version of the Pleasure model (see Pleasure Canoes, page 108–109). The canoe fits neatly into Chestnut history, as Bill wrote in his diary that he purchased the canoe on April 12, 1958, about the same time that Chestnut widened the sixteen-foot Pleasure forms.

The second canoe was more difficult to definitively place in Chestnut history. It most definitely was a Prospector, although it was well used, and the shape was rather distorted. (I couldn't help making the comparison to Patterson's description of one of his Chestnuts on the Nahanni River almost eighty years earlier.) Some of the canoe measurements didn't quite make sense when compared to those of the original form, but this was probably due to years of use. (Bill also had an eleven-foot Chestnut Featherweight.)

The Prospector was a very large canoe and would have suited Bill on some of his trips where his canoe was heavily loaded—he would carry a heavy canvas tent for example, quite unlike much of today's hi-tech lightweight camping gear. I am personally convinced he would have found a narrow Pal more fitting to the esteemed title of "best all-round canoe" if he travelled as light as most trippers do today. The bottom line was that he loved red Chestnuts, and he used the term Prospector, first used by Chestnut, perhaps as a generic term with which to spread his infectious enthusiasm.

My theory for what I took to be the misidentification of canoe models was that Bill had cut his teeth in advertising and his training carried over somewhat into the medium of film. He could hardly be expected to proclaim the world's best canoe a Pal or even a Deer or a sixteen-foot Pleasure model. Even though his first Chestnut, a sixteen-foot Pleasure model, was the canoe that cemented his love for Chestnuts, that name just didn't have the same appeal as the auspicious Prospector. I presented my theory to Becky. Was Bill, all these years, lying? Her response follows: "*Dad couldn't lie. The morality of lying was just not in his character, because of his religious background. On the other hand, Dad was not a stickler for details. He would get so caught up in his own enthusiasm that he could easily leave out little details, such as what particular model of canoe he was paddling at the time a photograph was taken.*"

Bill Mason, known to thousands of canoe enthusiasts, was characterized by unbridled enthusiasm. His exuberance and passion for life concealed his poor health. Bill used his well-loved Chestnuts as a medium to explore the driving forces of his life. Where Omer Stringer was pragmatic, Bill Mason was spiritual. Each has made a remarkable contribution to the sport and art of canoeing, and we are surely grateful for their gifts.

Bibliography

Adney, Edwin Tappan and Howard I. Chapelle. *The Bark Canoes and Skin Boats of North America.* Washington: Smithsonian Institution, 1964.

Alden, W.L. *The Canoe and the Flying Pros, or Cheap Cruising and Safe Sailing.* New York: 1877.

______. "The Perfect Canoe." In *Harper's,* vol. 56 (April 1878): 54–60.

American Canoe Association. Papers, including A.C.A. Yearbooks, in Library of New York State Historical Association, Cooperstown.

Baker, Bob. "How to Build Piccolo: A Seaworthy Sail and Paddle Canoe." In *Wooden Boat,* no. 35: 44.

Benedickson, Jamie. "Recreational Canoeing in Ontario Before the First World War." In *Canadian Journal of History of Sport and Physical Education,* vol. 9, no. 2 (December 1979): 41–57.

Bennett, Jill. *Canoe Builders of the Peterborough, Lakefield, Lindsay area.* Kanawa International Museum.

Bishop, Nathaniel H. *The Voyage of the Paper Canoe.* Boston: 1878.

Bray, Maynard. "The Incredible Herreshoff Dugout." In *Wooden Boat,* no. 14: 54.

Cameron, Dr. G. D. W. "Birth of the 'Peterborough' Canoe: Four Builders Start a Revolution." In *Wooden Canoe,* no. 9 (Winter 1982).

_______. *The Peterborough Canoe.* Peterborough Historical Society, 1975.

Chapelle, Howard I. *American Small Sailing Craft.* New York: Norton, 1951.

_______. *Boatbuilding.* New York: Norton, 1941.

Chestnut, Kenneth R. Letter to Mrs. Lillian Maxwell, New Brunswick Archives, 1952.

Cockburn, Robert. "Exploring Canada's Far North: A Bibliography." In *Wooden Canoe,* no. 15 (Summer 1983).

Crowley, William. *Rushton's Rowboats and Canoes: The 1903 Catalogue in Perspective.* The Adirondack Museum: 1983.

Davis, L. Jack. "Canoeing's Ugly Duckling: The Wood-Frame Canoe" and "Building a Puddle Paddler." In *Wooden Canoe,* no. 16 (Autumn 1983).

Douglas, C. M. "The Lone Canoeist of 1885." In *The Beaver,* Outfit 281, (June 1950): 38–41.

Drayton, Reginald. Mss. Diary of Reginald Drayton. Archives of Ontario.

Endicott, Abigail B. "The American Canoe Association, a Brief History." In *Canoe* (Official Publication of Canadian Canoe Association), vol. 1, no. 4 (June 1977).

Franks, C. E. S. *The Canoe and White Water.* Toronto: University of Toronto Press, 1977.

Frazer, Perry D. *Canoe Cruising and Camping.* New York: 1977.

Gardner, John. *Building Classic Small Craft.* Camden, ME: International Marine, 1977.

______. "Sailing Canoes Once Held a Brief Place in the Sun." In *National Fisherman,* (June 1977).

Hanson, John. "High Standards." In *Wooden Boat,* no. 13: 34.

Hearne, Samuel. *A Journey from Prince of Wales's Fort in Hudson's Bay to the Northern Ocean.* Rutland, VT: Charles E. Tuttle Company, 1971.

Hallock, Charles. *The Sportsman's Gazetteer and General Guide.* New York: 1877.

Hoffman, Ronald C. "The History of the American Canoe Association, 1880–1960." A Dissertation Presented to the Faculty of Springfield College. Springfield, MA: June 1967.

Hughes, Holly. "The Willits Brothers Canoes." In *Wooden Boat,* no. 55 (November/December) 1983: 82–86.

Johnston, Fred. "History of the Canadian Canoe Association." In *Canoe* (Official Publication of Canadian Canoe Association), vol. 1, no. 1 (February 1976).

______. "The Great Canadian Canoe was Made in the U.S.A.! or Where Has All our History Gone?" In *Canoe* (Official Publication of Canadian Canoe Association), vol. 1, no. 2 (June 1976).

La Brant, Howie. "The Principles of Canoe Design." In *American White Water Journal,* (Autumn 1962).

Love, Francis H. "Peterborough … Canoe Capital of the World." In *Forest and Outdoors,* vol. 45 (September 1949): 6–7 and 22.

MacGregor, John. *Our Brothers and Cousins: A Summer Tour in Canada and the States.* London: 1859.

_______. *A Thousand Miles in the Rob Roy Canoe on Rivers and Lakes of Europe.* 4th ed., London: 1866.

Manchester, Herbert. *Four Centuries of Sport in America.* New York: 1968.

Manley, Atwood with assistance of Paul F. Jamieson. *Rushton and his Times in American Canoeing.* Syracuse: Adirondack Museum/ Syracuse University Press, 1968.

Mason, Bill. *Path of the Paddle: An Illustrated Guide to the Art of Canoeing.* Toronto: Van Nostrand Reinhold, 1983.

Merriman, Lynn C. and Katherine E. Stewart. *The Builders of Wood and Wood-Cloth Canoes in Ontario, 1850–1976.* Kanawa International Museum, 1976.

Moores, Ted and Merilyn Mohr. *Canoecraft: A Harrowsmith Illustrated Guide to Fine Woodstrip Construction.* Camden East, Ontario: Camden House Publishing Ltd., 1983.

Morse, Eric W. *Fur Trade Canoe Routes of Canada Then and Now.* Toronto: University of Toronto Press, 1971.

Murray, Florence B., ed. *Muskoka and Haliburton, 1615–1875.* Toronto: Champlain Society, 1963.

New York Times. "The Canoe Regatta ... First Annual Regatta of the New York Canoe Club." In *New York Times,* October 20, 1872.

Norton, C. L. and John Habberton. *Canoeing in Kanuckia.* New York: 1878.

Osborne, A. C. "The Migration of the Voyageurs from Drummond Island to Penetanguishene in 1828." Papers and Records, Ontario Historical Society, vol. 3 (1901).

Patterson, R. M. *The Dangerous River.* Sidney, BC: Gray's Publishing Ltd., 1966.

Paulson, F. M. "Canoe Sailing Rigs." In *Field and Stream,* (August 1966).

Pinkerton, Robert E. "The Canoe: Its Selection, Care, and Use." In *Wooden Canoe,* no. 2 (Spring 1980): [reprint of introduction and chapter 1.]

Porteous, John. "Chestnut No. 1 in Canoes." In *The Atlantic Advocate,* (July 1977).

Raffan, James. *Fire in the Bones: Bill Mason and the Canadian Canoeing Tradition.* Toronto: HarperCollins, 1996.

"Retaw" [pseud.] "The Canadian Canoe." In *Forest and Stream,* vol. 29, no. 23 (December 1887).

Riviere, Bill. *Pole, Paddle & Portage: A Complete Guide to Canoeing.* Boston: Little, Brown and Company, 1969.

Roberts, Harry N. "On Canoe Construction." In *Wilderness Camping,* vol. 6, no. 6 (April/May 1977).

Roberts, Kenneth G. and Phillip Shackleton. *The Canoe.* Toronto: Macmillan, 1983.

Rogers, Mary Strickland. "The Peterborough Canoe." In *Peterborough, Land of Shining Waters, An Anthology.* Peterborough: (1967).233–35.

Rushton, J. H. *Pleasure Boats and Canoes, An Illustrated Catalogue.* J. H. Rushton, Canton, NY: c. 1899.

Rutstrum, Calvin. *North American Canoe Country.* New York: Macmillan Publishing Co, Inc., 1964.

Sears, George Washington ["Nessmuk"]. *Woodcraft.* New York: Forest and Stream Publishing Company, 1920.

Solway, Kenneth. "The Chestnut Canoe: A Canadian Legacy." *Royal Canadian Geographical Society,* 1984.

Stelmok, Jerry. *Building the Maine Guide Canoe.* Camden, ME: International Marine, 1980.

Stelmok, Jerry and Rollin Thurlow. *The Wood & Canvas Canoe.* Camden East, ON: Old Bridge Press, 1987.

Stephens, W. P. *Canoe and Boat Building.* New York: 1885.

Stephenson, Gerald. "John Stephenson and the Famous Peterborough Canoes." In *Peterborough Historical Society,* November 1987.

Stewart, Hugh. *The Story of the Chestnut Canoe.* (Paper, unpublished.)

Strickland, Samuel. *Twenty-Seven Years in Canada West.* Ed. by Agnes Strickland. 2 Vols. London: 1853.

Strobridge, Henry, L. "Modern Canoe Building for Amateurs." In *Outing,* vol. 24 (March/April 1894).

Taylor, J. Garth. "Canoe Construction in a Cree Cultural Tradition." Ottawa: National Museum of Man Mercury Series, 1980.

Teller, Walter Magnes, ed. *On the River: A Variety of Canoe & Small Boat Voyages.* New Brunswick, NJ: Rutgers University Press, 1976.

Thompson, David. *Narrative of… David Thompson.* Ed. by Richard Glover. Toronto: Champlain Society, 1963.

______. Mss. Diary of David Thompson. Archives of Ontario.

Tyson, O. S. *Sailing Canoes, a Brief History.* Published for American Canoe Association, 1935.

Vaux, C. Bowyer. "History of American Canoeing." In *Outing,* vol. 10 (June 1887): 259–69; (July 1887): 360–69; (August 1887): 395–414.

______. "The Canoeing of To-Day." In *Outing,* vol. 16 (May 1890): 133–37; (June 1890): 214–17.

______. "The Modern Single-Hand Cruiser." In *Outing,* vol. 22, (May 1893): 144–47.

______. "Canoeing." In *Outing,* vol. 16, (1890): 495.

Vesper, Hans Egon. *50 Years of the International Canoe Federation.* English edition. John Dudderidge, Florence, Italy: I. C. F., 1974.

Wipper, Kirk A. *Signs and Symbols.* Kanawa International Museum.

Index